BRITISH FINANCIAL MARKETS
AND INSTITUTIONS

BRITISH FINANCIAL MARKETS AND INSTITUTIONS

K.V. Peasnell

Wolfson Professor of Accounting and Finance, University of Lancaster

C.W.R. Ward

Lecturer in Finance, University of Lancaster

PRENTICE HALL

New York   London   Toronto   Sydney   Tokyo

First published 1985 by
Prentice Hall International (UK) Ltd,
66 Wood Lane End, Hemel Hempstead,
Hertfordshire, HP2 4RG
A division of
Simon & Schuster International Group

Printed and bound in Great Britain by
BPCC Wheatons Ltd, Exeter

British Library Cataloguing in Publication Data

Peasnell, Kenneth V.
    British financial markets and institutions.
    1.   Financial institutions—Great Britain
    I.   Title II.   Ward, Charles W. R.
    332.1'0941   HG186.G7
    ISBN 0-13-083213-8

---

3 4 5   92 91

To our wives and parents

Contents

Preface   xiii

Acknowledgements   xv

PART ONE   INTRODUCTION   1

Chapter 1   **Introduction to the Financial System**   3

Simple Model of the Economy   3
Financial Claims   6
Money and Credit   7
Financial Markets   10
Financial Institutions   10
Impact of Government   10
    Taxation   11
    Monetary and fiscal policies   11
Summary   11
Further Reading   12
Discussion Questions   12
Appendix A: Financial Markets   13
Appendix B: Financial Institutions   15

Chapter 2   **Flow of Funds in the Economy**   18

Sources and Uses of Funds   18
The Flow of Funds Matrix   22
Financing Patterns in Britain   27
Projecting Credit Flows   28
Summary   29
Further Reading   29
Discussion Questions   30
Problems   30

Chapter 3   **Financial Markets and Institutions**   32

Conflicting Requirements of Borrowers and
    Lenders   32
Services Provided by Intermediaries   34
Primary and Secondary Markets   36
Desirable Characteristics of Markets   40
    Primary Markets   40
    Secondary Markets   41
Hedging, Diversifying and Arbitrage   43

Criticisms of the City   46
Summary   48
Further Reading   48
Discussion Questions   48

Chapter 4   **Money, Credit and Interest**   50

The Creation of Money and Credit   50
Impact of Government Policies   54
Interest Rates   56
Inflation   57
Summary   58
Further Reading   58
Discussion Questions   58

PART TWO   ANALYSIS OF FINANCIAL MARKETS   61

Chapter 5   **Evaluating Financial Investments**   63

Time Value of Money   63
A Single Period Example   66
Compound Interest   67
Effective Rates of Interest   70
Valuation and Pricing   71
Varying Interest Rates   73
Summary   74
Further Reading   74
Problems   74
Appendix: Mathematics of Compound
    Interest   76

Chapter 6   **Short-term Money Markets**   80

Principles of Bill Discounting   80
The Discount Market   83
Parallel Money Markets   87
International Money Markets   90
Summary   91
Further Reading   92
Discussion Questions   92
Problems   92

Chapter 7   **The UK Securities Market**   94

Types of Trading System   94
Types of Securities Traded   96
Characteristics of Long-term Markets   97
Allocative Efficiency of the Stock Market   100
Operational Efficiency of the Stock Market
    102

Information-processing Efficiency   102
Regulation of the Securities Markets   104
Summary   105
Further Reading   106
Discussion Questions   106

Chapter 8   **Bonds and Their Valuation**   107

Issuers of Bonds   107
Characteristics of Traded Bonds   109
Maturity, Tax and Coupon   110
Running and Redemption Yields   114
Term Structure of Interest Rates   117
Hypotheses on the Behaviour of
  Interest Rates   120
Bond Clientele   121
Summary   122
Further Reading   123
Discussion Questions   123
Problems   124
Appendix: Calculation of Redemption Yields
  125

Chapter 9

Shares and Related Securities   126

Issue of Shares   126
Characteristics of Traded Shares   132
Methods of Valuing Shares   133
Share Price Behaviour   136
Portfolio Models   137
Share Clientele   139
Other Equity Based Securities   139
Summary   142
Further Reading   143
Problems   143
Appendix A: Discounted Earnings
  Models   145
Appendix B: Market Models   147

PART THREE   FINANCIAL INSTITUTIONS   149

Chapter 10   **The Impact of Financial Institutions**   151

Development of Financial Institutions   151
Taxation and Government Policy   154
Competition   156
Impact on the Markets   157
Classification of Institutions   158
Conclusion   159
Further Reading   159
Discussion Questions   160

Chapter 11   **Deposit-taking Institutions**   161

The Deposit Markets   161
The Banks   162
Other Licensed Deposit-taking Institutions
    164
The Operations of DTIs   165
     Portfolio composition   166
     Services provided   167
Bank Lending to Industry   167
Leasing   170
Taxation of DTIs   172
Summary   173
Further Reading   173
Discussion Questions   174

Chapter 12   **Insurance   Companies   and   Pension
                         Funds**   175

Cash Flow Inputs and Outputs   175
General Insurance   177
Risk Management in General Insurance   179
Life Assurance and Pensions   180
Principles of Investment Management   183
Public Policy Issues   188
Summary   191
Further Reading   191
Discussion Questions   191
Problems   192
Appendix: Actuarial Calculations   194

Chapter 13   **Other Institutions in the Financial
                         System**   197

Investment Intermediaries   197
Financial Intermediaries   205
International Institutions   206
Conclusion   207
Further Reading   208
Discussion Questions   208

PART FOUR   THE FUTURE   **209**

Chapter 14   **New Developments in the Financial
                         System**   211

New markets in Financial Instruments   211
Competitive Processes   212
Changes in Regulation   215
Future Shocks to the Financial Market System
    216

Conclusion   217
Further Reading   218
Discussion Questions   218

Glossary   219

Financial Tables   227
Present Value of £1   228
Present Value of £1 per Period   230
Terminal Value of £1 per Period   232

Index   235

Preface

This book is intended to provide a broad and balanced introduction to the principal British financial markets and institutions. It is suitable both for accounting, business and economics students and also for accountants, managers, investors and others interested in the workings of the financial system.

The book is designed for use in introductory business finance courses at the first or second year undergraduate level. Typically, these courses are attended by a wide variety of students, many of whom will take no further financial (or even business) courses. It is our belief that, at this level, students are best served by a course of study which emphasises the broad picture, the flows of savings and investment and the markets and institutions which exist to facilitate these flows, rather than on the financing and capital budgeting decisions of business firms. The book can be used in such courses as the main text, or as a supplement to a traditional business finance text.

There are a number of excellent texts on the British financial system available, but none is really suitable for the purposes we have in mind. A.D. Bain's book, *The Economics of the Financial System,* is intended for second or third year economics majors and therefore concentrates on public policy issues at the expense of technical detail. Jack Revell's *The British Financial System,* apart from now being somewhat dated, is too large a book for the typical introductory course, and heavy in descriptive detail but light on such matters as the pricing of securities. A number of monetary economics books provide good coverage of institutions and markets but the emphasis is invariably put on the implications for macroeconomic policy.

The book is divided into four parts. Part One provides foundations for the study of markets in the remaining parts. Readers with good background in economics will proceed rapidly through these chapters. Chapter 1 outlines the functions of the financial system, its relations to the real (i.e. non-financial) system and the characteristics of financial claims, markets and institutions. Chapter 2 examines the financial system from a flow of funds perspective. Chapter 3 provides some economic criteria for understanding the system. The concept of interest as the price of credit is introduced in Chapter 4.

Part Two of the book examines the money and capital markets. The tools of financial mathematics, presented in Chapter 5, are used to explain the principles of security pricing and investment choice in the remaining chapters. Money markets are covered in Chapter 6. Chapter 7 is concerned with outlining the main features of the markets for long-term securities. The pricing of bonds and equity shares is dealt with in Chapters 8 and 9, respectively.

The third part consists of four chapters which deal with the financial institutions. Chapter 10 outlines the forces which have shaped the institutions and the impact their investment policies are having on the financial markets. Institutions are classified into deposit-taking institutions, the major long-term investors and other institutions. They are dealt with under these headings in the next three chapters. The final part of the book considers recent developments and the changes which are likely to occur in the financial system in the future.

It is not possible to consider everything in a short, introductory textbook. A choice has to be made. The most significant omissions from this book are (a) capital budgeting and company financing patterns, and (b) international financial markets and institutions. The former is covered extensively in any conventional company finance textbook; the latter is a very complex topic, beyond the scope of an introductory textbook.

The complexity of the financial system is such that it is difficult to avoid swamping the reader with facts and figures, thereby letting the learning experience degenerate into mere fact-grubbing. We have tried to avoid this by providing a judicious mixture of fact and financial theory in the first part and then using this to provide structure to the treatment of the financial markets and institutions in the remainder of the book. Emphasising the pivotal role of interest rates in channelling savings, the mathematics of compound interest used by investment analysts are employed to throw light on the ways in which bills, bonds and shares are priced in the markets.

This approach has a number of advantages. It emphasises problem-solving of the kind conventional in the popular capital budgeting books but not to be found in British 'institutional' texts. This serves to integrate the institutional and analytical parts of finance from the outset of the student's studies. From the student's point of view, there is the added advantage that he not only learns 'facts and figures' about the markets and institutions, but skill at investment analysis is acquired as well. Annotated guides to further reading, discussion questions and problems are provided at the end of each chapter as aids to teachers and students. The text and problem material included in the book has been developed and classroom tested in a first year undergraduate course we have taught to accounting and other majors at the University of Lancaster for the last three years, and we are indebted to those students for the valuable feedback they provided to us. A separate Teacher's Manual providing solutions to the end-of-chapter questions and problems is available from the publisher.

Acknowledgements

We acknowledge with gratitude the helpful comments of our colleagues, as well as current and former students in the Department of Accounting and Finance, University of Lancaster. In particular we thank Patricia Berry, David Brown, John Cope and Paul Taylor who made a number of useful suggestions. Professor Edward Stamp suggested many improvements for which we are grateful. We also thank the following for their helpful comments on the institutional aspects of the text: Jonathan Miller (Fielding Newson-Smith), Stewart Millman (De Zoete and Bevan), David Revie (Legal and General Group), Paul Richards (Samuel Montagu & Co.) and David Salisbury (H. Schroder Wagg). We thank the *Financial Times* for permission to reproduce extracts.

Finally we are grateful to the Department of Accounting and Finance (University of Lancaster) and Department of Accounting (University of Sydney) for providing typing resources, and personally to Valerie Goulding, Rosemary Timperley, Susan Unsworth and Sheila Markham for their help in producing the typescript.

Acknowledgments

Part One
INTRODUCTION

Chapter One

Introduction to the Financial System

The City of London is one of the world's great financial centres; its markets and institutions are numerous and complex. It is therefore all too easy to overwhelm the uninitiated with facts and figures; obscuring the essential with a mass of detail. To avoid this trap, we start in this chapter with simple models of hypothetical economies in which the role served by finance is easy to grasp. After summarising the special properties of financial assets, money and credit, the chapter concludes with a brief section on the ways in which the government's actions affect the financial system. The principal British financial markets and institutions are listed in appendices to this chapter.

Simple Model of the Economy

A first step in constructing a simple model of the economy is to consider how an economy without a financial system would function. This is a somewhat artificial device because the financial system did not spring into its existing form overnight. On the contrary, various features of the financial system — notably money — came into being at the earliest stages of specialisation; the 'financial' and 'real' parts of the economy have grown up together. Nevertheless, we do take our financial markets and institutions for granted, so it is worthwhile trying to figure out how people would go about their daily business in the absence of a financial system.

For our purposes it is sufficient to divide this 'economy' into two parts or 'sectors'. The first sector, the *business sector*, produces goods and services wanted (directly or indirectly) by the second sector, the *household sector*. The household sector exchanges the resources under its control — property and labour power — for the goods and services created by the business sector. The definition of a household can, of course, differ from society to society. Households are assumed in this analysis to be the ultimate owners of all resources. (A third sector called *the government* has a very important part to play in the workings of the financial system, but will be ignored here for the moment.) Finally, we assume that this economy is closed, in the sense that no exchanges of goods and services occur with other countries. The innermost loop in Figure 1.1 depicts the flows in this imaginary two-sector economy.

Consider the choices open to a household in this economy. Commodities can be consumed, or exchanged for other commodities currently owned by other households. Alternatively, some or all of its commodities can be put to productive use in order to create other commodities which will be consumed in their turn. In the former case, exchanges have to be made by bartering with other households. If the choice is to transform resources through production, the household will have to create a business in which it can employ its resources or make them available to another enterprise in exchange for some of their output. Only this latter group of productive exchanges are captured in the inter-sector real resource flows shown in Figure 1.1.

The difficulties involved in trying to exchange commodities in mutually rewarding ways are considerable, but they are so obvious that there is hardly any point in elaborating them. Suffice to say that considerable time and effort must be devoted in a barter economy to searching out other households with whom trades can be done. The problems multiply in the case of production. A household which provides labour inputs to a business will often have to take the outputs received in exchange and try to exchange them for more desirable commodities. It is inevitable that pressure will grow to employ one or more widely circulating commodities as a standard unit of exchange, or *numeraire*, into which all commodities can be converted, in

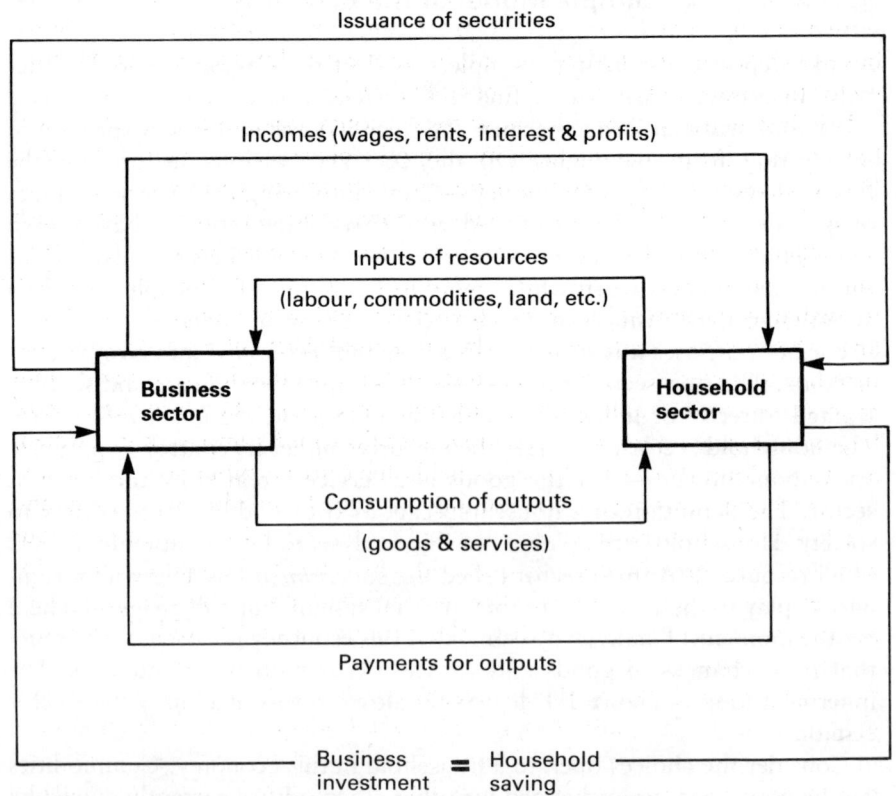

Figure 1.1   Flows in a Simple Two-Sector Economy

order to ease the search and divisibility problems which pure barter necessarily entails. The numeraire must be widely accepted as a means of settling obligations, and this means it must be in fairly fixed supply and homogeneous in quality if confidence is to be maintained in its exchange value.

Precious metals are ideal 'money commodities' from this perspective. If uncertainties concerning the quality and quantity of the money commodities persist to a great degree then it is very likely that barter exchanges will continue alongside monetary ones: money will be used to complete exchanges in those situations where the problems and costs of barter exchange are so great as to outweigh the uncertainties involved in accepting money in settlement.

The outcome of introducing monetary exchanges into the system is to create monetary as well as real flows in our simple model of the economy. Households can exchange their goods for those of other households and settle the transactions in cash. Businesses can buy inputs from other businesses in exchange for cash. Although these intra-sectors flows are important, ultimately all inputs come from the household sector and final outputs are consumed by households. These inter-sector real flows are settled in a monetary economy by proffering money. Thus monetary flows have to be 'added' to the real ones; these monetary flows are shown as inter-sector incomes and payments loops in Figure 1.1.

It is instructive to consider how these money-for-goods exchanges will have to occur if productive activity is to take place on any significant scale. In the case of simple, instantaneous-production enterprises there are no difficulties. The worker provides labour power and in return is paid in cash 'immediately' out of the revenues from (instantaneously) selling the firm's output. These wages can be exchanged for real goods and services immediately, if desired. Similarly, owners of land receive rents from farmers and other business users as and when it is used. Difficulties arise when the firm has to 'invest' in order to produce output; production is a roundabout process, so considerable amounts of time must elapse between the time of buying or hiring inputs and when revenues flow in. Examples of investment are to be found in agriculture — fields have to be ploughed and sowed months before the harvest; in mining — tunnels are dug with tools and machines which were previously created by the prior investment of labour and other resources and ore is quarried which has to be sold to others for further processing; and in industry — machinery and materials have to be bought weeks or months before the products can be sold. Investment involves waiting.

As long as there are sufficient wealthy individuals who are willing and able to wait, the two inner loops in Figure 1.1 adequately explain the flows in the economy. The providers of real inputs (labour, land and commodities) who are unable or unwilling to wait for payment are paid out of capital funds provided by the wealthy individuals. These capitalists or entrepreneurs take a share of the ultimate sale-proceeds because they are wealthy enough to be able to defer consumption and are willing to bear the risks involved in doing so.

The greater the scale of investment required, the fewer the number of households able to act as entrepreneurs. The greater the time between commitment of investment funds and the reaping of benefits then the greater the risks involved. Large scale and riskiness of investment require that capital be pooled. Sole proprietorships give way to partnerships, partnerships to corporate forms of business organisation. The financing process becomes more complex. Our simple model has to be augmented by the addition of the outermost loops of Figure 1.1 representing these flows of investment funds. The savings of the household sector are made available (lent) to the business sector and used to finance investment. In exchange for this finance, the business sector issues 'securities'. Securities can be thought of as rights to future benefits and take two basic forms: a promise to pay interest on certain dates and to repay the loan; or equity — a claim to a share of the after-interest-profits and ultimately the resources of the business after loans have been paid off.

Figure 1.1 can now be seen to depict an economy consisting of three connected subsystems: the real subsystem representing the flows of commodities; the monetary (or factor payment) subsystem charting the flows of incomes and payments for commodities; the investment subsystem. The financial system can be thought of in a very broad terms as being the monetary and investment subsystems together; a narrow view concentrates on the investment flows.

Financial Claims

The approach adopted above focussed on the creation and exchange of financial claims over a period of time. Another way of looking at a financial system is in terms of the quantities and types of various financial claims in existence at a point in time. Clearly the two are directly related one to the other: a flow over time measures the change in the stock of claims between the beginning and the end of the period.

A balance sheet is a useful means of depicting property and claims on property. The balance sheet may be constructed for a household, a company or any other institution in the economy. Generally, the term 'entity' is used to refer to any unit which owns or issues claims on property. If the property under the control of an entity can be identified, counted and somehow expressed in terms of money, these money values can be added together to yield a measure of the wealth of the entity. It is convenient for our purposes to distinguish here between real assets (RA) and financial assets (FA); the total 'worth' of the entity is therefore RA + FA. (How the assets are valued is of no concern here; they could be shown as the amounts it is estimated they would fetch if sold, what it would cost to buy them now or their original cost, or some mixture of bases.) There must be claims against this wealth: the entity owes money to others, i.e. it has financial liabilities (FL); the balance belongs to the owner of the entity and will be denoted as net worth (NW). We can combine these relationships in the form of a balance sheet equation:

$$NW + FL = RA + FA$$

or as

$$NW = (RA + FA) - FL$$

A balance sheet is nothing more than a financial statement on which assets are shown on one side and financial claims on the other, with the two sides totalling to the same amount in accordance with the balance sheet equation.

In principle, every entity in the country could be instructed to draw up a balance sheet at a specified date, say at the end of the calender year (31 December) or at the end of the tax year (5 April). In practice, only the government and corporate businesses normally do so; households and many unincorporated businesses do not. But suppose the command were to be issued and obeyed. There are thousands of business enterprises and millions of households; so it would be necessary to combine the balance sheets in some way if sense was to be made of the results. Sector balance sheets could be obtained by simply adding together the assets and claims of the constituent entities. The absence of balance sheet data for households makes the exercise a much more difficult undertaking in practice, and only limited and now very out-of-date results are available at present. (See J. Revell, *The Wealth of the Nation*, Cambridge University Press, 1967, for sector balance sheets for the years 1957–1961.) Government statisticians are currently engaged in trying to produce more up-to-date balance sheets for each sector.

The sector balance sheet data available at present reveal a number of interesting facets of the British financial system. The household sector is the ultimate owner of all private wealth; more interesting is the fact that it holds over half of all its wealth in the form of financial assets, and moreover its holdings of financial assets are greatly in excess of its liabilities. In short, the household sector is a net provider of funds to other sectors. By contrast, the business and government sectors both have borrowing greatly in excess of financial assets; they are net borrowers. As might be expected, the financial sector is light on real assets and its holdings of financial assets are approximately equal in amount to its financial liabilities. Financial institutions exist to channel funds from savers to lenders by issuing securities and acquiring financial assets with the proceeds.

Money and Credit

Money is the most basic financial claim, the one in which all others are usually denominated. Changes in the supply of and demand for money have immediate impacts on the prices of other financial claims.

Money can be thought of as serving three functions: as a unit of account, as a means of payment, and as a store of value. In developed capitalist economies, money is used in all three ways.

Money's unit of account function must be regarded as the most fundamental. Indeed, it is hard to see how any but the most simple of societies could do without unit-of-account money. This function is central to quantification and measurement in economic affairs. Even in a barter economy it is highly convenient to identify at least one commodity which can be used in the calculation of exchange values.

Although it is convenient to have a commodity which can serve as a means of payment, it is possible to use money passively, as a unit of account without using it to settle transactions. In the early days of the colonialisation of America and Australia merchants would often buy the produce of farmers at agreed money prices and settle the debt not in cash but by providing goods of equivalent money value. (When the goods provided to a farmer amounted to a smaller monetary value than those bought from him the balance would be carried over as a trading balance or 'deposit'; on other occasions the balance of exchange would leave the farmer with an 'overdraft' with the merchant.) The problem in the colonies was not the lack of a money commodity — in practice, several different currencies were often employed — but the lack of an adequate supply of notes and coins in circulation. However, in modern times the supply of money has usually been adequate for transaction purposes. The only barrier to its employment as a means of payment has been where its value has declined at a very rapid rate.

Money is important as a store of value. The availability of a convenient store of value serves to promote saving. Households save in order to enhance future consumption; in effect, they forego current spending for future spending. If money is not a good store of value then they must acquire real goods now and exchange them for cash (to be spent on other goods) in the future, and incur two sets of transaction costs in doing so. The more stable the purchasing power of money, the lower are the risks of saving.

The importance of money stems not from its use as a unit of account but rather from its means of payment and store of value functions. In a certain world it is hard to see why money would be needed. A bookkeeping barter system, of the kind employed in the early colonies, would suffice. But in an uncertain world people cannot always be relied upon to complete exchanges at future dates — they might be dishonest, reckless or be struck by unexpected misfortunes. It is not possible to anticipate without error the timing and amount of one's future consumption needs; risks multiply greatly if saving has to be effected in the absence of a store of value which can be readily converted into purchasing power. The main function of money in a modern economy is to provide a generalised means of payment to meet and alleviate the problems of exchange under conditions of uncertainty.

Money can be defined in a variety of ways. The narrowest definition is usually termed M_0 and consists only of notes and coins in public circulation, banks' till money and the balances held in their accounts at the Bank of England. M_1 consists of notes and coins in circulation with the public, plus current account bank balances in sterling held by UK residents. (Government statisticians exclude notes and coins in banks' tills and a proportion of cheques in transit between banks, in order to obtain a measure of the money which is actually being used to facilitate exchanges.) M_3, a broader definition of money, roughly consists of M_1 plus time deposits at UK banks and the deposits of public sector entities such as local authorities. Even broader definitions are possible: PSL2 for example includes net deposits at building societies and trustee savings banks.

Although it is possible to be precise about the functions of money, it is far from clear in practice as to which assets should be included in the definition of money. There is a large number of assets which fulfil some but not all of the functions of money. Examples include land, antiques and old paintings which can serve as stores of value but are not means of exchange; luncheon vouchers and other tokens which can be used as (limited) means of exchange, and even as stores of value, but are not units of account; and bank deposits and short-term money instruments which are not media of exchange but can easily be turned into cash.

In the conventional definitions of money (e.g. M_1 and M_3) the criterion of inclusion is speed and ease of conversion of the asset into currency (notes and coins). All other assets vary in the extent to which they possess moneylike qualities, i.e. in their *liquidity*. Financial claims are usually more liquid than non-financial assets; but there are many exceptions. (Shares in private companies, for example, are less readily turned into cash than are precious metals, or even many property assets.) It is helpful for some purposes to array assets along a liquidity spectrum, with notes and current account balances at the most liquid end, through to specialised kinds of business equipment, at the other (illiquid) end.

The borrowing and lending process can be thought of in terms of individuals and organisations varying their liquidity positions. Lending involves the surrendering of a liquid asset in exchange for a less liquid one. Since money can be used to buy an enormous range of goods and services whilst a promise to pay money in the future may not be acceptable to existing owners of goods and services, giving up liquidity implies a loss of flexibility. This sacrifice on the part of the lender is usually recompensed by a promise from the borrower to return a greater quantity of 'money' in the future than was lent initially. In other words, loanable funds command a 'price', usually described in terms of a *rate of interest*.

The significance of the monetary system in general and interest rates in particular on the workings of the financial system is discussed at greater length in Chapter 4. The mathematics of interest is the concern of Chapter 5.

Financial Markets

Financial claims have much in common with other assets. In particular, they can be bought and sold in markets in essentially the same ways as cars or real estate. New issues of securities are made in *primary markets* and old issues are traded in *secondary markets*. The roles played by financial markets in the promotion of saving and investment are described in Chapter 3.

One obvious way of classifying the different UK financial markets is in terms of the liquidity of the assets traded. The conventional division is between the money markets where the more liquid financial instruments are traded, and the securities markets, which handle the issuance and trading of stocks and shares. (See Appendix A for a brief description of these markets.)

Financial Institutions

Financial institutions are often referred to as financial intermediaries. As the name implies, financial intermediaries exist to smooth the flow of savings: borrowing funds from those individuals and firms with excess funds and relending these funds to other borrowers. They exist because they supply a useful service at a low cost. Financial institutions differ in a number of repects — in the terms they offer to lenders, in the ways they invest and lend out their funds, and in the ancillary services they provide. The main intermediaries are commercial banks, savings banks, building societies, finance companies, insurance companies and investment and unit trusts. Brief descriptions are provided in Appendix B.

Impact of Government

Mention has already been made of the importance of the government sector as a major borrower of funds. There are three other important ways in which the Government affects the workings of the financial system.

Regulation
In the UK, although the financial markets and institutions have imposed some self-regulatory discipline on their own actions, there has been a number of Commissions of Inquiry into various aspects of their operations. Governments of all hues have been concerned with maintaining the public's confidence in the soundness and probity of the financial system. To this end, numerous Acts of Parliament and administrative arrangements have been brought into being. The banks and insurance companies, in particular, are closely regulated. Government regulation largely takes the form of direct supervision (e.g. by the Bank of England, the Department of Trade, the Occupational Pensions Board, and the Registrar of Friendly Societies), or

the prescription and prohibition by statute of various financial arrangements and transactions, or by requiring public disclosure of information.

Another area of long-standing concern has been over the ways in which the markets and institutions channel funds to industry and commerce. The government-sponsored Committee to Review the Functioning of Financial Institutions, which reported in 1980, was the latest in a long line of inquiries into the financing of industry. Various special financing institutions, subsidies and taxation arrangements have been instituted to try to influence in particular ways the flow of industrial finance.

Regulations have been instrumental in shaping the financial system, but not always in the ways intended by the regulators. Perhaps the most striking example of the influence of regulation is provided by the international (so-called 'euro') money markets which operate outside the nationally regulated financial market systems and whose spectacular growth is attributed by most observers to the desire to avoid regulatory restrictions.

Taxation

The UK taxation system has had a marked influence on the country's patterns of savings and investment over the years. The tax rules are not neutral: they have stimulated the flow of savings into certain forms of investment at the expense of others. Investments which seem to be of comparable attractiveness on a pre-tax basis can look very different when tax is taken into account. The influence of taxation on the development of the financial system is dealt with in later chapters, notably in Chapter 10.

Monetary and Fiscal Policies

Government attempts to influence the behaviour of the economy have direct effects on the financial system. A distinction can be drawn between monetary policy and fiscal policy. Monetary policy is concerned with controlling the money supply. Fiscal policy is concerned with the aggregate levels of expenditures and taxes. The significance for the financial markets and institutions of these macroeconomic policy decisions of government are analysed in Chapter 4.

Summary

It is helpful in understanding how valuable is a service or product, to consider what would occur in its absence. In this introductory chapter, we therefore first looked at a model of the economy without a financial system. We then discussed the functions of money within the financial system, before looking at the government's part in the functioning of the financial markets.

Further Reading

1. J. Irving, *The City at Work* (Andre Deutsch, 1981). Provides a simple, up-to-date introduction to the financial markets and institutions intended for those considering careers in the City. Other useful introductions are: W.M. Clarke, *Inside the City* (Allen & Unwin, 1979); H. McCrae and F. Cairncross, *Capital City*, 2nd edn (Eyre Methuen, 1984).
2. *Report of the Committee to Review the Functioning of Financial Institutions* (the Wilson Report, named after the Chairman of the Committee, Sir Harold Wilson), Cmnd 7937 (HMSO, 1980). A 'must' for all serious scholars of the financial system; contains a great deal of detailed information. The volume of Appendices is a valuable source of data on the individual institutions and markets. Chapters 1–4 provide a good review of the history and structure of the system; see also chapters 21 and 25 for details of the regulatory arrangements.
3. J. Revell, *The British Financial System* (Macmillan, 1973). Although now rather dated, still an excellent source of data. Part A (Chapters 1–4) provides a helpful review of the main features of the system.
4. S. Mason, *The Flow of Funds in Britain* (Elek Books, 1976). Chapters 1–2 provide a useful review of the main features of the system.

Discussion Questions

1.1   What is the relationship between saving and investment, on the one hand, and lending and borrowing, on the other?

1.2   In what ways are financial claims like other assets, and in what ways are they different?

1.3   What is a balance sheet? What can you learn about inter-sector financial relationships from sector balance sheets?

1.4   Try to recall the main monetary transactions you have been involved in during the past month. Analyse the steps you would have had to take if the economy was a barter-based (rather than monetary) one.

1.5   Describe the three main functions of money. Discuss how well or badly each of the following assets would serve as a form of money: (i) cigarettes, (ii) cattle, (iii) jewellery, and (iv) IOUs issued by a major company.

1.6   Explain the reasons why an increasing share of the savings of the household sector in the UK is being channelled through financial intermediaries.

Appendix A
Financial Markets

Money Markets

The money markets provide the means for channelling wholesale funds from lenders to borrowers. The markets are highly specialised and are the more-or-less exclusive preserve of a limited number of large banks and other financial institutions operating at the wholesale end of the financial markets. Money market securities are of large denomination (usually ranging between £5000 and £1 million) and are often traded in huge blocks. The money markets have no physical market-place, transactions being largely conducted by telephone and telex.

The money markets can be divided into the discount market and the parallel money markets. The main difference between the two markets is that lending in the discount market is 'secured' by the Bank of England, i.e. liquidity is guaranteed, whereas in the parallel markets it is not.

The *discount market* consists of the discount houses and certain other financial institutions. These institutions, such as Union Discount and Alexander's Discount, borrow sterling on an overnight basis or a 'call' (i.e. on demand) basis, mainly from the banks, and invest the funds in Treasury, commercial and local authority bills and various short-dated securities. As the discount houses are always prepared to buy or sell Treasury bills and to borrow on call the surplus cash of the banks, the market serves to guarantee the liquidity of the banking system.

The *parallel money market* is essentially a market in unsecured instruments, in which interest rates of different instruments move closely together. Funds are generally placed by brokers acting for clients (such as banks, local authorities, building societies and industrial and commercial companies). The parallel markets can be divided into those which deal with sterling instruments and those dealing in 'eurocurrencies' — a term for international short-term securities denominated in currencies of countries other than where they are issued.

The workings of the money markets are considered in greater detail in Chapter 6.

Securities Markets

Capital market securities can be thought of as instruments issued with maturity dates longer than one year. The Stock Exchange is the principal trading market for long-dated securities in the UK. There are three types of capital market securities: (i) public sector and foreign stocks (the so-called gilt-edged market), consisting of British government and government guaranteed stocks, stocks issued by UK local authorities and public boards, and those issued by Commonwealth governments and the Republic of Ireland; (ii) company securities, comprising UK corporate loan stock, preference and ordinary shares and warrants and options of various kinds, plus the securities of overseas companies; and (iii) 'eurobonds' of UK and overseas companies.

The economics of the Stock Exchange are dealt with in Chapter 7. Chapters 8 and 9 explore the pricing of bonds and shares, respectively.

Other Markets

There are a number of other markets which warrant the adjective 'financial'.

The foreign exchange market: an inter-bank market in foreign exchange in which business is conducted on a wholesale basis by banks in different financial centres throughout the world, usually through brokers. Foreign exchange is the business of buying and selling one currency against another. Business in this market is done exclusively by telephone and telex. Deals are either on a 'spot' (meaning for immediate delivery) or on a 'forward' (i.e. for completion at the currently agreed price on a specified future date) basis.

Lloyd's is an international insurance market in which general (i.e. non-life) insurable risks are placed with Lloyd's underwriters through Lloyd's brokers. It had its origins in a London coffee house owned by Edward Lloyd in 1688 where shipowners, merchants and others with maritime interests gathered to accept part shares in risks, writing their names one under the other (hence the name underwriters). Lloyd's is the world's main insurance market and deals with four main kinds of business risk, namely, marine, non-marine (fire, etc.), aviation and motor.

The London Traded Options Market gives investors the opportunity to buy and sell share options in about twenty named companies such as Marks and Spencers or Beechams. Two types of option are traded: a *call option* which gives the holder the right to *buy* an ordinary share at a specified price, and a *put option* which gives the holder the right to *sell* an ordinary share at the exercise price. Traded Options are further discussed in Chapter 9.

The London International Financial Futures Exchange is the newest of all the UK financial markets, having opened for business in September 1982. LIFFE provides a means of hedging and speculating against movements in currencies, in short- and long-term interest rates, and in eurodollar interest rates. In principle, financial futures are no different to commodity futures which have been traded for many years.

Appendix B

Financial Institutions

Commercial Banks

Banks can be divided into two main kinds: the *deposit banks*, such as Midland and National Westminster, which maintain extensive networks of retail branches and operate the payments and cheque-clearing system (hence the term 'clearing banks'), and are the organisations which most people have in mind when they think of banks; and the *secondary banks* consisting mainly of the accepting houses[1] such as Barings or Rothschilds and overseas banks, each having relatively few UK branches, being only marginally involved in operating the payments mechanism and concerned primarily with the wholesale end of the deposit-taking business.

Savings Banks

These consist of the Trustee Savings Banks (TSBs), which are unincorporated societies providing banking services to the personal sector, and the National Savings Bank (NSB), a government service operating through post offices and providing simple savings facilities directed towards the modest personal saver. Virtually all the NSB's funds are invested in government securities. The TSBs used to be closely aligned with the National Savings movement, but since the removal of government controls in 1976 they have been rationalising their activities in order to compete more effectively with the commercial banks.

Building Societies

Building societies borrow directly from the household sector and lend to individuals buying their own homes. Building societies are mutual associations, i.e. they have no shareholders and instead are owned by their depositors. Their practice is to borrow funds on a very short-term basis and to lend long. Mortgage advances are secured against the property being purchased and the risk of loss is low. Building societies compete with the deposit banks for funds and vary the interest rates they pay to their depositors accordingly. The great majority of mortgage advances are made on a variable rate basis and the rates are altered from time to time in order to keep them in step with the rates the societies are having to pay their depositors. There are over 250 building societies in the UK, but most are very small, and mergers are causing the total number to shrink very rapidly. Five societies[2] occupy a dominant position, having extensive branch networks and accounting for over 50% of the total assets.

---

[1]   A bank concerned mainly with 'accepting' commercial bills of exchange, i.e. acting as a guarantor of bills. A bank with a high reputation will lend great credibility to a bill, enabling it to be sold at the finest rates in the discount market. Accepting houses therefore serve an important function in the discount market; they are to be distinguished from the discount houses, which borrow money and invest the funds in the discount market in bills and other short-dated securities thereby providing liquidity to the rest of the banking system.

[2]   The five largest are the Halifax, Abbey National, Nationwide, Leeds Permanent, and the Woolwich Equitable building societies.

Finance Companies

These consist of the finance houses and leasing and factoring companies. Finance houses are primarily involved in the provision of medium-term instalment credit to industry and consumers, traditionally taking the form of hire-purchase and credit sales, but now extended to include personal loans and even to the provision of banking services. Some finance houses are owned by other financial institutions or by manufacturing companies. Leasing companies are in the business of leasing capital equipment to business firms and public sector organisations. Leasing is a means of financing the use, rather than the purchase, of an asset, thus distinguishing it from hire-purchase or credit sale. Many of the leasing companies are subsidiaries of other financial institutions. A factoring company advances cash to a company in exchange for or on the security of its book debts. Factoring takes various forms and may involve the collection and credit control functions associated with the receipt of payment. Many factoring companies are bank subsidiaries.

Insurance Companies

The activities of insurance companies can be divided into long-term and general insurance, with long-term funds accounting for over 80% of combined funds. Long-term business consists mainly of life assurance and pension provision. Policyholders pay premiums to the company and are guaranteed either a lump sum (with or without profits) in the event of subsequent death or at maturity, or a regular annual income for some defined future period. With guaranteed premium inflows and predictable (in aggregate) future payments, there is little need for liquidity, so life assurance funds are able to invest heavily in long-term assets (bonds, shares and property).

General insurance business consists of fire, accident, motor, marine and other insurance and consists of contracts to cover losses within a specified period, usually 12 months. As liquidity is of greater concern in general insurance, a greater proportion of funds is invested in short-term assets; nevertheless the majority of general funds is invested in securities and property.

Pension Funds

Pension Funds are institutions which accumulate funds in order to meet the future pension liabilities of a particular organisation to its employees. Funds are normally built up from contributions paid by the employer and by its employees. Funds can be divided into two types: self-administered schemes, where the funds are invested directly in the financial markets; and insured schemes, where the funds are invested by, and the risk is covered by, a life assurance company. Pension schemes have enormous and rapidly growing funds available for investment in the securities markets. Together with the insurance companies, they comprise the major purchasers of company securities.

Investment and Unit Trusts

Investment trust companies are limited liability companies which invest mainly in the ordinary shares of other companies. The funds at their disposal are 'closed' at any point in time, in the sense of consisting of shares and loans issued and retained profits — hence they are often described as 'closed-ended funds'. Unit trusts are 'open-ended funds' which also invest in the shares of companies: the term open-ended fund refers to the fact that the resources at their disposal can vary greatly in short periods of time, depending on whether cash is going into the trust from the sale of 'units' or is going out because subscribers are selling their units back to the trust. The main function of both investment and unit trusts is to provide vehicles for diversified investment: individuals of limited means can invest in a trust and obtain a much more diversified portfolio than they could hold for themselves.

Other

There is a considerable variety of institutions in addition to the main categories mentioned above. They include various public sector agencies, such as the 3i group which invests in a wide range of British businesses; the Scottish, Welsh and Northern Ireland Development Agencies, which are intended to promote investment and employment in these areas, and to do so can make available finance and provide guarantees; the National Enterprise Board, which provides finance for industrial investment; and the Export Credits Guarantee Department, a separate government Department set up in 1919 to encourage exports by providing credit insurance to UK exporters. In addition, there is a growing number of financial institutions in the private sector which exist to provide venture and development finance for companies.

―――――Chapter Two―――――

Flow of Funds in the Economy

This chapter is intended to serve two separate but interrelated ends. The first is to present quantitative data about the savings–investment process. The second is to explain simply the logic of funds flow analysis and how the official financial statistics are put together to enable the readers to make sensible use of these sources in their own work.

The flow of funds accounts are of recent origin. The United States set the lead in the development of this form of financial statistics in the early 1950s, an example followed by many other countries in the following years. The impetus in the UK was provided by the Radcliffe Committee in 1959, and sector flow of funds accounts have been published on a quarterly basis in the *Bank of England Quarterly Bulletin* since September 1963.

The flow of funds accounts are generally regarded as an integral part of the national income and expenditure accounts. Like the national accounts, the flow of funds analysis is presented for a few, highly aggregated sectors. The choice of sectors greatly affects the use that can be made of the analysis because any intra-sector flows are generally omitted and only those transactions which pass across sector boundaries are presented. The four main categories employed in the national income and expenditure accounts are: the public sector consisting of the central government, local authorities and public corporations; the personal sector consisting not only of households but, due to the limitations of the statistics, including also unincorporated businesses and charities; the company sector covering industrial and commercial companies, the banks and other financial institutions; and the overseas sector comprising the imports, exports and financial transactions with foreigners. As so much financial business is done through specialised financial intermediaries, these institutions are distinguished from the company sector in the flow of funds accounts to form two sectors of their own — the 'monetary sector' and the 'other financial institutions sector'.

Sources and Uses of Funds

Flow of funds accounting provides a means of tracing the financial transactions of the different sectors. It traces financial transactions by recording the receipts that each sector obtains from the other sectors and the payments it makes to them. In effect, the statisticians try to construct from the available data what accountants normally describe as a 'sources and uses of funds statement' for each sector. When the sources and uses of funds statements for each sector are integrated with each other, a flow of funds matrix is obtained for the economy as a whole.

A sectoral sources and uses of funds statement could be constructed in a variety of ways, depending on the concept of 'funds' chosen for the analysis. Perhaps the most obvious funds concept to choose is 'cash', meaning cash-in-hand plus bank balances. In which case, a 'cash flow statement' would be prepared for each sector, recording the cash receipts from and payments to other sectors. Borrowing would be recorded as a financial source and lending as a financial use of funds.

At the opposite extreme, funds could be defined as 'net assets'. Net assets are the excess of the value of all assets owned over liabilities outstanding and are equal to the 'net worth' (NW) of the sector. Any transaction that increases NW is a source, and anything that decreases it is a use of funds. Sources of NW are 'income' and (in the case of the business sectors) new inputs of equity finance. Uses of NW are in the payment of taxes, dividends and other transfer payments, and in consumption. Financial transactions concerned with the acquisition of financial assets or the incurring of financial liabilities are excluded because they have no impact on NW. This concept of fund provides the basis of the national income and expenditure accounts.

The funds concept employed in practice is 'net financial assets'. Net financial assets (NFA) are equal to money and other financial assets (FA) less financial liabilities (FL). NFA are wider in scope than cash but narrower than NW. They serve to place primary emphasis on the workings of the financial sector of the economy.

The connection between the flow of funds accounts and the national accounts can best be appreciated in terms of the sector balance sheet equation introduced in the previous chapter. At a point in time, the stock of assets under the sector's control consists of real assets (RA) and financial assets and is exactly equal to the sector's financial liabilities and net worth:

$$RA + FA = NW + FL \qquad (2.1)$$

Net worth is, of course, only a residual and can be written as such:

$$NW = RA + (FA - FL)$$
$$= RA + NFA \qquad (2.2)$$

NW can increase through time in one or both of two ways. Firstly, the sector can save some of its income (Y). Put slightly differently, the change in net worth (ΔNW) could be due to the excess of income over consumption (C). Secondly the sector could have received from other sectors dividends or other transfer payments (T). (Transfer payments consist of gifts and other payments made without any corresponding product or service being received.) Taken together:

$$\Delta NW = (Y - C) + T \qquad (2.3)$$

Increases in real assets (ΔRA) are described as real investment or simply as investment (I). (In the absence of replacement investment the value of the stock of real assets will decline through time. Investment in excess of that required for replacement purposes is called net investment. Replacement and net investment, taken together, are labelled 'gross investment'. For purposes of exposition, the distinction between net and gross investment is ignored below.)

We are now in a position to explain the change in balance sheet values during an accounting period. Subtracting the earlier balance sheet from the later one we get

$$\Delta NW = \Delta RA + \Delta NFA$$
$$= I + \Delta NFA \qquad (2.4)$$

By substituting the expression for ΔNW, using (2.3) and (2.4),

$$Y - C + T = I + \Delta NFA$$

and rearranging, the flow of funds (ΔNFA) can be seen to equal to

$$\Delta NFA = (Y - C) - I + T \qquad (2.5)$$

This can be expressed less formally in words as:

$$\text{lending} - \text{borrowing} = \text{saving} - \text{investment} + \text{transfers}$$

The reconciliation between the sector flow of funds and sector income accounts is thus completed. The 'real' magnitudes, savings and investment, obtained from the income and expenditure accounts serve as the starting point for the flow of funds analysis.

The reconciliation is performed at an aggregate level by collecting the sector sources and uses of funds statements into a flow of funds matrix for the economy as a whole. Suppose we are dealing with a simple case with three domestic sectors:

- the personal sector
- the company sector
- the public sector;

and a sector representing the rest of the world:

- the overseas sector.

Let Y_1 be the factor incomes earned by persons (wages and salaries, rent etc.), Y_2 company profits, and Y_3 the profits of public corporations, C_1 be consumers' expenditures and C_3 government expenditures on goods and services; I_1, I_2 and I_3 are investment expenditures of the three sectors; transfers (interest payments, dividends, grants and taxes) between sectors are denoted T_1, T_2, T_3, and T_4. Finally X and M are the aggregate exports and imports, respectively. The results are given in the top part of Table 2.1, each column representing a particular sector's flow of funds.

Table 2.1   Flow of Funds Matrix for the Whole Economy

	Personal sector	Company sector	Public sector	Overseas sector	Total
Income	Y_1	Y_2	Y_3	$-X+M$	$Y-X+M$
Transfers (net)	$+T_1$	$+T_2$	$+T_3$	$+T_4$	0
Consumption	$-C_1$		$-C_3$		$-C$
Investment	$-I_1$	$-I_2$	$-I_3$		$-I$
Financial surplus/deficit	ΔNFA_1	ΔNFA_2	ΔNFA_3	ΔNFA_4	0
Notes & coin	ΔMA_1	ΔMA_2	ΔMA_3	ΔMA_4	0
Treasury securities	ΔTA_1	ΔTA_2	ΔTL_3	ΔTA_4	0
Company securities	ΔCA_1	ΔCL_2	ΔCA_3	ΔCA_4	0
Totals	ΔNFA_1	ΔNFA_2	ΔNFA_3	ΔNFA_4	0

The inter-sector transfers sum to zero, as logic dictates they must. Similarly, the sum of the financial surplus and deficits is shown to be zero also, reflecting no more than that the financial liabilities of one sector must be the financial assets of another.

The final column of Table 2.1 can be rearranged into the conventional national accounting identity:

$$Y = C + I + X - M$$

This expression states nothing more than that national income is equal to domestic consumption and investment plus the balance of foreign trade.

The task that remains to be done in constructing a sector sources and uses of funds statement is to analyse the changes in financial assets and liabilities which go to make up the financial surplus or deficit for the period. Consider again the simple four-sector case. Suppose both the public and the company sectors issue financial claims. The change in government liabilities consists of treasury securities (ΔTL_3) and money, i.e. notes and coin. We do not distinguish between the different kinds of company sector securities, simply denoting them as ΔCL_2. These changes in liabilities have their counterbalancing changes in assets, ΔTA, ΔMA and ΔCA. The increases and decreases are shown in the bottom half of Table 2.1.

The changes in holdings of a particular kind of financial asset or liability sum to zero, as can be seen by reading across each row. For a particular sector, the changes in net financial assets can be decomposed into the changes in its holdings of the financial assets of other sectors and in the financial claims it issues.

The introduction of financial sectors causes no difficulties, and follows exactly the same lines as set out above.

The Flow of Funds Matrix

The Bank of England and the Central Statistical Office (CSO) publish a great deal of flow of funds data. In this section attention is concentrated on the all-sectors flow of funds matrix (officially designated the 'financial transactions matrix') reported annually in the 'Sector Financing' article of the June issue of the *Bank of England Quarterly Bulletin*.

The financial transactions matrix for 1983 is presented in Table 2.2. Although the table is larger and more complex than the hypothetical one shown in Table 2.1, the structure is the same. There are six sectors but, owing to data inadequacies, the monetary sector and other financial institutions are merged together in the top part of the table. The public sector is analysed further into central government, local authorities and public corporations in the first three columns; the matrix proper consists of columns 4–10. The top and bottom parts of the table reconcile in the sense that the numbers in line 5 tally exactly with those obtained by adding lines 39 and 40. The totals of each of the first five lines have their counterparts in the national income statistics prepared by the CSO. Each line in the financial assets and liabilities part of the matrix (lines 6 – 38) should of course sum to zero.

There are many deficiencies in the data used to compile the national income and flow of funds accounts. Government statisticians do not have access to bookkeeping systems containing complete records of all the financial transactions. Instead they have to make use of a great variety of sources of greatly differing coverage and quality. Gaps and errors of all kinds abound.

The residual error column and the balancing item row in Table 2.2 are the direct consequences of these data deficiencies. The figure for national income should be equal to that for national expenditure but, in practice, the two do not match. The unexplained difference constitutes the residual error.

The differences between the sector surpluses and deficits and the corresponding identified financial transactions are shown as balancing items for the various sectors. These necessarily add up to the residual error, and arise largely from the imprecise measurement of the national income and expenditure accounts. Hopefully, the financial transactions are of greater reliability than the sizes of the balancing items seem to warrant: for every financial asset there is a financial liability somewhere else and, where the data sources provide different numbers, those considered most reliable are used. It is therefore generally safer to use the figures for financial transactions (line 39) than those for financial surplus/deficit (line 5) as a measure of net borrowing or lending for a particular sector. The problem is particularly acute in the case of the company sector where the balancing item is £4 billion, i.e. almost two-thirds of the financial surplus.

An examination of the financial assets and liabilities section reveals a bewildering variety of financial claims being traded in the markets. The lines are grouped in order of the sector which issued the financial claims: the public sector, consisting of the various instruments issued by the central government and the securities of local authorities and public corporations; the borrowings and lending of the monetary sector and other financial institutions; the liabilities of the company sector; the private sector, limited to the net savings channelled into life assurance and pension funds plus miscellaneous domestic instruments; and investment flows into and out of the country. The final line (line 38), labelled accruals adjustment is a 'pseudo security' in the sense that it represents outstanding but not yet invoiced liabilities to income tax, interest, etc., rather than financial claims issued by a particular sector.

The table can be used to glean a number of interesting details about the flow of funds in 1983. The public sector is the biggest borrower, with a deficit of £11 billion to finance. The overseas sector is also a net borrower. The company sector, traditionally a net borrower, provided £2½ billion in 1983. The personal sector provided funds amounting to £10 billion for the year. It is helpful to examine each column in turn in order to ascertain the borrowing and lending profiles of the sectors.

Most of the public sector deficit is accounted for by the issuance of British government securities (line 8). The picture for the other big borrower, the overseas sector, is a bit more complicated: its deficit of £1¼ billion being the difference between two large items, namely acquisition of sterling time deposits (line 21.2) more or less offset by foreign currency borrowings from the banks (line 21.3), plus numerous other financial flows. Overseas flows are highly volatile from one year to the next and are responsive to interest and currency exchange rate differentials between countries. Personal sector savings are invested in a variety of instruments — most notably in the form of deposits in banks and building societies (lines 21 – 22) and in life assurance and pension funds (line 33). The personal sector borrowed £14.7 billion for house purchase (line 27). The company sector deposited £6 billion with the banks, offset by bank borrowings of nearly £3 billion and issues of new securities of £1 billion; outflows of company funds abroad were more or less exactly balanced by direct investment in the UK from abroad.

It can be instructive to read across the rows as well as down the columns. Of the £9.5 billion increase in issues of British government securities, 73%

Table 2.2   Flow of Funds Matrix 1983

	Line	Central government	Local authorities	Public corporations	Public sector	Monetary sector	Other financial institutions	Industrial and commercial companies	Personal sector	Overseas sector	Residual error
Capital account											
Saving	1	− 4,974	+ 2,650	+ 7,080	+ 4,756		+ 6,398	+ 24,835	+ 16,977	− 2,049	—
Taxes on capital and capital transfers	2	− 1,322	− 484	+ 618	− 1,188		− 335	+ 475	+ 1,048	—	
less:											
Gross fixed capital formation at home	3	− 2,458	− 2,886	− 8,098	− 13,442		− 5,704	− 15,103	− 11,441		
Increase in value of stocks and work in progress	4	− 435		− 451	− 886		− 85	− 3,528	− 571		
Financial surplus +/deficit −	5	**− 9,189**	**− 720**	**− 851**	**− 10,760**		**+ 274**	**+ 6,679**	**+ 6,013**	**− 2,049**	**− 157**
Changes in financial assets and liabilities *Assets: increase+/decrease−* *Liabilities: increase−/decrease+*											
Notes and coin	6	− 822			− 822	+ 129	—	+ 117	+ 583	− 7	
Market Treasury bills	7	− 154		+ 122	− 32	− 29	+ 75	− 47		+ 33	
British government securities	8	− 9,490	+ 18	+ 4	− 9,468	+ 229	+ 6,669	+ 353	+ 1,314	+ 903	
National savings	9	− 2,975	+ 2	+ 18	− 2,955		+ 11	+ 83	+ 2,861		
Certificates of tax deposit	10	+ 101		− 105	− 4	+ 33	+ 25	+ 78	+ 24		
Net government indebtedness to Banking Department	11	+ 157			+ 157	− 157					
Northern Ireland central government debt	12	− 12			− 12	− 7	− 1		+ 20		
Government liabilities under exchange cover scheme	13	+ 88	− 3	− 85	—						
Other public sector financing:											
Non-marketable debt	14.1	− 215		+ 322	+ 107	− 107	− 12				
Short-term assets	14.2		+ 15	− 1	+ 14			+ 8	+ 5	+ 1	
Issue Department's transactions in commercial bills	15	− 725			− 725			+ 725			
Government foreign currency debt	16	+ 37			+ 37					− 37	
Other government overseas financing	17	+ 100			+ 100					− 100	
Official reserves	18	− 603			− 603					+ 603	

Local authority debt:									
Temporary	19.1	+ 26	– 88	– 4	– 66	+ 83	– 45	– 27	+ 72	+ 17
Foreign currency	19.2	—	– 78		– 78					– 78
Sterling securities	19.3		+ 233		+ 233	+ 254	– 4		+ 24	+ 7
Other sterling debt	19.4	+3,678	–1,363	– 7	+ 2,308	–1,748	+ 156	– 37	– 365	+ 2
Public corporation debt:									
Foreign currency	20.1			– 101	– 101	+ 115				– 14
Other	20.2	+1,646	– 46	–1,364	+ 236	– 227	– 4		+ 15	– 20
Deposits with banks:									
Sterling sight	21.1	+ 11	+ 36	+ 44	+ 91	– 4,369	+ 324	+ 1,396	+ 2,138	+ 420
Sterling time	21.2	+ 13	+ 3	—	+ 16	– 8,590	+ 1,931	+ 2,086	+ 931	+ 3,626
Foreign currency	21.3	– 4	+ 10	+ 10	+ 4	– 22,020	+ 499	+ 1,834	+ 167	+ 19,858
Deposits with building societies	22					+ 694	–11,928	+ 740	+10,489	+ 5
Bank lending (excluding public sector):									
Foreign currency	24.1					+20,392	– 790	– 616	+ 73	–19,059
Sterling	24.2					+10,829	– 1,498	– 2,086	– 4,992	– 2,253
Credit extended by retailers	25			+ 21	+ 21			+ 140	– 161	
Identified trade credit:									
Domestic	26.1	– 5		– 508	– 513			+ 701		
Import and export	26.2	– 233		– 23	– 256			+ 75	+ 188	+ 181
Loans for house purchase:									
Building societies	27.1		– 292	+ 213	– 75	+ 3,597	+11,041		–11,041	
Other	27.2	+ 4	+ 5	+ 31	+ 470		+ 153		– 3,675	
Other public sector lending	28	+ 434						+ 60	+ 25	– 435
Other lending by financial institutions	29						+ 1,129	– 505	– 624	
Unit trust units	30						+ 608		+ 608	
UK company securities	31	– 515		+ 34	– 481	+ 60	+ 2,371	– 1,095	– 2,335	+ 1,480
Overseas securities	32	—		—	—	+ 2,773	+ 3,310	+ 580	+ 450	– 7,113
Life assurance and pension funds	33	– 58			– 58		–13,945		+14,003	
Miscellaneous domestic instruments	34	—					+ 101	+ 27	+ 74	—
Direct and other investment abroad	35					– 282	+ 3	+ 4,062		– 3,783
Overseas direct and other investment in United Kingdom	36	+ 566		+ 29	+ 595	– 209	– 143	– 3,880		+ 4,232
Miscellaneous overseas instruments	37				+ 740		+ 96	– 698		+ 199
Accruals adjustment	38	+ 960	– 459	+ 239		+ 4	+ 274	– 1,200	+ 182	
Financial transactions	39	–7,990	–2,007	–1,131	–11,128	+ 939	– 1,508	+ 2,582	+10,343	– 1,228
Balancing item	40	–1,199	+1,287	+ 280	+ 368	+ 843		+ 4,097	– 4,330	– 157

— nil or less than £½ million.

Source: *Bank of England Quarterly Bulletin*, June 1984.

was taken up by financial intermediaries. As might be expected, the lion's share (90%) of the additional foreign currency deposits with the monetary sector was accounted for by the overseas sector. Less predictable, almost half of the increase in sterling bank lending was taken up by the personal sector. The increment in company liabilities of £1.1 billion was augmented by personal sector net disposals amounting to £2.3 billion; other financial institutions increased their holdings of these assets by £3.3 billion.

A difficulty with a flow of funds matrix containing the amount of detail of Table 2.2 is that it is difficult to see the wood for the trees. It is possible to reduce the amount of detail by adding together some or all of the within-sector lines. An example is provided in Table 2.3. In this table each row represents the *net* increase or decrease in the financial claims issued by a sector and the net acquisitions or disposals of other sectors of the instruments created by that particular sector. A noticeable omission from the table is a line representing the claims issued by the personal sector; but there are no claims which 'belong' unequivocally to the personal sector, and the omission is not of great importance given that the sector is overwhelmingly composed of surplus units.

A number of features of Table 2.3 warrant comment. The extent of the public sector's reliance on financial intermediaries has already been noted; the aggregated statistics reveal it to be almost as dependent on the personal sector (mainly because of the latter's acquisitions of government securities and national savings deposits). The monetary sector borrowed heavily from companies and overseas in order to lend to the personal sector. Companies placed large amounts of money in financial institutions (monetary and other) and obtained funds from abroad.

A single funds flow statement affords limited opportunity to form views

Table 2.3   Financial Transactions Between Sectors, 1983

Issuing sector	Matrix lines	Public sector	Monetary sector	Other financial sector	Company sector	Personal sector	Overseas sector
				£ millions			
Public	6 – 20	– 11,674	– 1,940	+ 6,566	+ 1,081	+ 4,553	+ 1,414
Monetary	21, 24	+ 103	– 3,758	+ 466	+ 2,614	– 2,017	+ 2,592
Other financial	22, 25 – 30 33 – 34	– 411	+ 4,291	– 14,259	+ 1,118	+ 9,510	– 249
Company	31 – 32	– 481	+ 2,833	+ 5,681	– 515	– 1,885	– 5,633
Overseas	35 – 37	+ 595	– 491	– 236	– 516	—	+ 648
Accruals	38	+ 740	+ 4	+ 274	– 1,200	+ 182	—
Financial transactions	39	– 11,128	+ 939	– 1,508	+ 2,582	+ 10,343	– 1,228

Source: Derived from Table 2.2.

about the pattern of financing in Britain. To make sense of the data they have to be compared and contrasted with other pieces of information, related to trends over time, and so on. In the next section we identify some of the major features and patterns in saving and investment in Britain.

Financing Patterns in Britain

Since the mid-1970s saving and investment in Britain has fluctuated from year to year but has typically absorbed less than 20% of the Gross Domestic Product (GDP). Investment traditionally exceeded saving, the shortfall being financed by borrowing from abroad, but in recent years investment has exceeded saving resulting in outflows of capital. Saving and investment in Britain have been considerably lower than in countries like Japan, France and Germany, and slightly higher than in the USA.

The personal and company sectors have traditionally generated practically all the UK's savings, but the trends in the savings of each (expressed as a percentage of GDP) follow different patterns. Personal sector saving has been increasing steadily, from 6% in 1963 – 67 to 9% in 1978 – 82. On the other hand, the company sector's savings stayed constant (with fluctuations) at about 8% over the corresponding period. The difference in trends of the financial surpluses and deficits of the two sectors is even more marked: the personal sector's financial surplus as a proportion of GDP rose from 2% in 1963– 67 to 5% in 1978 – 82; the company sector, on the other hand, fluctuated from surplus to deficit, its average surplus in each period being less than ½% of GDP.

Personal saving has increased greatly over the major part of the last 20 years. In the period 1956 – 62 personal saving accounted for about 6% of personal disposable income. This had risen to 15% by 1980 (although it has fallen away since, being down to 11% in 1983). Much of this increase was invested in money assets such as cash and deposits. The increased investment in money assets seems to be due in no small measure to the need for households to maintain the purchasing power of their money balances in inflationary times. (As the prices of goods and services increase with inflation it is necessary to hold larger amounts of money to pay for them.) The fall in inflation since 1980 could explain the subsequent decrease in the personal saving ratio. Inflation is part of the reason for the increased spending on life assurance and pensions, but it is not the major reason since there are considerable tax advantages to this form of investment. Equity shares have traditionally been regarded as a good hedge against inflation, but nevertheless the personal sector has been a steady net seller of company securities for over thirty years — a reflection of the tax advantages accruing to investment in houses, life assurance, pensions and certain kinds of government securities, and the corresponding disincentive to investment in company securities which do not offer these tax benefits.

Undistributed income is an important source of company finance, but this has generally not been sufficient to fund the sector's investment in fixed assets and inventories. (Investment has been a fairly stable proportion of total funds over the years, except that there was a marked decline in inventories during the recent depression.) The shortfall in finance has been made up largely by bank borrowing, particularly in recent years. Issues of ordinary shares and long-debt account for a very small proportion of new finance; indeed new debt issues dried up completely in the mid-1970s.

A great deal of attention has been given to the Public Sector Borrowing Requirement (PSBR) in discussions about the management of the economy in recent years. It can be thought of as a measure of the finance raised by the public sector in the markets. The PSBR is equal to the sum of the public sector's financial deficit, its lending, and certain other financial transactions not connected with the authorities 'open market' operations. A clear picture of which financial transactions are included in the PSBR figure and which are excluded can be obtained from Table 2.2: if the elements in the public sector in Table 2.2 are summed for lines 6 to 20.2 inclusive it will be found that they total to the amount of the 1983 borrowing requirement, £11,674 million. An examination of Table 2.3 reveals that the PSBR is the net amount of claims issued by the public sector.

The PSBR accounted for $2\frac{1}{2}\%$ of the GDP in the period 1963 – 67 but this had grown to about 4% by the period 1978 – 82. The public sector's needs for finance far outstrip those of other sectors; as already noted, these needs are largely met by the issue of government securities. The impact of these operations on the capital markets is enormous, with trading in British government and UK local authority securities accounting for over three-quarters of the monetary value of all Stock Exchange transactions. Nevertheless, though the impact is considerable, the average value per *transaction* is much higher than for other securities. Thus public sector securities account for less than one-fifth of the *number* of transactions and an equivalently minor proportion of the market *value* of outstanding securities.

Unlike the other domestic sectors, decision-making in the public sector is highly centralised. The bulk of the sector's financial needs are raised centrally. For example, over the period 1976 – 80 the central government financed 85% of the PSBR. Although the public corporations account for about one-quarter of the PSBR their borrowings amount to only 5% of the total.

Projecting Credit Flows

The flow of funds accounts provide valuable data about what is happening in the financial markets. They are now widely used in the forecasting of interest rates. Official forecasts, in flow of funds form, are constructed jointly by the Treasury and the Bank of England several times a year. These forecasts provide a view of interest rates, monetary aggregates and the financial positions of the various sectors consistent with the national income forecast. Much work in this area is also done by economists employed in the financial community (stockbrokers, banks, etc.), and by academic researchers.

Interest is the price of credit (loanable funds). Like other prices, when demand for the product (credit) increases or its supply decreases, interest rates rise; and vice versa when the opposite conditions prevail. Forecasts of the components of the supply and demand for credit can therefore form the basis of forecasts of movements in interest rates.

The advantage of the flow of funds matrix is that it provides a means of keeping the component forecasts in touch with one another. Checks can be instituted for plausibility and consistency.

Summary

Flow of funds accounting provides a means of tracing the financial transactions of different sectors. We can see that the public sector has been the biggest borrower and that the personal sector has been the principal source of funds. By carefully examining the flow of funds matrix we can determine what kinds of financial claims are issued, by whom, and who takes them up. Not only is this kind of information useful in determining what is happening in the financial markets but it provides a basis for integrating forecasts.

Further Reading

1. A.D. Bain, *The Economics of the Financial System* (Martin Robertson, 1981). Chapter 1 provides a succinct flow of funds based analysis of the financial system. The analysis is extended to deal with the personal, company, public and overseas sectors in Chapters 6 – 9 respectively.
2. S. Mason, *The Flow of Funds in Britain* (Elek Books, 1976). As the title implies, flow of funds analysis serves as the basis for the author's examination of the financial system.
3. M.E. Polakoff and T.A. Durkin (eds.), *Financial Institutions and Markets*, 2nd edn (Houghton Mifflin, 1981). Concerned with the American financial system, but Chapter 2 provides an excellent (balance sheet oriented) explanation of flow of funds concepts. Chapter 25 examines the role of funds flow analysis in the forecasting of interest rates in America.
4. Bank of England, *United Kingdom Flow of Funds Accounts: 1963 – 1976* (May 1978). Provides a useful account of the official flow of funds accounts plus detailed time-series.

5. Central Statistical Office, *National Accounts Statistics: Sources and Methods* (HMSO, 1968). Provides detailed information on the methods used to compile the national accounts. For details of the financial accounts, see Chapter 14.
6. A.D. Bain 'Surveys in Applied Economics: Flow of Funds Analysis', *Economic Journal* (December 1973). An advanced treatment of flow of funds analysis.
7. M. Yanovsky, *Anatomy of Social Accounting Systems* (Chapman and Hall, 1965). Provides a useful comparison of the national accounting systems of different countries. Chapter 4 deals with flow of funds systems.
8. Central Statistical Office, *Guide to Official Statistics*, No.4 (HMSO, 1982). Chapter 14 provides a detailed guide to the numerous published statistics concerned with the business sector and the financial institutions and markets.

Discussion Questions

2.1 Explain what is meant by the term 'net worth'. What can cause net worth to increase or decrease? Why must the change in net worth be equal to the sum of real investment and net lending?

2.2 Must the actual real investment of an individual sector of the economy be equal to its saving? Show how, in the absence of an overseas sector, actual real investment for the whole economy must be exactly equal to its saving.

2.3 Account for why the creation of internally held debt makes no difference to the wealth of the country. What happens if some of this debt is acquired by foreigners?

2.4 Discuss the following statement: 'Since the financial deficits and surpluses of difference sectors must be exactly offsetting, it makes no difference if the deficit of one sector (e.g. the public sector) increases.'

Problems

2.5 Find the error in the following simplified matrix of financial transactions between sectors (ignore accruals and unidentified items):

		Sector		
		1	*2*	*3*
Issuing sector	*1*	− 38	+510	−472
	2	+120	+ 15	−165
	3	− 19	+ 62	− 43
Surplus/deficit		+ 63	+587	−680

2.6 Consider a simple three-sector economy, consisting of households, companies and banks. There is no government or overseas sector. Shown below are balance sheets assumed to have been drawn up at the beginning and end of 1983, for each sector.

	31.12.82	31.12.83
Personal sector		
Real assets	50	55
Bank deposits	140	160
Shares in firms	50	40
Shares in banks	160	160
	£400	£415
Net worth	£400	£415
Company sector		
Real assets	350	370
Bank deposits	60	60
	£410	£430
Bank loans	200	220
Net worth	210	210
	£410	£430
Banking sector		
Shares in firms	160	170
Loans to firms	200	220
	£360	£390
Deposits	200	220
Net worth	160	170
	£360	£390

Income for the personal sector consists of wages of £300 for the year of which £290 was consumed and £5 devoted to investment in real assets. The company sector earned £305 in sales revenues, paid out £300 in wages and the profit was paid over as dividends to the personal sector. The banks made a profit of £10.

Required: Prepare a flow of funds matrix for the year 1983.
Comment on the results.

2.7   Using Table 2.2 describe the main sources and uses of funds for the personal and company sectors, respectively.

2.8   Using Table 2.2, determine which sectors have financial surpluses and which have deficits in 1983. Identify the major acquiring and issuing sectors of the following financial claims: company securities; investment abroad; British government securities; loans for house purchase; bank deposits.

---Chapter Three---
Financial Markets and Institutions

In Chapter 1 we point out that one function of the financial system is to improve the business and consumption opportunities available to individuals and organisations. The use of money both as a unit of account and as a means of payment greatly increases the possibilities of mutually satisfactory exchanges of goods and services. By providing a cheap store of value, money also promotes saving. In turn, the existence of financial markets and institutions greatly expands opportunities to transfer consumption from one period to another in mutually satisfactory ways. Financial institutions and markets promote saving and investment by providing the means of saving, of gathering savings together, and of making them available to borrowers. In this chapter we identify how this process is meant to work and establish criteria for evaluating the workings of financial markets and institutions.

Conflicting Requirements of Borrowers and Lenders

Borrowers and lenders often want different things. The business and government sectors of the economy are generally net borrowers; households are net savers. Businesses borrow in order to buy capital equipment and property or to finance inventories. Government borrows in order to finance its deficits. Households save for a variety of reasons: to accumulate enough cash to meet large payments (purchase of a car, tax bills, holidays etc.) as they fall due; to transfer income through time (mainly to provide for retirement); to meet unforeseen events. Businesses and government are few in number, relative to households, and need to borrow large sums, often for long periods of time. A specialised building or heavy engineering unit might cost millions of pounds and have an expected useful life of ten to fifteen years. Similarly, roads and bridges are very expensive to build and last for many years. Sales and tax revenues which ultimately finance these investments stretch far into the future.

On the other hand, households are many in number and commonly save in very small amounts. An individual's life span is approximately seventy years, but the time available for saving is much less. The first twenty years are typically years of negligible income and little concern for the future. These are followed by years of increasing earnings accompanied, however, by heavy expenditure on homes and consumer durables. During this period the need by the family to spend money on consumption may also be at its maximum. Thus for many, long-term saving begins in earnest only when the children are grown up and retirement looms nearer. Because of this type of pattern in earnings and savings, the ability of individuals to plan their long-term savings will be limited. For those preparing for their retirement, long-term saving may be restricted to a period of less than ten years. For savings created to even out payment flows or for precautionary motives the horizon will be much shorter.

The problem is obvious. Many borrowers want to borrow large sums for long periods of time, whereas many savers accumulate funds in very small amounts and only want to lend for short periods of time.

Much business investment is risky in nature. Firms invest large sums in the development of new products which may either not materialise, or be too costly to produce, or for which demand may not be forthcoming. Similarly, unforeseen inventions might suddenly destroy the markets for newly established products, newly acquired foreign assets might be nationalised, and so on. Anyone who lends money to business enterprises has to recognise that all or part of the money might be lost.

Individuals might not be willing to take such risks. If their wealth is limited, they might be ruined by such losses. In the absence of mechanisms to bridge this risk gap, they are likely to prefer either to consume instead of saving or to keep their savings in less risky forms, such as cash or selected real assets.

Finally, lenders and borrowers can be kept apart because they perceive it unprofitable to do business. A saver can always keep his savings in cash; in doing so, the options to consume or to snap up more profitable investment opportunities are kept open. As long as the costs of protecting the cash from loss are negligible, savers will always demand a positive money-return from lending. (It is not necessarily the case that the expected return must be positive in real terms, i.e. when allowance is made for the expected changes in the purchasing power of money through time. The expected real return in inflationary times may often be negative. Although it may be possible to earn a positive real-return by buying real assets or even consumer goods which might be expected to maintain their real value in inflationary periods, the opportunities for this type of action are limited for small savers.)

The demand for funds depends on the relationship between the cost of acquiring funds and the profits which are expected to be earned by the borrowers. If the rate of interest rises, firms will be unwilling to maintain the volume of their borrowing unless the profits they expect to make from employing the borrowings also increase. The profits must be sufficient to pay not only the interest but the cost of searching out lenders (transaction costs). Transaction costs will be greater the more there are divergencies between the requirements of borrowers and lenders with respect to loan size, term to maturity and riskiness of the loan. In the absence of special mechanisms, a firm which wants to raise, say, £1 million, might have to collect £100 loans from 10,000 different households, with all the attendant advertising, postage and other expenses (including the opportunity cost of management time involved). Alternatively, the firm will have to compete with other firms with similar needs for the funds of wealthy savers, thereby driving up the rates of interest which these wealthy individuals are able to charge. (In equilibrium we would expect these two sources of loanable funds to be equally expensive, the extra transaction costs involved in the many-small-savers option being equal on average to the extra interest payable to the wealthy investors.)

The conflict between borrowers and lenders concerning the term to maturity of loans can be accommodated (at a cost) in one of two ways. Firstly, the firm can borrow money on a short-term basis, seeking new funds as and when the existing loans are repaid. Thus, if a firm wants to borrow a specified sum for ten years, it can borrow for two years on five separate occasions, each two years apart, using the proceeds on each new loan to repay the old one. The trouble with this procedure is that the firm will incur transaction costs on five separate occasions.

The other way of overcoming the maturity mismatch is by offering a much higher rate of interest for longer term loans. It might not be possible, of course, to obtain sufficient loanable funds of ten year maturity; but there might be takers for, say, five year loans. This would result in the saving of three lots of transaction costs. (Again, in equilibrium, the two methods would be expected to be equally expensive, on average.)

Lenders will have to be recompensed for the risks involved. If the funds are collected from small-scale savers in as large bundles as those individuals are able to offer, the savers will face the risk of losing their entire savings if the firm should be unable to repay its debt. The firm will have to pay very high interest rates on the loans to compensate the savers for the high risks-of-ruin they face. Should the firm be unwilling to pay this interest rate, it may attempt to seek out less risk-averse (perhaps wealthier) savers or to subdivide further the minimum size of the loans obtained from each investor. Heavy costs can be involved in either procedure, as already noted. The only alternative is for the firm to borrow money on a preferential basis, agreeing perhaps to protect the lenders from loss by offering specific security, such as a mortgage secured on some readily marketable asset of the firm (e.g. land and buildings).

It is the function of financial institutions and markets to afford means by which the above impediments to marshalling and using savings can be overcome or minimised. In the absence of such mechanisms the incentive to save and the means to invest are likely to be a good deal less.

Services Provided by Intermediaries

As we pointed out in Chapter 1, there is a considerable variety of financial institutions which exist to stimulate and smooth the flow of savings. They have all come into being either to take advantage of economies of scale in the financial process or to reduce the uncertainties (and hence the costs) of saving and investing.

Businesses can (and do) seek funds directly from the public by advertising.

They can and do approach individuals or other firms known to have excess funds. Both methods are expensive. It is necessary to know or to find out to what kinds of deals savers are most likely to respond. Acquisition of this kind of knowledge is not costless. Moreoever, firms do not need to raise new finance every day; they are intermittent acquirers of funds. In an institution-less world, savers will find themselves equally disadvantaged. Those with excess funds will have to look through advertisements or ask friends, and get in touch with the firms concerned. This is costly in time if not in money. If an individual has £50 which he wants to lend for one month then it might not be worth the effort. The existence of institutions to which savers and lenders alike can always turn is likely greatly to reduce the search costs incurred by both parties. If the institution is one with many retail outlets (high street branches) with whom one is in regular day to day contact, so much the better. Commercial banks are, of course, the most familiar financial intermediary, maintaining extensive networks of retail outlets.

The main services offered by financial intermediaries are:

■ *The collection and parcelling up of the savings of surplus units into larger loan packages for the deficit units.* (Banks and building societies take deposits of often very small amount from individual savers and make advances sometimes of very great amounts to individual or commercial borrowers.) In this process, the intermediaries can rely to a considerable extent on the assumption that the many small lenders will be unlikely simultaneously to withdraw their deposits; but the possibility cannot be discounted entirely. If for some reason, there is an abnormally large number of withdrawals, the intermediary has to be operating on a large enough scale to absorb the withdrawals. This can be done easily only if there are loans maturing frequently. If the intermediary is small, the risk of withdrawal can only be covered by keeping a large percentage of its funds in cash or other assets which can be quickly converted into cash.

■ *The transmutation of claims.* In other words, borrowing money on a short-term basis and lending long-term. (Perhaps building societies provide the most striking example of this transmutation function, borrowing effectively on demand and lending to home buyers on as much as a twenty-five year repayment basis.) Of course, the acceptance of funds for short periods does not necessarily imply that the funds will be withdrawn. Small savers are often not very sensitive to financial investment opportunities and tend not to switch their funds quickly from one institution to another. It is therefore quite possible for a short-term deposit to be left for a long period. Similarly the loans made on a long-term basis may well be repaid before they become due. In the case of building societies, borrowers will usually not stay in the same house for the full term of the mortgage; building societies therefore find that the loans are repaid in much less time than twenty-five years. In any event, the 'law of large numbers' applies to financial flows, withdrawals of savings being offset by the funds inflows provided by new depositors.

■ *Spreading of risk by taking (often small amounts of) savings from many different savers and lending to a variety (portfolio) of firms.* A small-scale saver could lend to no more than a single firm. If that firm defaults then all the saver's investment is lost. A bank can rely on the laws of probability virtually to guarantee that bad loans will be offset by good ones, thereby offering the saver a risk-free investment opportunity. (Various formal and informal insurance arrangements ensure that this low-risk investment is for all practical purposes actually risk-free.) To gain from economies of scale in this activity, the intermediary must lend or invest the funds in a range of businesses or activities. There would be no safety in an intermediary lending its funds to a number of firms operating in the same line of business. Intermediaries which do not attempt to spread their portfolios believe that their specialist knowledge of the markets in which they operate will enable them to obtain rewards that will more than compensate for the increase in risk. (An investor who lends to this kind of institution must do the diversification personally, or carry the risk.)

■ *Reduce transaction costs to borrowers and lenders.* As suggested above, intermediaries may attract funds simply by siting branches in locations through which potential customers are passing. One example of this is the use made of the Post Office by the government in borrowing from individual savers in the form of savings certificates and securities. The convenience and central location of Post Office branches may well have substantially reduced the transaction costs involved in financing the public sector.

■ *Provide insurance and financial advice services of various kinds.* Sometimes, the intermediary will offer a financial service merely as one way of attracting custom. In other cases, specialist agents set up in business with the express purpose of providing a service aimed to reduce the search costs of the individual. Thus there are insurance brokers who will advise on the range of insurance products or mortgage brokers who will arrange loans for individuals even in periods of 'mortgage-starvation'.

Primary and Secondary Markets

In a capitalist society the existence of financial markets can greatly ease the process of exchanging loanable funds for financial claims. A firm that wants to borrow money can go to the market in the knowledge that those with funds to lend will be there. The process is made easier still if specialist traders habitually attend the markets, buying and selling financial claims (loans) on their own account, thereby smoothing over days on which trading is thin or when there is an excess of potential borrowers or lenders.

Further economies are achieved if agents and brokers can be employed who will (for a commission) enter the market on the customer's behalf to buy and sell securities. If the brokers provide investment advice and can be contacted via branches or through intermediaries (e.g. a bank) so much the better. The market serves borrowers and lenders alike by reducing the search costs which each has to incur to get in touch with the other.

The market does not always have a physical location. A market for loanable funds might consist of nothing more than a list of known dealers who can be contacted by letter or telephone. The UK Securities Market (the Stock Exchange) is an example of a market which has both physical trading sites and a highly developed system of trading (see Chapter 7). The Discount Market is another traditional financial market (see Chapter 6), but one which operates without a physical site; representatives of the discount houses each day keep in close contact with the leading banks, either by telephone or personal visits, to ask whether each bank wants to lend or to call back money already lent.

A distinction needs to be drawn between two types of financial market. A *primary market* is a market which deals in 'new issues' of loanable funds. Transactions in primary markets result either in the creation or in the extinction of financial claims. The creation of a new loan causes the transfer of cash from a lender to a borrower in exchange for a financial claim on the latter. The claim is extinguished when cash (usually of greater amount than lent) has been repaid to the lender.

A *secondary market* is a market for 'old issues'. Transactions in secondary markets do not create or extinguish financial claims; cash does not pass between borrowers and lenders. What happens is that old issues change hands. The borrower remains unaffected by the transaction but the lender transfers his rights of repayment to another.

The main economic function of the secondary markets is to support the operations of the associated primary (or new issue) markets by providing liquidity to lenders. In the absence of a developed secondary market an individual saver might be very unwilling to lend out money for long periods of time (except at rates of interest no borrowers can afford to pay). Suppose the lender falls sick or becomes unemployed. If the lender has invested all his or her savings in an unmarketable interest-bearing bond maturing in ten years' time, there is no way of consuming anything other than the interest earned on the savings. However, if there is an active secondary market, the lender can sell the bond to someone else, thereby restoring his stock of liquid assets. There is no guarantee, of course, that the lender will receive back in sale proceeds the full amount: the proceeds may be greater or smaller, depending on the current prices of bonds of this type.

Secondary markets also contribute to the efficiency of the primary market by providing pricing information. In the share market, for example, the current prices of traded securities significantly reduce the problem of setting a price on new issues (i.e. primary market operations). Similarly, the provision of information from the secondary market will also influence the attitude of potential participants in primary markets (e.g. housebuilders may take close interest in reports of the demand for existing houses).

Figure 3.1 illustrates the connections between the primary markets and their associated secondary markets. Not all primary markets have associated secondary markets: securities are issued for which there are no secondary markets; the securities are not negotiable. On the other hand, for every secondary market there must exist, or have existed, an associated primary market.

The distinction between primary and secondary markets is not unique to financial markets. The same distinction can be drawn in the markets for physical goods. There is both a market for new and for used cars. In the primary car market, newly-manufactured cars are sold; in the secondary market, used cars are bought and sold.

It is possible for a physical good to be sold or a financial security to be

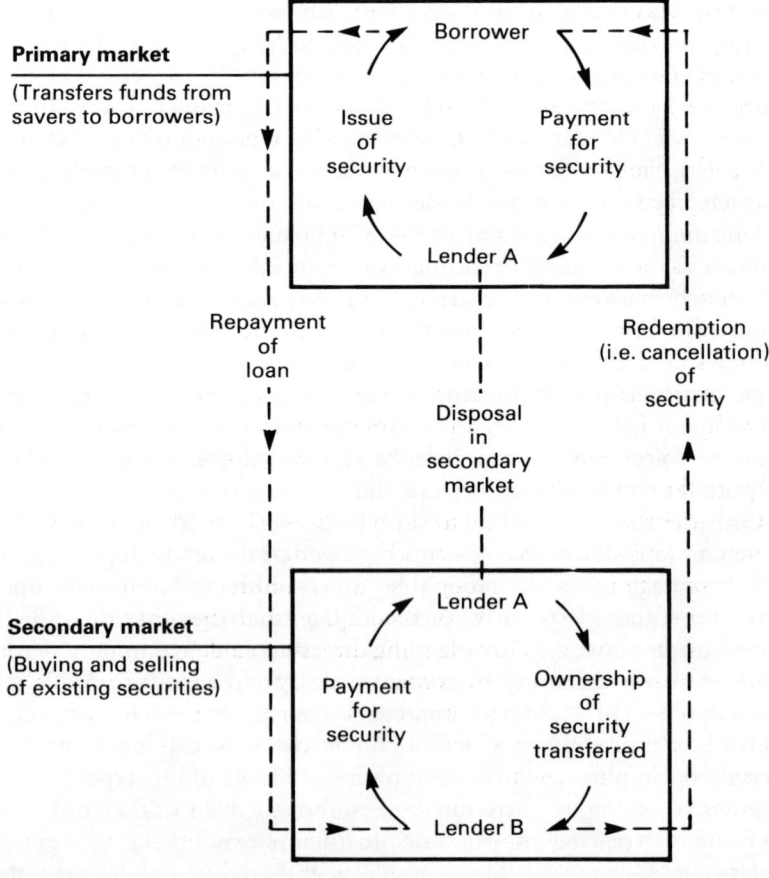

Figure 3.1 Primary and Secondary Markets.

issued in a primary market which subsequently (virtually or even completely) ceases to function, in the sense that new goods/new issues dry up. Striking examples are to be found in the markets for farm land and the paintings of old masters. The creation of new farm land is limited to countries still exploiting formerly unused land. In the UK, there has been a substantial and continuing loss of farm land to other uses: we might liken this to a negative primary market. With old master paintings, the primary market is by definition non-existent, although a few entrepreneurial artists might amorally rectify the lack of primary markets by forgery!

A similar phenomenon exists in certain financial markets. The primary market for corporate long-term bonds dried up in the 1970s in Britain, although old bond issues continued to be actively traded. The mismatch in activity levels of the primary and secondary markets for securities is not usually quite so marked, but it is considerable. Trading in new issues of ordinary shares, for example, is variable in frequency (and lumpy in monetary value). But trading in old corporate issues is very active; though the monetary value of money transactions is not always very great, on average about one-sixth of ordinary shares changes hands in a year. Trading in British Government securities is very active, in both the new and old issue markets. Turnover in old British Government securities in 1981 amounted to over twice the market value of the stock outstanding.

Some confusion surrounds the economic function of the secondary markets. The fact that much trading occurs in these markets, sometimes in circumstances where the associated primary market appears to be defunct, often leads journalists and others to conclude that the activities of these secondary markets are bringing about a misallocation of resources. The observation that pension funds, for example, invest very large sums of money in old issues of shares or empty buildings has led to the charge that these institutions are 'letting industry down' by not investing these monies *directly* in industry (via the primary markets for corporate finance). However, problems such as these are rarely as simple as they are represented by popular commentators.

Consider the choices open to savers who wish to invest. They can lend the money to an institution, such as a bank, or they can invest it in the markets. The first option can be thought of as an indirect way of investing in the markets, so we will set it to one side. Consider the market option. Here a saver has the choice of either lending directly to a deficit unit via the primary markets or of purchasing an existing security in the secondary markets. If he buys an old security then the previous holder of the security will receive cash which he can use either to spend on consumption goods and services or to plough back into the financial markets. Only if the money is spent on imports or in the acquisition of foreign assets are the proceeds lost to the economy. (Even then the loss may be a temporary one, to be offset later by orders from abroad for British goods to be paid out of the import proceeds, or by dividends.)

In a monetary economy, the distinction between saving and investment (via lending) is a real one. Savings can always be held in the form of cash and cash-like assets (e.g. precious metals). To lend is to forego liquidity. In order to stimulate long-term lending it is necessary to provide the means by which lenders can restore liquidity without calling in their loans. This is the function of the secondary markets.

Desirable Characteristics of Markets

Whenever funds change hands as a result of voluntary exchanges, financial markets can be said to exist. But some markets function better than others. It is helpful to have criteria which can be used to evaluate the efficiency of markets.

Primary Markets

The most pressing need of users of primary markets is that they should be able to do business with each other at *low cost*. If dealers' commissions and stamp duties, for example, are a significant proportion of the funds borrowed then the effective rate of interest paid on loans will be very high, thereby reducing the demand for loanable funds. So one test of the economic value of a primary market is the average proportion of the borrowed funds consumed in transaction costs.

Another way in which a primary market can help is if it is tied to a secondary market and so *provides negotiable securities*. The main value here is in minimising the interest compensation sought by lenders.

It follows that a primary market should operate in such a way that it *minimises disruptions to the secondary markets*. Suppose each new issue of loans caused dramatic falls in the prices of old issues, perhaps because each new issue more than marginally increased the total stock of a particular type of security. The effect of new issues might then be to decrease the price and hence the liquidity of old issues; but it is the liquidity of old issues which encourages lenders to subscribe for new issues. Following this line of argument, it would seem to be desirable that the secondary market's transactions be much greater (in value and volume) than the primary one's.

Finally it is desirable that the primary market should operate in such a way that *savings are directed to the most productive firms* (be allocatively efficient). This is desirable from the viewpoint of lenders, obviously, because they want to maximise the returns and minimise the risks of lending (more accurately, they seek optimum trade-offs between return and risk). Faced with dealers who, by accident or design, have a habit of putting them in touch with firms which yield low returns or default with excessive frequency, investors will either take their funds elsewhere, increase the interest compensation they require, or impose severe restrictions on the kinds of business in which they will invest.

It is also desirable from a social point of view that savings should flow to the most productive firms. The problem gets more complicated when viewed from this angle because the definition of productivity from a social perspective may be different from that taken by lenders. Lenders may not care whether the firms to whom they lend are monopolists, pollute the atmosphere or engage in illegal activities, but other groups in society might. It is possible for there to be conflict between the objectives of the individual decision makers and the wishes of society. The problem can even exist within a group of investors: pension funds, for example, invest money in order to provide pensions for their members but may find that some of their members demand that the funds are not invested overseas or in a competing firm in the same sector. Whilst these decisions may, if sufficiently widespread, affect the relative issue costs, it is not clear that the result should be interpreted as being allocationally inefficient.

There are very definite limits to the extent to which it is possible for markets to bring about the optimal allocation of funds. Mistakes occur because of ignorance. Ignorance can be reduced, but only at a cost. Beyond a certain point, it is not worthwhile obtaining more information about potential borrowers; the extra benefits are less than the additional costs. It is often not worthwhile acquiring new information because market prices reflect the information known to different transactors. This process is greatly facilitated by the existence of a secondary market; in these circumstances the condition and prospects of borrowers will be monitored on a regular basis.

Secondary Markets

The purpose of a secondary market is to enable holders of securities to convert them into cash without undue loss. This is most likely to happen if the market is an active one. There are two ways of viewing 'activity':

■ In terms of the *depth* of the market. This refers to how closely bunched the buy and sell orders for a security are around the last sale price. A 'sell order' is an instruction from the owner of a security to a broker to sell. In some cases, this order will be conditional on the security climbing above a specified price. A 'buy order' is an instruction to buy. Again this may be conditional on the security price falling below a specified level. Suppose the last trade occurred at £105 and there are ten buy orders between £103 and £104, and five sell orders between £106 and £107. The price cannot decline much below £105 before a buy order prevents it falling further; and it cannot rise very far before sell orders come into effect. A deep market ensures that prices are not too volatile.

■ In terms of the *breadth* of the market. A market is said to be broad when there is a large number of different types of investors buying and selling securities. The reasoning here is that a broad market is unlikely to be characterised by marked excesses of buy or sell orders because different investors will have various reasons for transacting and will form different expectations. A broad market should exhibit less price volatility.

Price volatility is undesirable to the extent that it increases uncertainty about the eventual pay-offs from holding securities. Risk-averse savers will tend to prefer to hold short-maturity instruments rather than rely on having to sell long-dated ones in a very volatile market. Thus the availability of deep, broad secondary markets helps to bring savers and lenders together. Nevertheless, there are limits to the possibilities of reducing price volatility: new information is bound to result in price movements — who would pay the same amount for a bond paying 5% per annum as a newly issued one offering 10%?

Another important consideration is the *efficiency* of the workings of the secondary market. Three aspects of efficiency can be identified: *allocative efficiency, operational efficiency* and *information-processing efficiency*. Allocative efficiency has already been discussed. Secondary markets are not directly involved in the transmission of funds from savers to borrowers, so it does not make strict sense to talk of the allocative efficiency of the secondary markets. Nevertheless, a secondary market can make a difference to the allocative functions of the primary market in two ways: by not disrupting the smooth workings of the primary market, and by providing a better and more regular flow of information to lenders about the current conditions and future prospects of borrowers. This boils down to arguing that the secondary markets should be operationally and informationally efficient.

A market is said to be operationally efficient when there is only a small difference between the net proceeds from selling a security and the total cost of buying the same security. Dealers in securities make their living by trying to buy securities for less than they sell them for. At a particular moment, a dealer will quote a buy–sell *spread*. The more active the market, the less the spread will be. Brokerage costs are incurred by all buyers and sellers of securities: the brokerage costs of a purchase have to be added to the buy price in determining the total acquisition costs; the brokerage costs are deducted from the sale price to get the net sale proceeds. The greater the difference between gross acquisition costs and net sale proceeds, the more expensive it is for lenders and borrowers to do business in the primary market, or for holders of old securities to restore liquidity without loss in the secondary market. Spread and buy–sell brokerage costs, taken as a proportion of price, provide another measure of the efficiency with which securities can be converted into cash.

Information-processing efficiency refers to the extent to which the prices of securities reflect what is currently known about the likely future pay-offs from investing in those securities. In a market which is fully information-efficient all buyers and sellers must bargain on an equal footing. Some investors might be more informed than others, but they cannot use this to their advantage (and to the disadvantage of the less informed) because the prices of securities fully reflect everything which is currently known. By contrast, in a market which is information-inefficient the informed investors can take advantage of the uninformed and reap abnormal gains in the process. An example of information-inefficiency would be where someone knew that a particular company was about to announce the discovery of valuable mineral deposits when others did not; this individual could buy the securities of the firm in question from unsuspecting holders in the confident knowledge that the price would shoot upward after the announcement. In an efficient market, information gets to the market and is absorbed into the price structure through the actions of all the participants in aggregate; there is no monopoly of information.

In an active securities market there will always be individuals on the look-out for opportunities to make abnormal profits. Their operations can be relied upon to promote the information efficiency of the market. Of course, if transaction costs are considerable then differences in prices can exist which cannot be traded away. Information efficiency is thus tied up with operational efficiency.

These criteria are essentially static in nature. The workings of the primary and secondary markets are considered at a point in (or over a short interval of) time. From a dynamic viewpoint, it would be interesting to consider the ability of the financial system to adjust to changes in external circumstances, such as changes in the tax system; the creation, alteration and dismantling of exchange control regulations; alterations in patterns of savings and investment over time; the impact of international economic shocks (the sharp rise in the price of oil in the mid-1970s, defaults on debts by one or more countries, etc.). A financial system which is capable of adjusting to changes such as these, if necessary by introducing new markets and institutions, without major disruptions to the savings transmission process, must be judged to be dynamically efficient, regardless of its static efficiency.

Hedging, Diversifying and Arbitrage

Financial institutions and markets are the products of uncertainty. In a certain world, there would be no need for a financial system as such. Money would be needed only as a unit of account; it would not be required to serve as a means of payment nor as a store of value. Everyone would know about everyone else's circumstances, opportunities and future actions. Transactions could take place on a credit or bookkeeping basis. Investment could take place without fear of loss. Saving would take account of the prices which are certain to prevail in the future, in the knowledge of future lifespan, circumstances and wants of the saver. But uncertainty changes everything.

Financial institutions and markets provide the means with which individuals can try to cope with uncertainty in a capitalist economy. Risk cannot be avoided entirely as far as society is concerned, but it can be reduced or shifted from one individual to another.

Certain risks can be eliminated by *pooling or diversification*. This aspect of risk avoidance is summed up in the old saying, 'don't put all your eggs in one basket'. Instead of putting all one's savings into the securities of one firm, an investor can spread his savings across a variety of businesses. If his funds are insufficient to do this, he can invest in a firm which itself has very diversified business interests, or in a unit trust which collects the savings of many small-scale investors and puts the funds into a diversified portfolio. A bank is another such institution providing diversification services, and so are pension funds and insurance companies. The financial system provides many and varied means of avoiding diversifiable risks.

Not all risks are diversifiable. The profits of firms move together, to some considerable extent, through boom and slump, and therefore variations in their profits and cash flows cannot be offset entirely by diversification across a portfolio of firms. Ultimately, the common movements in profits and share prices of firms are traceable to interdependencies between parts of the economy and between the economies of different nations. The fortunes of whole nations can be destroyed by war or bad harvests. The collapse of the international banking system could bring about the destruction of international trade. These risks can be shifted from one individual to another, but they cannot be removed entirely.

The financial system provides many opportunities for shifting risks. Examples include:

- The issuance of different classes of securities. In addition to raising ordinary share capital, a firm can issue fixed-interest-paying bonds, the security of which might be guaranteed by pledging assets. The fixed interest charges and prior claims of the bondholders make the ordinary shares more risky. The effect is to shift virtually the whole of the risk of the business on to the shareholders. The ordinary shareholders will of course be expecting extra returns, compared to the bondholders, to compensate for the extra risks carried.

- The creation of 'futures' markets. A British businessman has to settle a large debt in America in dollars in three months' time and is worried about the dollar–sterling exchange rate moving against him in this period. He can 'hedge' (or protect himself) against this outcome by purchasing a futures contract that will reflect changes in the exchange rate. Thus if the rate of exchange moves against him, his futures contract will rise in value so that when sold, he will receive sufficient dollars to settle his debt. If, on the other hand, the exchange rate moves in his favour, the futures contract will fall in value but this will be offset by the increase (in dollar terms) of the value of his sterling assets. Overall, therefore, the hedging operation will minimise the risk of exchange rate changes.

There are limits to the possibilities of hedging and diversifying, limits which are themselves the products of uncertainty. Uncertainty which takes the form of *asymmetry of information*, i.e. where one party knows more than another, can result in *moral hazard* (i.e. a temptation to cheat on a bargain) and *adverse selection* (e.g. a tendency for only poor risks to seek insurance cover).

For example, a risk-averse individual might want to insure against all risks of loss of property (e.g. against losses caused by fires, thefts, accidents) but would be unable to find an insurer willing to write all the contracts involved. If an insurer covers all risks the insured has no incentive to take care, so the insurer will accept only part of the losses. Similarly, a company will find that there are limits to the amounts of capital it can raise in the form of bonds: buyers of the bonds will be afraid that if the amount of debt gets too high then the chances of their being able to get their money back in the event of bankruptcy are greatly reduced; this risk is increased in hard times because, as the company's troubles worsen, the prospect of any gains accruing to shareholders diminishes, everything going to bondholders, giving manager–shareholders little incentive to give of their best.

Transaction costs limit the scope of the market as well. As transaction costs increase, the incentive to issue and to take up new securities, or to create new kinds of securities, diminishes. Transaction costs are themselves largely the products of uncertainty, for they arise in large measure from the need to seek out information. Financial markets and institutions create information, but information costs money, so there are limits to the gains from further extension and elaboration of the financial system.

Transaction costs impede the equilibriating process. Equilibrium is achieved when identical securities (meaning those securities offering the same average returns and the same risk) sell at the same price (the 'one price' law). If two securities are identical in all respects other than price then one would anticipate there being a demand for the cheaper of the two. In equilibrium excess demand will be zero. The process which brings about this equilibrium is *arbitrage*. Prices are out of equilibrium when profits can be made from 'arbitrage profits'. Suppose there are two securities, A and B, both offering £10 p.a. in perpetuity, but A sells for £100 and B for £80. An investor could buy one unit of B and thereby acquire an annual income of £10. But he could also sell one unit in A, thereby taking on the liability to pay an annual income of £10. The net annual cash flow would therefore be zero, yet the investor has paid out only £80 for B and received £100 for A. He has made an immediate arbitrage profit of £20. This arbitrage profit would disappear, however, if the transaction costs involved in selling the unit of A and buying B exceeds the £20 difference in price between the two securities. Transaction costs can cause a breakdown in the 'one price' law.

Criticisms of the City

There are many impediments to the transmission of savings; but left to their own devices, borrowers and lenders are able to find ways of doing business together. Incentives exist to set up financial markets and intermediaries which greatly smooth the financing process. Government tries to assist in a variety of ways: by providing an effective system of property rights; by maintaining a sound monetary system; by controlling operations in ways designed to maintain lenders' confidence in the financial markets and institutions; by insisting that companies provide shareholders and other investors with audited financial statements. The net result of these private initiatives and government support is that Britain possesses a financial system of great size and complexity, one offering diverse means of putting the nation's savings to work.

The economic ideal is a system of *perfect* and *complete* markets. In a perfect market, all participants are equally informed and all are price-takers (i.e. they cannot, by their own individual transactions, influence the market price); there are no impediments to the smooth working of the market, e.g. no transaction costs or taxes. Furthermore it should even be possible to sell the good or service 'short', e.g. in many stock markets, investors can sell shares which they do not own, with the intention of buying them later before delivery. Markets can be described as complete when all sources of income can be traded, where it is possible to arrange one's affairs such that one can bear as much or as little risk as wished, and where it is possible to borrow and lend as much as required to achieve one's desired pattern of consumption through time. Where markets are perfect and complete, all individuals can get the most benefits from their endowments of wealth; but when there is *market failure*, restrictions on contracting exist and fewer combinations of consumption patterns are possible.

The analysis in the preceding sections of this chapter might lead the reader to believe that the operations of the City are universally regarded with favour. But the markets are neither perfect nor complete. Many criticisms of the UK financial system have been voiced and numerous changes and reforms have been proposed. Some concern the way in which the major investing institutions are rapidly acquiring large share-holdings in British industry; this is taken up in Chapter 10. Another concerns the Stock Exchange trading system; see Chapter 7. We also deal in Chapter 7 with the problem of the regulation of the securities markets, another area which has attracted much attention in recent years. But the two most serious criticisms deal with the provision of finance for industry.

It has been argued that the financial system is, in effect, biased against small businesses. The Macmillan Committee pointed out in 1931 the difficulties which small firms often encounter in raising finance. The difficulties which have most frequently been cited are (i) the inability of small firms to go to the capital markets and (ii) the possibly excessive caution displayed by the banks in assessing the risks involved in lending to new businesses. The issue was taken up again by the Wilson Committee, and the Committee made a number of recommendations (see Cmnd. 7503, March 1979), including the establishment of a Small Firm Investment Company and the creation of a publicly underwritten loan guarantee scheme.

There are two ways of viewing this problem. One is to treat the (alleged) bias against small businesses as an instance of 'market failure'. The market could be failing in either one or both of two senses. It could be that small businesses are being charged more for loans than is commensurate with the risks and costs involved. However, there is no evidence that financial institutions which do provide finance to small firms make excess profits from doing so. In any event, it is hard to see how such excess profits could continue: other institutions would simply move into the field.

Market failure could perhaps be argued to take the form of small businesses conferring 'external' benefits on society, e.g. in the form of creating jobs, preserving local communities, promoting innovation. As these benefits would, presumably, accrue to others and not to the small firm generating them, they would not be reflected in the firm's profit and hence would not command a price in the financial markets.

Another argument is that the tax system currently distorts the allocation of funds away from the business sector, and from small firms in particular, into pension funds, building societies and similar financial institutions; so countervailing 'favouritism' is called for. Special provision for small business financing would be one such countervailing force.

An alternative way of viewing the concern over the 'Macmillan Gap' is not as an instance of market failure, but as the expression of a desire to further the welfare of small-scale business proprietors as a social class in preference to that of others. In short, a transfer of wealth (in the form of subsidies) is being proposed.

This line of thought brings us to the second major line of criticism which has been advanced against the City. This criticism centres on the distribution (and locus of control) of wealth in society. Financial markets and institutions exist to facilitate the exchanges and transformation of claims to wealth, and as such respond to the wishes of the owners of property. The complaint here is not that the financial system is 'inefficient' but rather that its behaviour is not in accordance with the wishes of the property-less classes. Proposals have been made by the Labour Party: to control certain forms of wealth (e.g. by directing insurance companies and pension funds to invest via a National Investment Bank in British industry[1] and in government securities); to limit the outward flow of capital (which is

---

[1] For a detailed consideration of this proposal, see the 'Note of dissent' attached to chapter 20 of the Wilson Report signed by the chairman and the union members of the Committee to Review the Functioning of Financial Institutions.

likely to occur when a future Labour Government tries to socialise aspects of the economy) by the reimposition of exchange controls; to bring certain financial institutions (e.g. the clearing banks) into public ownership; and to redistribute wealth via taxation.

Summary

Financial markets and institutions match together the requirements of borrowers and lenders in a variety of ways: by reducing transaction costs; by transmutation of claims; by spreading risks; by providing insurance and financial advice; by providing liquidity and information; by enhancing consumption and investment possibilities; and by making possible risk-sharing and risk-shifting.

Further Reading

1. J. Revell, *The British Financial System* (Macmillan, 1973). Chapters 3 and 4 provide useful factual detail about the markets and institutions.
2. A.D. Bain, *The Economics of the Financial System* (Martin Robertson, 1981). Chapters 1, 3 and 4 provide a rigorous account of the economic theory of financial systems, and chapter 15 'scores' the UK system against a variety of economic criteria. Prior exposure to economic theory is called for.
3. *Report of the Committee to Review the Functioning of Financial Institutions* (the so-called Wilson Report, named after the chairman of the Committee, Sir Harold Wilson), Cmnd. 7937 (HMSO, 1980), Chapters 3 and 13. More up to date than Revell.
4. M.E. Polakoff and T.A. Durkin (eds), *Financial Institutions and Markets*, 2nd edn (Houghton Mifflin, 1981). This book is over 700 pages in length and provides excellent coverage of virtually every aspect of the American financial system. Chapters 1, 12, 31 and 32 deal with the theoretical aspects of institutions and markets.
5. E.V. Morgan *et al.*, *City Lights: Essays on Financial Institutions and Markets in the City of London* (Institute of Economic Affairs, 1979). Consists of four papers dealing with the savings process; efficiency of the capital market; the commodity and future markets; the international markets. Very readable.
6. Labour Party Financial Institutions Study Group, *The City: A Socialist Approach* (Labour Party, 1982). A clearly argued critique of the British financial system from a socialist perspective.

Discussion Questions

3.1   What is the distinction between a primary financial market and a secondary market? Is it possible to have a primary market without a secondary market? A secondary market without a primary market? Give examples.

3.2   Discuss what is required for a secondary market to function well.

3.3 What is the relationship, if any, between financial intermediation and economic growth?

3.4 Discuss the following statement:
"Financial institutions provide means of minimising the costs of collecting information and of dealing in the financial markets. If these costs were the same for all, then there would be no need for financial institutions; a system of financial markets would suffice."

3.5 The cost to a firm of raising new finance can be broken down into two elements: the interest charged (or profit expected) by the lender and issue costs (including stamp duties). The net return to a lender consists of the interest charged to the borrower, less (i) any tax deducted from the interest and (ii) costs incurred in making the loan. Explain the ways in which economic forces can be expected to equalise: (a) the total costs of all sources of finance to a particular firm; (b) the net returns which a lender can expect to get from different investments (of the same riskiness).

3.6 Explain the significance of 'depth' and 'breadth' of a market. Give examples of markets which you think are likely to score poorly in terms of depth and breadth.

3.7 Explain the distinction between allocative efficiency and information-processing efficiency. Is it possible for the financial markets to be judged to be allocative efficient but not informational efficient, or vice versa?

3.8 How highly would you rate the market for home-purchase loans (mortgages) in the UK, in terms of allocative, operational and informational efficiency?

3.9 Suppose two individuals have inherited £1000 each. One individual is very risk-averse, and the other is by nature a gambler. Outline some of the ways in which these two individuals might invest their money, and the ways their choices might differ. How different would your answers be if each inherited £100,000, rather than £1000?

3.10 Discuss the following statement:
"We have seen how the financial institutions derive substantial power from their ability to provide or withhold funds from different activities. This power has a political dimension in that it enables the institutions to influence government policy through the markets for government debt and foreign currencies, and through formal and informal channels. The interests which the City defends by these means are identified with high interest rates, a high and stable exchange rate, free movements of capital and an environment of what the financiers would call 'political stability'. These interests run counter to the needs of industry and employment; and there is substantial evidence that the poor performance of UK industry is due in part to the dominance of financial interests over policy making." (Labour Party Financial Institutions Study Group, *The City: A Socialist Approach*, Labour Party, 1982, p. 22).

Chapter Four

Money, Credit and Interest

The purpose of this chapter is to consider some of the ways in which macroeconomic factors influence the workings of the financial system.

The Creation of Money and Credit

Phrases like 'the government prints money' are commonplace in financial circles and they can easily give rise to the impression that the Bank of England directly supplies the British economy with money. In practice, the process of governmental control of the stock of money is much less direct than this implies. All the operational definitions of money include assets other than notes and coin. In even the narrow M_1 definition, notes and coin forms but a small part of the total. Most M_1 money is created by banks. While it may be correct to say that the Bank of England influences and even tries to control money creation, a clear picture requires a fuller description of how banks, non-bank financial intermediaries, households and businesses, and the authorities interact in the process.

In Britain, the main component of the money supply is bank current account balances (demand deposits). Demand deposits qualify as money because they are accepted as the final settlement of a debt. Demand deposits arise in three ways. In the first a demand deposit is created when a customer pays in currency or a cheque. No money is created because the inflow already consists of money. The second method of creating a demand deposit is when a customer of the bank shifts money from a time deposit (savings account) into a demand deposit. In this situation, the supply of money increases because non-money has been turned into money. This source of monetary increase is likely to be of short duration and can easily be followed by reverse shifts from demand deposits to time deposits.

The third and major way in which banks increase demand deposits is by acquiring financial assets. Whenever a bank acquires a financial asset, by buying a security or making a loan, spending power is injected into the system. If a security is purchased, a cheque is issued by the bank which will usually be paid into a demand deposit in this or another bank. If a loan is made by the bank, a demand deposit is created immediately. In either case, the total supply of money has increased, since no one else's money has decreased as a result of the transaction.

Although the banks are largely responsible for the creation of M_1 money, their ability to expand demand deposits is not without limits. Their freedom of action is circumscribed by the authorities in a variety of ways, as we shall see below. Government controls aside, considerations of prudent bank portfolio management set bounds to the possibilities of creating more and more money by buying securities or advancing loans to customers. The continued acquisition of financial assets is a risky business for a bank, for there is always the possibility of a large number of depositors wanting to withdraw their funds at the same time and the bank not having the cash to pay them. The larger the bank and the more varied its customers, the less likely is such an event to occur. Banks know from experience that it is prudent to keep a proportion of their assets 'in reserve', in the form of highly liquid assets (cash, near-cash assets such as money lent on call, and deposits with the Bank of England). The existence of these 'reserve requirements' limits the amounts of money banks can create. Individual banks are limited by the amount of their reserves over requirements — by their excess reserves.

The process of bank money creation can best be appreciated via a simple example. Suppose there are just two banks in the economy, A and B, both of which aim to keep 10% of deposits invested in the form of reserves with the balance in higher yielding loans. A and B have deposits of £100 each. A's deposits are invested in the desired proportions of £10 in reserves and £90 in loans, but B has £20 in reserves and only £80 in loans. B therefore advances £10 of its reserves as loans; loans and deposits will therefore initially rise by £10. But the customers who have received the loans will purchase goods by writing cheques on their account at B. Suppose for simplicity these funds are used to buy goods from A's customers and hence find their way into deposits in A. Cash has flowed into A's tills and its reserves now amount to £20. But A only needs 10% of its deposits (now £110) in reserve, i.e. £11, so it makes further loans of £9. Suppose those find their way into B's tills. B now has excess reserves of £8.1 And so the adjustment process continues, until the deposits of A and B together have increased from their initial level of £200 to £300, at which point no further bank portfolio revisions will be called for. Thus, B's excess reserves of £10 will eventually bring about a ten-fold increase in demand deposits, i.e. in money. The *money multiplier* is the reciprocal of the banks' reserve ratio, here assumed to be 10%. Inflows of funds to the banks enable them to create credit up to ten times the magnitude of the inflow.

Outflows of funds destroy credit in analogous fashion. In terms of our example, if B had found itself with a £10 shortfall of reserves this would lead it to cut back loans and this will have a draining effect on the demand deposits of both banks. Equilibrium will be restored when the initial joint deposits of the banks of £200 have fallen to £100.

Reserve ratios determined for precautionary motives are based on experience and judgement and could vary between banks and over time. But reserve ratios imposed by decree on banks by the government via its 'central bank' are very different in character. They serve of course the purpose of preserving the stability of the banking system and safeguarding the interests of savers; however the main intention of such regulations is to facilitate control of the economy.

The usefulness of reserve asset regulations to the government can be seen readily enough via the simple two-bank economy example. Recall that the existing reserve ratio, now assumed to be centrally imposed, is 10%. Deposits in the two banks have increased to £300. Assume the central bank is concerned about this increase in the money supply and therefore increases the reserve ratio from 10% to 12½%. Reserves are currently 10% of deposits, i.e. £30; they must rise to 12½%, so an extra £7.5 of reserves are required. The banks will have to cut back on loans to achieve this result. As the money multiplier is now 8 (the reciprocal of the reserve ratio of 12½%), these adjustments to bank portfolios will reduce demand deposits by eight times the original increase in required reserves, i.e. by $7.5 \times 8 = £60$. In other words, the central bank has been able to reduce the money supply by £60 by the simple device of increasing by decree the reserve asset ratio.

We will pick up the question of the role of government in the money creation process again. A more pressing issue, though, is the impact of monetary impulses on the financial institutions and markets, and to this matter we now turn.

The commercial banks are immediately and obviously affected by changes in the money supply. As we have seen, their everyday asset management decisions directly influence the money supply; conversely, inflows and outflows of bank funds, for whatever reason, stimulate asset portfolio revisions by the banks. A corollary of the banks' central role in the money creation process is that their operations are closely overseen and regulated by the central bank. We shall see in Chapter 11 that over the past decade banks have lost ground to non-bank financial intermediaries in the competition for personal sector deposits; the banks argue that government controls have greatly constrained their ability to compete for deposits. Certainly there can be no doubt that banks' operations are more closely regulated than are those of the non-banks and this must have hampered them.

The effect of monetary changes is soon felt by other parts of the financial system. For example, an increase in the money supply augments the stock of loanable funds thereby tending to put downward pressure on interest rates. A fall in interest rates on new loans and securities increases the attractiveness of existing securities and hence drives up the prices of bills and bonds. The increase in money balances might have some effects on the real economy as well, and these will in turn impinge on the financial system. Cash is a nil-return asset so individuals can be assumed to economise their holdings of it. A process of substitution into other assets, real as well as financial, and into consumable expenditures will occur as invididuals try to make better use of excess cash. This will put upward pressure on production and on prices. In turn, price inflation will reduce the attractiveness of money-denominated financial securities, thereby driving down their prices and putting upward pressure on interest rates. To the extent there is any impact on production (or the relative prices of goods and services), share prices will react accordingly.

The net effect of monetary impulses is to send shock waves through the financial system, particularly if the monetary changes are unanticipated. The effect of changes in the money stock on the real economy is currently an issue of great controversy in macroeconomics, one with considerable implications for government policy and hence for the financial system.

Economists divide on the question of the significance of the money supply. At one extreme, there is a Keynesian school of thought which argues that changes in money stock have no effect on real income or output in either the short-run or in the long-run. Keynesians consider that the demand for money is very sensitive to changes in the yields on alternative financial assets and hence the demand for money is both unpredictable and unstable. Economic activity responds to variations in credit flows and rates of interest. As the demand for money is unstable there is no point in attempting to control its supply, for any variation in its supply will simply alter interest rates rather than economic activity. Real investment is not very responsive to changes in interest rates, but depends on expected changes in output. To the Keynesian, fiscal policy is the most effective instrument of economic management.

At the other extreme, there is a monetarist school of thought which contends that the demand for (and velocity of circulation of) money is a stable and predictable function of permanent (i.e. the trend in) incomes and is therefore insensitive to the yields on alternative financial assets. As the demand for money is stable and insensitive to interest rate changes, any restriction in its supply will deprive people of liquidity and restrict their real expenditures. If the money stock is allowed to grow much faster than the rate of growth in economic activity, then the eventual result will be inflation and not the stimulation of economic growth. To the monetarist, the central task of economic management is that of matching the supply of money with the demand for money.

There are many issues in dispute between Keynesians and monetarists. Perhaps the most crucial, as far as financial economists are concerned, is the question of the substitutability between money narrowly defined (M_1) and other financial assets. This question arises as a direct consequence of the rapid growth of non-bank financial intermediaries (see Chapter 10). It can be argued that these intermediaries do not possess the money-creation capacity of banks but are merely money brokers. The deposits they obtain in competition with the banks eventually find their way back into the banks' tills. Nonetheless, if non-bank deposits are sufficiently liquid instruments that they may serve to replace money to such an extent that personal sector expenditure is maintained in the face of a monetary squeeze, then monetary policy could be made ineffectual. Conversely, if other financial assets are not good money substitutes then a monetary policy concerned to control the supply of a narrowly defined, 'high power' monetary base can be expected to be efficient (in the sense of having a strong and direct impact on aggregate spending).

The evidence on this issue is unclear. Some researchers have found that bank time deposits, and deposits of building societies are good substitutes for money, whereas others have produced evidence suggesting that they are not. There does seem to be some evidence to indicate that part (but only part) of the demand for money is accounted for by variations in interest rates.

The growth in non-bank intermediaries might well have complicated monetary policy in another way. Even if it is accepted that non-bank intermediaries are brokers rather than creators of money, there remains the distinct possibility that increasing non-bank intermediation has increased the velocity of circulation of money and hence weakened the link between aggregate expenditure and the money supply.

Impact of Government Policies

There have been a number of important changes since the Second World War in the methods the authorities have employed to regulate the British economy. These changes have been of great significance for the workings of the financial system.

Macroeconomic management in the UK during the 1950s and 1960s was governed by Keynesian principles. The primary economic goal was to maintain employment. The main constraint was the balance of payments; the exchange rate was fixed. Economic management consisted largely of trying to steer a course between too much aggregate demand, which would put the balance of payments into serious deficit and hence drain away the official reserves, and too little demand, which would cause unemployment to rise.

The main instrument was fiscal policy. If the balance of payments went into crisis, spending power was removed from the economy by either easing back on public spending or by increasing taxes (or both). As a result unemployment would rise. As soon as the official reserves had risen to a satisfactory level, spending power would be injected into the economy by a budget which either increased government spending or cut taxes.

Monetary policy was not non-existent but was largely concerned with the problems of financing the government borrowing requirement and with the commitment to a fixed exchange rate. The money stock was not a target. Monetary 'control' consisted mainly of quantitative ceilings on lending by banks and non-banks and variations in interest rates. The latter was accomplished in large measure by changes in the Bank Rate (later renamed the Minimum Lending Rate, or MLR), which was the rate the Bank of England in its capacity as lender of last resort charged the discount houses for re-discounting bills (see Chapter 6).

In 1971 the credit controls were swept away with the introduction of the reforms known as 'Competition and Credit Control'. Reliance was placed instead on control via a reserve assets system. The aim of the reforms was to encourage competition between financial institutions. The philosophy was that by encouraging competition the authorities could influence monetary aggregates through manipulating interest rates. The money supply was adopted as an indicator of monetary policy but was not made the primary instrument of policy.

The reserve assets system did not provide an effective means of controlling the monetary base. The problem was that the discount houses could, in effect, create money by borrowing on a call basis from the banks and use the funds to acquire bills, Certificates of Deposit and other short-dated assets; the call money was treated by the authorities as a reserve asset and hence could provide the basis for further bank lending. Thus the banks and discount houses had the ability to create reserve assets at will, a factor which led to a general disenchantment with the system.

Greater emphasis began to be placed on the money supply. The practice of announcing money supply targets began in 1976. The monetary aggregates chosen as targets are usually either M_0 or M_1 (i.e. one of the narrowly defined monetary indicators) and M_3. How the Bank of England attempts to control the money supply is not entirely clear. Some believe that it concentrates on the 'demand side' by manipulating the interest rate. Others argue that the Bank emphasises the 'supply side' in the sense that it identifies and tries to control the component parts of the money supply. Of course, demand and supply side control are not mutually exclusive possibilities. The variables which interact to produce a change in the money supply present an enormous variety of policy options to the authorities.

Another recent development has been the publicising of public expenditure targets. This is consistent with supply side control, for the Public Sector Borrowing Requirement (PSBR) is a large component of the Bank's definition of M_3 money stock:

$$M_3 = PSBR + L + X - D \qquad (4.1)$$

where L is sterling lending to UK private sectors, X is external and foreign currency flows to the private sector, and D is sales of public sector debt to the non-bank private sectors. By restricting growth in the PSBR (a component purportedly directly under central control) growth in M_3 can be slowed. Growth of the PSBR increases the supply of M_3 money because the expansion of net governmental spending (i.e. excess of spending over tax receipts) finds its way into bank deposits, unless this increase in the PSBR is financed by increased sales of debt to non-bank private sectors. In this latter situation, the increase in bank deposits caused by the growth in the PSBR is exactly offset by a decline in deposits occasioned by private sector purchases of government debt.

Monetary policy is intended to influence financial behaviour. However, the actual effects have not always been those intended. Examples include:

attempts to discourage bank lending to property companies in 1972 merely made it profitable for insurance companies to lend to them instead; control of M_3 has tended to cause a switch in deposits away from banks and into building societies; attempts to control the supply of money by selling government debt to the non-bank private sector have pushed up interest rates to the point where it could be argued that private sector debt is 'crowded out'.

Interest Rates

Interest rates play a central role in the workings of the financial system. Interest can be thought of as the price of loanable funds. Other things equal, the higher the interest rate (the price) then the greater the supply of and the less the demand for loanable funds. Equilibrium is achieved at that rate which serves to balance supply and demand.

Interest is viewed somewhat differently by Keynesians and monetarists. Keynesians view money primarily as an asset rather than a medium of exchange and asset choice as essentially the sacrifice of liquidity. If cash is exchanged for bonds then the investor's ability to respond to favourable business opportunities is diminished. Interest is the price demanded by the market for sacrificing liquidity, i.e. it is a reward for bearing risk of a particular kind. Interest rate changes are therefore of great importance in the conduct of monetary policy and in the transmission of monetary effects to the real sector.

To the monetarist, interest is the reward demanded for deferring consumption. Emphasis is placed on the medium of exchange function of money. Investment requires the foregoing of current consumption. Equilibrium is achieved when the rate at which each individual is willing to exchange consumption now for consumption later is equal to the market rate of interest and when the market rate of interest is equal to the marginal rate of return available on business investment.

These competing viewpoints can be reconciled as follows. The rate of interest offered by a particular instrument can usefully be thought of as consisting of two components. The first part is the return offered on an appropriate riskless asset; it is a reward for foregoing consumption. The second element is the loading for risk. Viewed in this fashion, we can throw some light on the differences in the rates of interest or yields on various financial instruments. Reasons include:

■ *Term to maturity*. In normal circumstances we would expect long-term liabilities to pay higher rates of interest than short-term ones, partly because of the bias of lenders to short-term securities noted in the previous chapter, but also because of the risk to lenders of having to liquidate long-dated securities prior to maturity if they should unexpectedly need the cash. The risk is entailed because variations in interest rates over time might imply that security holders could sell their holdings only at a low price.

■ *Risk proper*, which can be thought of as variability of expected yields. In the case of a bond the interest rate and redemption value are usually fixed, so risk boils down to either the probability of default or exposure to future interest rate changes (a function of term). With equity shares, dividends and final liquidation values are inherently uncertain.

■ *Transaction costs and taxes*. The rates of interest charged to borrowers must cover transaction costs and taxes.

Inflation

Inflation has had a marked impact on the financial system. Inflation in the UK and elsewhere was negligible in the 1950s and 1960s, but became a serious problem in the 1970s. The increasing emphasis on monetary control during this decade was caused in large measure by the apparent failure of traditional Keynesian methods of economic management to cope with inflationary pressures.

Inflation has affected the demand for loanable funds. Company profits failed to keep pace with inflation, in part due to the attempts of the authorities to control inflation, and this reduced the willingness of the business sector to invest. Coupled with this, the steep rises in interest rates in the 1970s resulted in a drying up of new issues of corporate bonds. Profit retentions also declined sharply. Increasing reliance was placed on short-term financing, in particular bank overdrafts.

Patterns of savings were also affected. We saw in Chapter 2 how personal saving as a proportion of personal disposable income rose from 6% at the beginning of the 1960s to 15% in 1980. Holdings of liquid assets increased, a reflection in part of the erosion of the real value of these assets caused by inflation and also of the increased economic uncertainty (the precautionary motive). The composition of personal saving has also been influenced by inflation, as individuals tried to invest in assets which would rise in value with inflation. Traditionally, equity shares had been regarded as a good 'hedge' against inflation, but this ceased to be the case. Investment was increasingly placed in property assets — principally home dwellings.

Inflation affects the level of interest rates. Savers can be expected to try to protect themselves from the ravages of inflation. Suppose an individual is only willing to save if a 2% real return is forthcoming. If he or she anticipates that inflation will be 10% in the coming year then he will need at least 12% to be 2% better off in real terms in a year's time. Other things equal, we should find money interest rates increasing in this fashion to reflect changes in inflation, assuming the market is able to anticipate the rate of inflation correctly. To the extent that inflation also changes the propensities to save and to borrow then the real rate (2% in our example) might change as well.

Summary

Macroeconomic factors influence the workings of the financial system in a variety of ways. Of central importance is the way changes in the supply of money cause banks to change their asset portfolios, put pressure on interest rates and (if unexpected) alter expectations. Government attempts to influence the workings of the real economy have a direct impact on the financial markets and institutions, the impact depending on the regulatory device employed.

Further Reading

1. A.D. Crockett, *Money: Theory, Policy and Institutions* (Nelson, 1973). Provides a very thorough treatment of monetary theory and practice in the UK. The treatment of practice has inevitably been overtaken by recent developments.
2. K.W. Wilson, *British Financial Institutions* (Pitman, 1983). The book is primarily concerned with the growth of non-bank institutions and the increasingly important role they play in the financial system, but it also provides a very thorough and up-to-date review of the history and state-of-the-art of British monetary policy in Part Two.
3. A.D. Bain *The Economics of the Financial System* (Martin Robertson, 1981). Chapters 5 and 8 deal with interest rates and the impact of inflation, respectively, and are highly recommended.
4. C.A.E. Goodhart, *Money, Information and Uncertainty* (Macmillan, 1975). A thorough treatment of modern monetary theory. Requires good background in economics. The demand for money is dealt with in the first three chapters; Chapters 8, 9, 12 and 13 are concerned with monetary policy.
5. *Report of the Committee to Review the Functioning of Financial Institutions* (Wilson Report), Cmnd. 7937 (HMSO, 1980), Chapters 1–4. Provides a clear review of the history of monetary control and the main features of the system.

Discussion Questions

4.1 Explain how banks are able to create money. What limits are there on the money-creation capacities of banks?

4.2 Explain the distinction between money and credit.

4.3 Discuss the ways in which an unanticipated increase in the money supply could be expected to affect the financial system.

4.4 Compare and contrast Keynesian and monetarist views on the effectiveness of trying to influence the level of economic activity by controlling the money supply.

4.5 What has been the main character of changes in methods of monetary control in the past two decades?

4.6   Discuss the following proposition: 'Control of the money supply does not carry with it any implication about control of the PSBR. An increase in the PSBR can be contained within a given money stock by either increasing the sales of public sector debt to the non-bank private sectors, by a reduction in inflows of foreign currency or by a reduction in bank lending.'

4.7   Explain why there are variations in the rates of interest offered on different financial assets. Does the existence of these rate variations necessarily imply that some assets are 'better buys' than others?

4.8   What is the distinction between the expected real rate of interest and the expected money rate of interest? Explain why the difference between the two rates need not necessarily be equal to the observed rate of inflation.

Part Two

ANALYSIS OF FINANCIAL MARKETS

Chapter Five

Evaluating Financial Investments

We have seen in the previous chapter how the rate of interest can be thought of as the price of loanable funds. Rates of interest serve to balance savings and investment in the economy. The rates charged for funds differ according to maturity, liquidity, riskiness and costs of flotation. Funds go to the highest bidders, due allowances being made for perceived differences in risks and costs of lending.

The purpose of the present chapter is to show how individual actors in the financial system can use information about interest rates and prices of securities in decisions to lend, borrow and invest funds. We begin by exploring the concept of the time value of money and its relationship to interest rates and then use the concept to develop a number of key financial variables. Mathematical formulae are developed in the Appendix to this chapter and are illustrated with applications in the text.

Time Value of Money

The concept of the *time value* of money can be summed up in the maxim: '£1 today is worth more than £1 tomorrow'. This maxim is based on the observable fact that idle money can be invested in the financial markets to yield a positive rate of interest. Thus £1 can be invested at interest today and the investment will grow to more than £1 tomorrow.

That money has a time value is readily apparent when the decision is to borrow funds in order to invest now in the prospect of gains tomorrow. Interest is an out-of-pocket cost; the borrower is bound to consider whether the payments from the investment are likely to exceed the interest incurred. Similarly, if the decision is whether to borrow funds to enhance current consumption, the borrower can hardly fail to weigh the increase in current consumption against the loss of future consumption thereby entailed. In both cases, £1 now is obtained only at the cost of more than £1 in the future. The cost of finance is given by the market borrowing rate of interest.

In other circumstances an out-of-pocket cost is not incurred; rather account has to be taken of the loss of benefits involved in not being able to take up an alternative opportunity. To apply one's funds to one purpose, e.g. to invest it in company shares or to keep it in a current account to finance transactions, is to pass up the opportunity of lending it at interest in the market. The *opportunity cost* here of holding cash or investing in financial assets is the market lending rate of interest.

The time value of money can be equal to the rate of interest for borrowing or for lending, depending on the circumstances. Either the borrowing rate must be greater than or equal to the lending rate or borrowing must be rationed (otherwise it would be possible to borrow and lend without limit and amass a fortune in the process).

In the event of restrictions on borrowing, investment beyond a certain point will not be possible. When capital is thus rationed the time value of money will be equal not to the borrowing rate (because more borrowing is not possible) but to the rate of return on the *most attractive investment foregone* through lack of funds. For example, suppose an individual has £100 savings and three investment projects, A, B and C, each requiring £50 outlay and offering the prospect of 15%, 20% and 10% annual rates of return, respectively. The logical decision would be to invest in projects A and B but to reject C. The time value of money invested in A and B would seem to be the 10% rate of return offered by the rejected project C, for if an extra £50 *had* been available then 10% is the annual rate of return which would have been earned on the incremental investment. If the 10% yield on the marginal project C is less than the lending rate then the opportunity cost of funds is of course given by the lending rate: the cost of investing in A and B is not now the foregone opportunity of investing in C (for this is not the best alternative use of funds) but is the loss of returns from lending.

We have identified two possible measures of the time value of money. The first is the market rate of interest, and this measure can be divided into two subordinate market measures — the borrowing rate and the lending rate. The second measure is applicable only in conditions of strict capital rationing and defines the time value of money as the return on the most attractive investment opportunity passed over because of lack of funds. Circumstances will dictate which of the two monetary measures is appropriate to a particular decision problem.

These monetary measures of the time value of money are suitable for use in making decisions about what business investment opportunities will give the best payoff over time, and also whether borrowing or other means of raising capital (e.g. by issuing new shares) to finance new investment is worthwhile. Analogous measures are appropriate in decisions about how much an individual should consume now and how much he or she should save or dissave. A decision to save is essentially one to consume less now in order to consume more in the future — and dissaving is the reverse. An 'impatient' individual will want considerably more than £1 of extra consumption tomorrow to warrant giving up £1 today. In other words, this individual places a high time value on money, he has a high *personal rate of time-preference*. On the other hand, someone who is keen to provide for the future will have a low personal rate. In contrast with market rates, personal rates are unobservable and unique to each individual. Market rates do enter into the consumption–saving decisions of individuals because of the impact on borrowing and lending. Indeed, the market rate of interest can be viewed as a weighted average of the personal rate of individuals.

The connection between market and personal rates can be seen as follows. Assume for simplicity a world where all future events are known with certainty, where there is only one market rate of interest, and where all individuals can borrow or lend freely at this single rate. Suppose individual X's personal rate of time-preference is less than the market. This means that X is more willing than people in general to trade current consumption for future consumption. X would feel better off by reducing current consumption by lending at interest. After lending some money X will become less willing to lend yet more money. In other words, X's personal rate of time-preference will have increased. The optimal position will be reached when X's personal rate is equal to the market rate. Given that personal rates are unobservable, it seems likely that the consumption–saving decisions of individuals will be taken more on the basis of subjective trade-offs than on the results of financial calculations. Nevertheless, in principle, consumption–saving decisions involve the use of the time value of money concept in exactly the same way as do business decisions.

The concept of personal time-preference rates can be extended from the individual to society as a whole. In the same way as there is a rate of trade-off between current and future consumption for a particular individual, so one can think of there being a *social rate of time-preference*, expressed somehow through the political institutions of the country, which can be thought of as the rate of increase in aggregate consumption in the future which will be sufficient to induce society to reduce current consumption by £1.

Clearly the choice of an appropriate measure of the time value of money can be a complex one and must depend on the problem to hand. The only general principle which can be set forth is that the measure employed should reflect the cost of applying funds to the particular purpose under consideration. 'Cost' can mean the cash outlays on interest to be incurred, or the returns lost from not being able to invest in (say) bonds or another project, or the rate of sacrifice of future consumption required, or whatever. We will concentrate on the conventional business problems of valuing financial instruments, investments and financing options.

In a certain world with perfect capital markets firms and individuals alike would be able to borrow and lend at the same risk-free rate of interest. But as already noted in the previous chapter, uncertainty and market imperfections can result in not one but many market rates of interest. In markets dominated by risk-averse investors, interest rates will contain a 'loading' for risk, the amount of the loading varying from financial instrument to instrument according to the perceived degree of risk. Transaction costs can cause borrowing and lending rates to diverge. For further insight into the problems of computing market rates and valuing financial instruments, see Chapters 8 and 9.

In order to undertake a financial valuation exercise, two kinds of data are required. The first kind consists of estimates of the *extra* cash inflows and outflows which are expected to occur if the project goes ahead. If, for example, the project consists of a decision to purchase say a government bond, then there will be an immediate outlay being the purchase price of the bond, followed by inflows of interest coupons at half-yearly intervals, plus the repayment of principal (i.e. contractual redemption value of the bond) if it is expected to be held to maturity, or the anticipated market sale-proceeds if it is to be sold prior to redemption. The second datum required is an estimate of the time value of money.

Armed with these data, the problem becomes one of combining them into a measure of investment worth. In order to grasp the logic involved we start with a simpler problem than the bond valuation example, one involving only a single period's delay in payoffs.

A Single Period Example

Suppose you are owed £1000 by a firm which is hard pressed for cash at the present moment and, though willing and able to settle up now, has offered to pay you an additional £100 if settlement is deferred for one year. Assuming you are fully confident of the firm's ability to meet its obligations next year, should you take the £1000 now or £1100 in 12 months' time?

The first question to be answered is, what could you do with £1000 extra right now? Suppose the best use would be to invest it in a bank at 8% p.a. One way of deciding whether to defer settlement would be to see how much £1000 would grow to in a year's time if invested at 8%:

$$£1000 \ (1.08) = £1080$$

As this sum is less than the sum offered, you should agree to defer settlement. Put differently you will be £20 richer in a year's time: the 'net terminal value' (NTV) is £20.

Another way of approaching the problem would be to try to find the investment P which would exactly grow to £1100 in one year's time:

$$P \ (1.08) = £1100$$

Solving for P gives

$$P = (1100) \ (1.08)^{-1}$$
$$= £1018.52$$

This P can be thought of as the 'worth' or 'present value' (PV) of the future sum £1100. As P is greater than the sacrifice required, the 'net present value' (NPV) of $1018.52 - 1000 = £18.52$ is positive and deferment is indicated.

A third statistic is the 'internal rate of return' (IRR). The IRR is the rate of interest which will equate the £1000 with the £1100 one year later:

$$£1000 \ (1 + IRR) = £1100$$
$$IRR = 0.10 \ (10\%)$$

This 'internal' rate can be compared with the market opportunity rate of 8% foregone. As the IRR is the greater, it is worthwhile deferring settlement.

In this simple example, these three measures all give the same signal to the decision-maker, and the choice of which to use here is immaterial. Each measure tells us a slightly different story. NTV indicates the impact of the investment on wealth at a future date. NPV can be thought of as the impact on present wealth. The IRR is a rate of return which can be compared with the time value of money.

Compound Interest

In order to extend our analysis to cope with multi-period investment problems it is necessary to have some understanding of the economic logic of compound interest. The relevant mathematics appears in the appendix to this chapter.

Consider again our simple credit example. Suppose the offer is not to pay £1100 in one year's time but rather to delay its payment for two years. Would you be better off?

To compute the NTV we must invest the present sum for two years. After one year it has grown to £1080 at 8%. Suppose this sum could be invested for a further year at 8%. So

$$\text{NTV} = 1100 - 1080\ (1.08)$$

Actually we would normally calculate this in the form

$$\text{NTV} = 1100 - 1000\ (1.08)^2$$
$$= -\text{£}66.4$$

As final wealth will be diminished, deferment should not be accepted.

To find the NPV we solve for P in the following expression and subtract the initial £1000 sacrifice:

$$P\ (1.08)^2 = 1100$$
$$P = (1100)\ (1.08)^{-2}$$
$$= \text{£}943.07$$

so NPV = 943.07 − 1000 = − £56.93, and initial wealth is diminished.

The IRR can be found from either the NPV or the NTV formulations. We use the latter:

$$1000\ (1 + \text{IRR})^2 = 1100$$
$$= 0.0488\ (4.88\%)$$

This is below the cost of capital of 8% so deferment will leave us worse off.

Extension to problems involving multiple cash flows is a simple matter. Denote the cash flow at time t by C_t. If C_t is negative (i.e. $C_t < 0$) then a

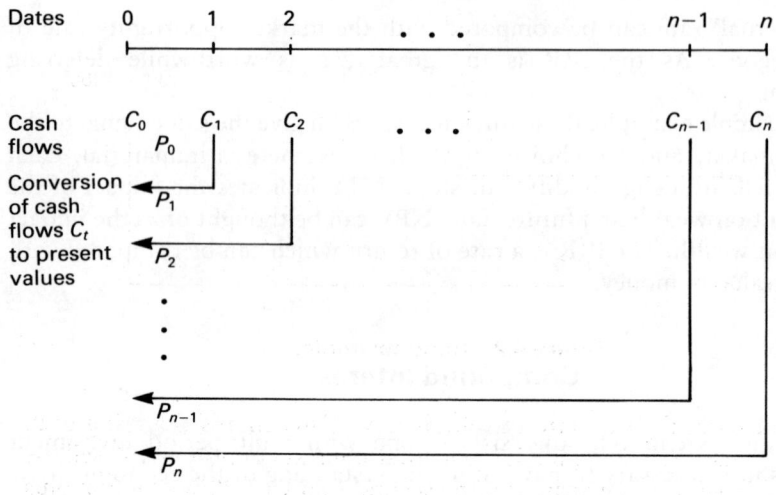

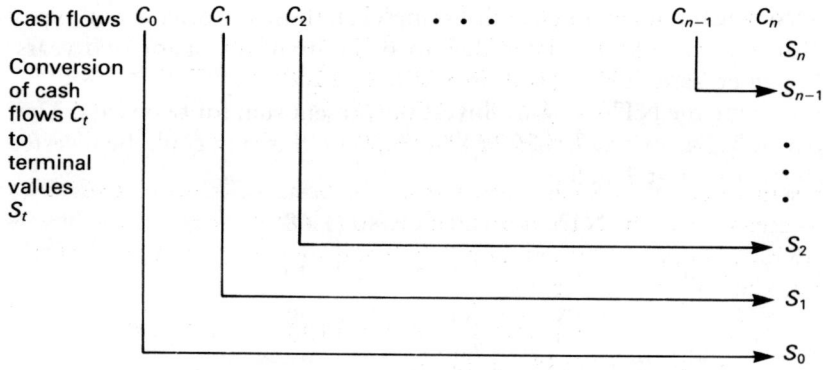

Figure 5.1   Time Diagrams for Valuing Cash Flows.

payment is expected; conversely if $C_t > 0$ a receipt is anticipated. *In order to carry out a valuation exercise all these cash flows must be converted into equivalent values of a common date.* The date selected could be now — in which case all flows are expressed in present values; or it could be at the end of the series — hence each flow is converted into a terminal value; or it could be any other *single* date. See Figure 5.1 for a time diagram depicting the PV and TV alternatives. Once each cash flow has been converted to the equivalent value at the given date, the conventional arithmetical operations of addition and subtraction can be carried out.

Consider a simple example. A bond pays interest of £100 at the end of each year. The bond is to be redeemed at the end of two years for £1000. Its current market price is £950. Suppose you could invest your money elsewhere at 12% p.a. for each of the next two years. Is it worthwhile buying the bond?

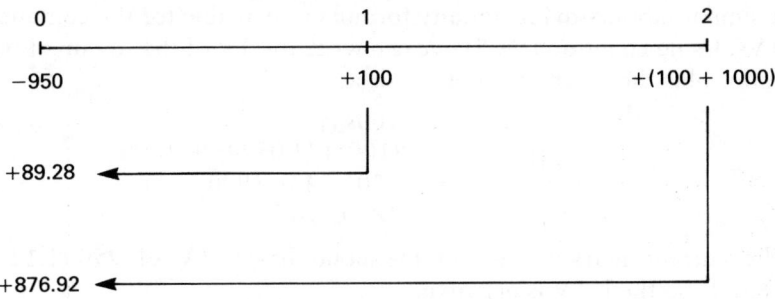

Figure 5.2   Bond Example.

The most natural *focal date* to take is now. This entails replacing each cash flow by its PV. See Figure 5.2. The first interest coupon of 100 will be 'discounted' back for one year, and the second year cash flow (coupon plus redemption proceeds) for two:

$$
\begin{aligned}
\text{NPV} &= C_0 + C_1 (1 + i)^{-1} + C_2 (1 + i)^{-2} \\
&= -950 + 100 (1.12)^{-1} + (100 + 1000) (1.12)^{-2} \\
&= -950 + (100) (0.8928) + (1100) (0.7972) \\
&= -950 + (89.28 + 876.92) \\
&= -950 + 966.20 = £16.20
\end{aligned}
$$

The present value of the cash inflows from the bond amounts to £966.20, which is greater than the current price of £950, so it looks to be a good buy.

The IRR can be found by setting NPV=0 and solving (by trial and error) for the unknown interest rate i:

$$
\begin{aligned}
\text{NPV} &= -950 + 100 (1 + i)^{-1} + 1100 (1 + i)^{-2} = 0 \\
i &= 0.13 \ (13\%) \ \text{approx.}
\end{aligned}
$$

The IRR is greater than the time value of money, so purchase is indicated.

Suppose the bond has twenty years to run. The twenty equal £100 coupons have to be converted to twenty separate (and unequal) present values. A lot of tedious arithmetic is involved. Fortunately, in the case of constant cash flows, when $C_1 = C_9 = \ldots = C_{20}$, it is possible to use a simple annuity formula, given by equation (5A.7) in the Appendix. Applied to the present problem, we have

$$
\text{PV} = 100 a_{\overline{20}|.12} + 1000 (1.12)^{-20}
$$

The value of the annuity factor $a_{\overline{20}|.12}$ can either be obtained from financial tables or be computed directly:

$$
\begin{aligned}
\text{PV} &= (100) (7.4694) + (1000) (0.1037) \\
&= 746.94 + 103.70 = £850.64
\end{aligned}
$$

which is considerably less than the current market price of £950. The twenty year bond is a very poor buy.

A similar labour-saving annuity formula is available for the computation of TVs. Using equation (5A.8), we can write the TV of the stream of twenty coupons plus the redemption proceeds as

$$
\begin{aligned}
TV &= 100s_{\overline{20}|.12} + 1000 \\
&= (100)(72.0524) + 1000 \\
&= 7205.24 + 1000 \\
&= £8205.24
\end{aligned}
$$

The current market price of the bond has a TV of $950(1.12)^{20} = £9163.98$, so the NTV is negative.

The annuity formulae can save a lot of tedious calculations when trying to estimate the IRR of a long cash flow series. Suppose we set the PV of the cash inflows equal to the current market price,

$$
100a_{\overline{20}|i} + 1000(1 + i)^{-20} = 950
$$

and try out various rates of interest i to see if this equation holds. At $i = 0.106$ (10.6%) the left-hand side comes to £950.94, which is near enough to £950 for practical purposes. So IRR = 10.6% which is less than the 12% cost of capital.

Effective Rates of Interest

Compound interest logic is not always strictly adhered to in practice; in consequence it is often easy to draw the wrong conclusions. In particular, so-called *nominal* rates of interest are commonly quoted in the financial markets. The use of nominal rates can make comparisons between investment and financing options very difficult.

Suppose you are faced with two mutually exclusive investments, A and B, each of which will cost £100 to acquire and will generate an income of £10 per year. The only difference between the two is that the income from A is received at the end of each year whereas that from B comes in two equal six monthly instalments. The interest rate reported in the financial press is the same for both and is arrived at by dividing the annual income by the investment outlay = $10 \div 100$ = 10% p.a. An interest figure which takes no account of frequency of payment during the year is known as a nominal rate; so that 10% quoted is a nominal rate.

However, A and B are not equally attractive. Each year, part of the income of B is received sooner than A's, and £1 today is worth more than £1 tomorrow. The nominal rate would therefore seem to be misleading. What is needed is another rate of return concept which can be used in comparing alternatives — an effective rate of return.

Consider how £1 invested in B would grow. Every half-year interest of 5% is paid. Thus, after six months the investment would have increased to £1.05. If the interest of £0.05 is ploughed back to earn 5%, the investment will have grown to

$$
(1.05)^2 = £1.1025
$$

by the end of the year. Hence the total amount of interest will be £0.1025 during the year, i.e. 10.25% p.a. A proper comparison between A and B can be made using their effective rates of interest of 10% and 10.25%, respectively.

A third investment, C, also paying interest of £10 p.a. but at quarterly intervals, can be handled in the same way. The quarterly rate of interest offered on C is $10\% \div 4 = 2.5\%$. £1 invested at 2.5% per quarter would grow to

$$(1.025)^4 = £1.103813$$

by the year-end, i.e. has a prospective effective yield of 10.38% p.a.

The effective rate increases with greater frequency of compounding. In the limit, where interest is paid continuously, the effective annual rate would become

$$e^{0.10} - 1 = 0.1052 \ (10.52\%)$$

See equation (5A.15).

Many countries, including Britain, have introduced 'truth in lending' laws which compel money lenders and consumer credit organisations to disclose the effective rate of interest charged on loans. But in other areas of finance nominal rates are still widely quoted.

A distinction can be made between nominal interest and simple interest. A nominal interest rate is calculated as if all interest were paid or charged at the end of each year. In effect, compounding is assumed to occur once a year. On the other hand, simple interest is computed only on the principal; interest is *not* charged on past interest charges (i.e. there is no compounding).

Whether interest is charged on a simple or compound basis can make some difference during the course of even a single year, as we have seen in our previous example. Money invested at simple interest grows a *constant* amount each year, whereas invested compound it grows exponentially. For example, £1 invested at 10% increases as follows:

year	=	0	1	2	3	4	...	20
simple interest	=	1.00	1.10	1.20	1.30	1.40	...	3.00
compound interest	=	1.00	1.10	1.21	1.33	1.46	...	6.73

Over short periods the differences are small, but they increase dramatically for longer maturities.

Valuation and Pricing

It is interesting to contemplate a state of affairs in which the investment, financing and perhaps even savings decisions of individuals and firms can be represented in terms of the logic of compound interest. Individuals increase their savings from current income if the prospective yields on investments exceed their personal rates of time-preference. They compute the PVs of alternative investment opportunitites and choose those which are greater than or equal to the purchase price; they sell investments where PV is less than price. Firms compute the NPVs of investment projects and select those where NPV>0, raising additional finance where necessary. If there was general agreement about future cash flows from different securities then market prices would fall into line with market transactors' estimates of PVs. More realistically, there may often be considerable disagreement about payoffs; in which case prices would settle at the marginal transactors' estimates of PV. Either way, the equilibrium market price of a security can be depicted in present value terms.

The PV formula (equation (5A.4)) provides insight into the market pricing process. A share or a bond can be thought of as an entitlement to a series of n future cash payments, $C_0, C_1,...,C_n$, each of which has a price of its own — $P_0, P_1,...,P_n$, respectively. The price of the complete security, PV, must be equal to the sum of the prices of the constituent cash flows:

$$PV = P_0 + P_1 + ... + P_n$$

(If this additivity principle does not hold then opportunity exists to make profits by selling overpriced securities and buying underpriced ones.) The price P_t of the component cash flow C_t is of course obtained by discounting at the (assumed constant) market rate of return i:

$$P_t = C_t (1 + i)^{-t}$$

The discounting factor $(1 + i)^{-t}$ can be thought of as the price at time 0 of £1 at time t. For example, with $i=15\%$ and $t=5$, the current price of a dividend or interest coupon of £1 in 5 years' time is £0.497; a payment of £1 at $t=6$ will have a current price of £0.432.

It is worth noting that short-term money instruments are sometimes valued by a different (but equivalent) procedure. The present value is computed by deducting ('discounting') a proportion d of the final proceeds:

$$P = S - dS$$
$$= S(1-d)$$

in the case of a 12 month bill. In contrast, the PV procedure employs the market rate i:

$$P = S (1 + i)^{-1}$$

There is a direct relationship between i and d; see equation (5A.12). It makes no difference of course which method is applied, as long as it is applied consistently. In practice, the discounting is done on a simple rather than compound basis, i.e.

$$P = S (1-nd)$$

For example, a three-month £1000 bill will be discounted at 12% p.a. on a simple basis to

$$P = 1000 (1 - \tfrac{1}{4} \times 0.12)$$
$$= £970$$

Varying Interest Rates

We have assumed throughout this chapter that the time value of money is constant from period to period. This need not be so either in theory or in practice. We have already pointed out in the previous chapter that one of the reasons why interest rates vary from instrument to instrument is because securities vary in the term to maturity. A one-year bond might offer a different rate of interest than, say, a two-year one. This subject is taken up in Chapter 8. It is sufficient for our present purposes to note the implications of interest rates varying through time.

Suppose we are trying to estimate the present worth of an investment offering £100 in each of the next two years. We discover that if we want to borrow money for one year it will cost 10%; if a further year's finance is required it will cost 14.03% in year two. We can use these rates as follows. First, we discount year two's receipts back to year one at 14.03%,

$$\frac{100}{1.1403} = £87.696$$

and add the result to the year one receipts. Second, we discount this sum back to the present at 10%,

$$\frac{100.000 + 87.696}{1.10} = £170.63$$

This procedure is equivalent to discounting the flows back at the rates appropriate to each period:

$$PV = \frac{100}{1.10} + \frac{100}{(1.10)\,(1.1403)}$$

$$= £170.63$$

There is of course no obvious problem in discovering the year one rate of 10%. It is the one-year *spot rate* and can be found by looking at the yield on one-year bonds. But how do we find the year two rate of 14.03%? One way is to find the spot rate on a two year no-coupon bond and compare this with the one-year spot rate, as follows. (No-coupon bonds are needed in order to avoid reinvestment problems.) Suppose we find that the yield (the IRR) on a two-year bond will amount to $(1.12)^2 = £1.2544$ in two years' time. If we invested £1 in a one-year bond, this will grow to £1.10 after one year. In order to be indifferent between investing (i) in a two-year bond, and (ii) in successive one-year bonds, the one-year rate in year two must be 14.03%:

$$(1.10)\,(1.1403) = 1.2544$$

Hence 14.03% is the *forward rate* which is implicit in the two-year spot rate of 12%.

A corollary of this relationship between spot rates and implied future rates is that we could have used 10% as the discount rate for the first of our cash receipts and 12% for the second in our example above and have produced exactly the same result:

$$PV = \frac{100}{1.10} + \frac{100}{(1.12)^2}$$

$$= £170.63$$

The two cash receipts of £100 are treated here as distinct claims to be 'priced' (i.e. discounted) quite separately.

Summary

This chapter has discussed the methods used to analyse and value financial assets. In explaining the time value of money, alternative methods have been shown to be consistent. Thus if two investment opportunities are compared by discounting the cash flows back to one focal date, the same order of preference will be revealed if evaluation takes the form of compounding forward the cash flows to a terminal focal date. In later chapters these methods are applied to the valuation of specific securities such as shares, and to other types of asset such as insurance policies.

Further Reading

1. F. Ayres, *Theory and Problems of Mathematics of Finance* (McGraw-Hill, 1963), Chapters 1–14. Short on economic concepts but provides a thorough treatment of the basic techniques of simple and compound interest in what amounts to a programmed-learning format.
2. R. Cissell, H. Cissell and D.C. Flaspohler, *Mathematics of Finance*, 5th edn (Houghton-Mifflin, 1978). A more wordy and less mathematical alternative to Ayres.
3. M. Bromwich, *The Economics of Capital Budgeting* (Penguin, 1977). Provides an excellent and highly readable explanation of the economic principles of investment. The mathematics are treated lightly and there are few numerical examples and no problem sets. The first five chapters deal with basic principles, the remaining chapters being concerned with the problems of business investment and financial management.
4. R.A. Brealey and S.C. Myers, *Principles of Corporate Finance* (McGraw-Hill, 1981). Contains a very thorough treatment of financial decision-making, with extensive coverage of economic and computational aspects and numerous problem sets.

Problems

5.1   Assume that you are given the choice between £100 now and £100 one year from now. Which would you choose? Explain. Assume that you could invest money at 10% p.a. How large would the amount one year from now have to be for you to be indifferent between the two choices?

5.2   The time value of money is 5% p.a. Compute the present value of £100 (a) received one year from now; (b) received at the end of five years; (c) received at the end of 20 years. Compute these values again using 20 years from now as the focal (i.e. valuation) date.

5.3   Assuming a 10% rate of interest, compute the present value of a series of five payments of £100 a year: (a) the first to commence in one year's time; (b) to commence immediately.

5.4   Estimate the present market value of a ten year bond which has a face and maturity value of £1000 and pays interest annually at 3%. The first interest payment is one year from now. The current market yield on bonds of this type is 12%.

5.5   You are owed £1000 by A. A wants to ease the strain of repayment by spreading it out over four years in equal instalments — the first now and the remainder at yearly intervals. If money is worth 15% to you, what should be the amount of each payment?

5.6   In the text it is shown that when the time value of money is 12% a £1000 two-year bond paying interest at 10% has a present value of £966.20, whereas a 20-year 10% £1000 bond is worth only £850.64. This seems contradictory, given that the second bond offers 18 more interest coupons than the first. Explain.

5.7   You approach a money lender for a loan. He tells you that he charges interest each week at the rate of ½%, i.e. 26% per year. If interest is charged as stated, what is the effective annual rate?

5.8   You are planning to buy a house and need a mortgage of £20,000. The mortgage is to be of the conventional 20-year repayment type, repayments to be made in equal monthly instalments commencing in one month's time. A building society states that it will charge interest at 16% p.a. whereas your bank quotes a rate of 1¼% per month, i.e. an effective rate of 16.0755% p.a. But on further inquiry you discover that they compute repayments differently. The bank computes the monthly repayment using the monthly interest rate of 1¼%. The building society calculates an annual repayment figure on the assumption that repayment occurs at the end of each year and then divides this figure by twelve to arrive at the monthly charge. Calculate the payments required by each and explain why they are different.

5.9   A £10,000 ten-year bond pays interest twice-yearly at 10% nominal. Its current market price is £7055. Find by trial-and-error the effective rate of return currently yielded by the bond.

5.10   A £100,000 bill maturing in 9 months' time is discounted at 16% p.a. simple. What is the bill's current market price? What is the implied (a) simple and (b) compound rate of interest on the bill?

5.11   Assume year to year interest rates for years one to three are 10%, 11% and 12% respectively. What should be the yields on no-coupon bonds maturing in (a) one, (b) two and (c) three years time?

Mathematics of Compound Interest

Let i be the compound rate of interest per period, P be the principal (i.e. amount of money at the beginning) and S be the amount of the sum invested. After one period the investment P will have grown by the addition of interest iP to

$$S = P + iP$$
$$= P(1 + i)$$

If the increased sum $P(1 + i)$ is left to earn interest for yet another period, the amount will grow by the addition of interest on both the principal and the interest already earned:

$$S = P(1 + i) + iP(1 + i)$$
$$= P(1 + i)^2$$

After n periods the amount will have grown to

$$S = P(1 + i)^n \tag{5A.1}$$

Suppose we already know the final amount S to be received n periods hence and want to know what it is worth now. Clearly the present value of S is the principal P which could be invested now such that it will grow to S after n periods. To find P all we have to do is solve (5A.1) for P, by multiplying both sides by $(1 + i)^{-n}$ (or equivalently, by dividing both sides by $(1 + i)^n$):

$$P = S(1 + i)^{-n} \tag{5A.2}$$

These results can be generalised without difficulty to deal with more complicated patterns of cash flows. Suppose an investment offers the prospect of cash receipts of amounts $C_0, C_1, C_2, \ldots, C_n$, occurring at the end of periods $0,1,2, \ldots, n$, respectively. Each receipt can be invested at compound interest up to the end of period n by separately applying equation (5A.1):

$$S_t = C_t(1 + i)^{n-t}, \qquad t=0,1, \ldots, n$$

The terminal value TV of the investment at n is obtained by adding together the amounts of the separate cash flows:

$$TV = S_0 + S_1 + \ldots + S_n$$
$$= C_0(1 + i)^n + C_1(1 + i)^{n-1} + \ldots + C_n$$
$$= \sum_{t=0}^{n} C_t(1 + i)^{n-t} \tag{5A.3}$$

Present values can be obtained by application of (5A.2) to each cash flow in turn:

$$P_t = C_t(1 + i)^{-t}, \qquad t=0, 1, \ldots, n$$

The present value (PV) of the series is obtained by application of the fundamental Additivity Principle of finance, i.e., by adding together the present values of the separate elements:

$$
\begin{aligned}
\text{PV} &= P_0 + P_1 + \dots + P_n \\
&= C_0 + C_1 (1 + i)^{-1} + \dots + C_n (1 + i)^{-n} \\
&= \sum_{t=0}^{n} C_t (1 + i)^{-t}
\end{aligned}
\tag{5A.4}
$$

Simpler versions of equations (5A.3) and (5A.4) can be developed when the cash flows take the form of an *annuity*, i.e. when all the cash flows are of equal sign and amount (or grow or decline in a mathematically regular fashion). For our purposes it is sufficient to concentrate on *ordinary annuities*. An ordinary annuity is a series of n equal and equally spaced payments starting at the end of the first period:

$$
C_0 = 0 \text{ and } C_1 = C_2 = \dots = C_n = C
$$

The PV of an ordinary annuity can be written as

$$
\begin{aligned}
\text{PV} &= C (1 + i)^{-1} + C (1 + i)^{-2} + \dots + C (1 + i)^{-n} \\
&= [(1 + i)^{-1} + (1 + i)^{-2} + \dots + (1 + i)^{-n}]\, C
\end{aligned}
$$

Following traditional actuarial practice, we put $v = (1 + i)^{-1}$ and write out the geometric progression in square brackets in more compact form:

$$
a_{\overline{n}|\,i} = v + v^2 + \dots + v^{n-1} + v^n
\tag{5A.5}
$$

Multiplying the left-hand side of (5A.5) by $(1 + i)$ corresponds to dividing by v. Thus $a_{\overline{n}|\,i}\,(1 + i) = 1 + \dots + v^{n-1}$ and subtracting (5A.5) from the result yields

$$
a_{\overline{n}|\,i}\,(1 + i) - a_{\overline{n}|\,i} = 1 - v^n
$$

so

$$
a_{\overline{n}|\,i} = \frac{1 - v^n}{i}
\tag{5A.6}
$$

The PV of an ordinary annuity can therefore be reduced to a simple formula:

$$
\begin{aligned}
\text{PV} &= C a_{\overline{n}|\,i} \\
&= C \left[\frac{1 - v^n}{i} \right]
\end{aligned}
\tag{5A.7}
$$

The TV of an ordinary annuity can be obtained by multiplying (5A.7) by $(1 + i)^n$

$$
\begin{aligned}
\text{TV} &= C a_{\overline{n}|\,i}\,(1 + i)^n \\
&= C s_{\overline{n}|\,i}
\end{aligned}
\tag{5A.8}
$$

where

$$
s_{\overline{n}|\,i} = \frac{(1 + i)^n - 1}{i}
\tag{5A.9}
$$

The annuity formula most commonly employed in investment work is (5A.7). (Relevant formulae for other annuities can be derived straightforwardly from (5A.7) and (5A.9) and are therefore not developed here.)

For some financial instruments interest is charged not at a specified rate i on the principal (or present value) P but as a proportion d of the final amount S. Suppose the instrument has only one period to go before maturity. Its present value with one period to run is P and during the period the instrument increases in value by the amount of discount dS:

$$P + dS = S$$
$$P = S(1-d) \qquad (5A.10)$$

In order to find the value of the instrument two periods before maturity it is only necessary to apply the discount rate d to the value one period later, given by (5A.10):

$$P + dS(1-d) = S(1-d)$$
$$= S(1-d)^2$$

More generally, for an instrument with n periods to run to maturity the present value is

$$P = S(1-d)^n \qquad (5A.11)$$

The relationships betwen d and i can be obtained by comparing the two present value formulas, (5A.2) and (5A.11). Setting them equal and solving yields an expression for i in terms of d,

$$i = \frac{d}{1-d} \qquad (5A.12)$$

and another for d,

$$d = \frac{i}{1+i} \qquad (5A.13)$$

Obviously, $d<i$ because d is computed on the final value S and i is on the present value P where $P<S$.

This brief review of the mathematics of compound interest is concluded with an examination of the implications of variations in the frequency of compounding. Interest on a bond is usually payable semi-annually; for many types of loans it is charged monthly. Interest rates are almost invariably quoted on an annual basis, even when interest is charged more (or less) frequently than once a year. In many financial markets the annual rate quoted is a *nominal* one, meaning one which simply takes the total amount of interest paid during the year as a proportion of the amount invested, no account being taken of the returns which could be gained from reinvesting interim interest payments. Proper comparison of instruments with different payments frequencies requires the use of effective annual interest rates.

Suppose interest is added at equal intervals m times per year. (If $m=2$, interest is added twice yearly; if $m=4$, interest is on a quarterly basis, and so on.) We denote the nominal rate of interest by r. The *effective rate of interest* is therefore given as the amount of interest which would accumulate during 12 months on a compound basis when interest at the rate r/m is added m times and reinvested:

$$i = [1 + (r/m)]^m - 1 \qquad (5A.14)$$

The pay-off on a security offering interest at the rate of $100i\%$ once at the end of the year will be the same as that on another in which interest is added m times during the year at the rate of $100(r/m)\%$ on each occasion.

For a given nominal rate r, the result of increasing the frequency of compounding is to produce a larger effective rate i. In the limit with m approaching infinity, compounding becomes continuous and (5A.14) becomes

$$i = \lim_{m \to \infty} [1 + (r/m)]^m - 1$$

$$= e^r - 1 \qquad (5A.15)$$

where e = 2.718 is the base for natural logarithms, a constant.

The PV and TV formulas for an ordinary annuity, (5A.7) and (5A.8), can be changed to deal with the case where payments are made continuously rather than at the end of each year and are presented below without proof:

$$PV = C\left[\frac{1-e^{-n}}{r}\right]$$

(5A.16)

$$TV = C\left[\frac{e^{n}-1}{r}\right]$$

(5A.17)

Chapter Six

Short-term Money Markets

The short-term markets for finance are characterised by large size, quick speed of reaction and low transaction costs. Based mainly on telephone contact between dealers, the markets invariably operate on verbal agreements for deals which usually individually account for millions of pounds. The markets are less formally established than the longer-term capital markets but have more than compensated for their informality by their vigorous expansion. In discussing the operations of the markets and the instruments which are traded, we have first to consider the ways in which profits are reported in buying and selling short-term 'money'.

Principles of Bill Discounting

In the previous chapter, we discussed the principles of simple and compound interest and showed how they could be used to compare the payment of money at different times. In the short-term money markets the life of a loan or security is usually less than one year, so perhaps it is not surprising that the comparisons are conventionally made using simple interest and the related concept of simple discount. (We have already considered compound discount in Chapter 5.) To illustrate the relationship between the two concepts, take the example of a bank loan that is taken out at the beginning of the year for £880 with the promise to repay, at the end of the year, the sum of £1000. This transaction can be analysed from the lender's point of view as promising a return at the beginning of the year of (1000 − 880)/880 or an interest rate of just over 13.6% on the bank's initial 'investment' of £880. Alternatively, we describe the difference between 1000 and 880 as *the discount* and estimate the *discount rate* to be (1000 − 880)/1000 or 12% of the maturity value.

Another example will show how the discount rate is estimated if the loan is taken out for less than one year:

> A firm is owed £5000 by a commercial customer and is faced with an immediate need for cash. It offers to accept £4900 if payment is made immediately rather than at the end of the month. Calculate the interest and discount rates implicit in this offer.

In this example, the firm is effectively borrowing £4900 for one month, and paying interest on the loan. In simple interest terms, the present value is given by

$$P = \frac{5000}{(1 + r/12)}$$

where r is the annual rate of interest. But the present value is known to be 4900 so we can write

$$4900 = \frac{5000}{(1 + r/12)}$$

and solve for r to find

$$r = 0.245 \text{ or } 24.5\% \text{ p.a.}$$

The discount is the £100 difference between the initial payment and the final amount. The discount rate is found by dividing the discount by the sum owed and then annualising the result. In simple interest and discount terms, the annualising is achieved by multiplying the discount by 12 (the discount is obtained if payment is brought forward 1 month). Thus,

$$d = \frac{100}{(5000/12)}$$

$$d = 0.24 \text{ or } 24\% \text{ p.a.}$$

We can generalise these examples by letting P = the initial value, S = the maturity value and n = the time (in years) between the payments or receipts. The interest rate r is given by

$$r = (S - P)/Pn \text{ p.a.} \tag{6.1}$$

Whilst the discount rate is given by

$$d = (S - P)/Sn \text{ p.a.} \tag{6.2}$$

Alternatively we can express the present value of the loan either in terms of the interest rate or the discount rate by rearranging the above expressions:

$$P = S/(1 + rn) \tag{6.3}$$
$$P = S(1 - dn) \tag{6.4}$$

Finally we can equate these values to express the discount rate in terms of the interest rate,

$$d = r/(1 + rn) \tag{6.5}$$

The usefulness of these expressions can be seen by examining the *Bank of England Bulletin* which presents yield statistics on various short term investments. Treasury bills, for example, are reported to have been sold at an average *discount rate* of, say, 10% p.a. whilst local authorities' three month loans may be reported as yielding an *interest rate* 10 $7/8$%. It is not easy to see which is the most profitable investment since they are reported in different units. But by using expression (6.5) we can calculate that the discount rate equivalent to the local authority loan of 10.875% is

$$d = 0.10875/(1 + 0.10875 \times 0.25)$$
$$= 0.1059$$

Comparing this discount rate of 10.59% with the 10% from the Treasury bills reveals that the local authority bills are yielding a discount of about ½% above the Treasury bills.

Usually the prices quoted in the bill markets will be in terms of the discount. Thus a £100,000 Treasury bill may be bought at a 10% discount rate to mature in 91 days time; the buying price will therefore by (6.4) be

$$P = 100,000 (1 - 0.1 \times 91/365)$$

Thus $P = £97,506.80.$

An investor will buy the bill for £97,506.80 and in 91 days time can collect £100,000 on maturity to earn the 10% discount rate. The market price will rise from £97,506.8 to £100,000 as maturity draws nearer. Suppose however, that the interest rate falls sometime during the life of the bill; the price of this bill will tend to rise faster than the market had anticipated. Perhaps the investor will want to sell the bill after 50 days has passed to realise the unanticipated profit. The market may be quoting a discount rate of 8 per cent. To calculate the price of the bill, the investor can use expression (6.4) thus:

$$P = 100,000 (1 - 0.08 \times 41/365)$$
$$= 99,101.4$$

The realised return on his investment can now be calculated using expression (6.1) thus:

$$r = (99,101.4 - 97,506.8)/(97,506.8 \times 50/365)$$
$$= 0.1194 \text{ or } 11.94\% \text{ p.a.}$$

In other words the seller has earned a profit equivalent to a simple interest return of 11.94% p.a.

The buyer of the bill who plans to hold the bill until it matures in 41 days time will earn interest of $100,000 - 99,101.4$ or £898.60, which will represent a return of

$$r = (100,000 - 99,101.4)/(99,101.4 \times 41/365)$$
$$= 0.08072 \text{ or } 8.07\% \text{ p.a.}$$

We can check this calculation by converting this interest rate back into a discount rate by (6.5). Thus

$$d = 0.08072/(1 + 0.08072 \times 41/365)$$
$$= 0.08$$

which accords with the discount rate used to price the bill in the same market. Note that in calculating these rates we have used the convention of a 365 day year. In many markets, especially in Europe, a 360 day year is assumed. Having looked at the simple ways in which the short-term investments can be analysed, we pass onto the markets and their operations.

The Discount Market

The Bank of England, in managing the government's financing, has raised money from selling government bonds (see Chapter 8) and short-term Treasury bills. In recent years, however, for reasons which will be discussed below, the amount raised by Treasury bills has declined substantially. This decline has affected most of the operations of the short term *discount market* which has been the channel through which the Bank has chosen to communicate its policy decisions to banks and other investors. Although the Bank of England continues to use the discount market for its day-to-day policy operations, the decline in the number of Treasury bills issued has necessitated its dealing in other types of short-term instruments which will be discussed later in the chapter.

Traditionally, the discount market existed as a buffer between the Bank and other commercial banks. The discount houses would borrow money for very short periods and effectively lend to the Bank of England by buying Treasury bills. The Treasury bills would be issued by the Bank usually for 3 month terms, at weekly intervals; at any time, the discount houses would be holding a portfolio comprising Treasury bills of various maturities, financed largely by 'overnight' or other short-term loans from the commercial banks. Should the banks have failed to renew their loans, the discount houses were allowed to sell any unfunded Treasury bills back to the Bank of England (or to borrow cash from the Bank if it was thought that the cash shortage was temporary).

By this operation, the Bank could if it so wished, smoothly increase interest rates, first by causing the commercial banks to suffer a shortage of cash and then reinforcing this shortage by helping the discount houses to cope with the induced lack of funds only at higher rates of interest. To ensure that this policy would work, the Bank could rely on the agreement by the discount houses to buy any Treasury bills not taken up by other investors. Thus the bank could always, if necessary, issue more Treasury bills than could be funded by commercial loans from the banks if it wished to 'drive' the discount houses into the position of asking for help.

The sale of Treasury bills has in the past been central to the way in which the Bank of England influences the market. Each Friday, the Bank announces the amount of Treasury bills that will be offered for sale the following week. Investors, including the discount houses, then submit offers for the bills, specifying the price at which they will buy and the numbers of bills required. Bills are allotted first to the highest bidder, then down the prices bid until all the bills offered have been sold. The Bank then announces the results of the tenders (see Table 6.1).

Table 6.1   Bank of England Treasury Bill Tender (22 June 1984)

Bills on offer	£100m	Top accepted rate of discount	8.8843%
Total of applications	£331.5m	Average rate of discount	8.8563%
Total allocated	£100m	Average yield	9.06%
Minimum accepted bid	£97.785		
Allotment at minimum level	28%	Amount on offer at next tender	£100m

Source: *Financial Times,* 25 June 1984.

From this report, it will be realised that Treasury bills are sold at different rates depending on the price of each individual tender. In the example, reported, the minimum accepted bid of £97.785 will correspond to the top accepted rate of discount, that is (by 6.2))

$$d = (100 - 97.785)/(100 \times 91/365)$$
$$d = 8.8843\%$$

Similarly, the average rate of discount of 8.8563% will correspond to a tender of £97.792 (by 6.4)). The two differences in rates may seem small but in tenders involving tens of millions of pounds, these small differences may have a substantial effect. It will also be seen that the tender involves considerable uncertainty in that only just over a quarter of the offers made were accepted and that the tenders offering the minimum accepted bid of £97.785 were allotted only 28% of the number of bills required.

Although Treasury bills continue to be sold weekly, their importance has declined relative to commercial bills. This decline stemmed from a desire on the part of the government to control and restrict the supply of money in the UK economy. To attain this, the bank sold large amounts of long-term government bonds to private and corporate investors who paid for the bonds by drawing on their accounts held in the commercial banks. In turn this resulted in the loss of cash by the commercial banks to the Bank. The quantity of money was thus greatly restricted and the government's borrowing requirement was in the event more than covered by the sale of the long-term securities. This 'over-funding' thus led to a dramatic fall in the issue of Treasury bills and the almost paradoxical situation in which the Bank had to find some way of alleviating the chronic shortage of cash in the short-term money markets. Traditionally, of course, the shortage would be helped by buying back Treasury bills, but the small stock of outstanding Treasury bills precluded this tactic. As a matter of policy the Bank decided to offer through the discount market to buy, or lend cash on, commercial bills (bills of exchange). Although there have been strict constraints on the type of bill bought, the volume of bills held by the Bank has increased substantially, and by the end of 1983 amounted to over £7 billion.

The *bill of exchange* is a traditional method by which industrial and commercial firms obtained their short-term finance, especially those concerned in international trade. There are, in practice, two ways in which similar documents can originate. The conventional *bank bill* is 'drawn' (i.e. created) by a creditor company on a debtor (perhaps because the debtor has bought goods) and the liability is 'accepted' by a bank or discount house which will guarantee to pay for goods being supplied by the creditor. *Acceptance credits*, on the other hand, are drawn by the debtor company and are 'accepted' by a bank or discount house which will guarantee to pay the amount owing if the debtor defaults.

Bank bills can be further classified as 'eligible' or 'ineligible'. Eligible bills are those which have been accepted by banks such as Midland, Bank of America or Deutsche Bank and thereby become eligible for purchase by the Bank of England. Ineligible bills will be perceived to be either less secure or less marketable than their eligible counterparts.

Eligible bills can be sold to the Bank of England by the discount houses when they find their other sources of finance are inadequate. In effect, eligibility depends on an eligible bank accepting the bill; traditionally the list of eligible banks was limited but the number increased dramatically in August 1981 to over 100 when the Bank of England announced changes in its method of carrying out monetary policy through control of the money market.

Currently, the Bank may announce that it will buy or sell bills daily. In some cases, the Bank will announce that it will buy bills which will be resold at a later date, or may only lend money to the discount houses. In recent years there has been an increasing emphasis on market transactions. In order to let the market influence or even determine the pattern of interest rates, the Bank will frequently only operate in bills which are due to mature in the very near future. In the classification adopted by the Bank, there are four bands of maturity: 0–14 days, 15–33 days, 34–36 days and 64–91 days. The Bank usually confines its dealings to bands 1 and 2.

The Bank also takes account of the risk and maturity of bills in fixing the terms under which the discount houses operate. Because of the nature of their business financing, discount houses are inherently risky: they borrow on a very short term basis and lend over a longer term, all on a small capital base. Typically, the discount houses borrow and lend up to thirty times their own capital. Much of their funds is provided by the recognised banks, all of which place a specified proportion of their assets with the discount market.

The discount houses' solvency in volatile markets depends on the Bank of England's role as lender of last resort, and it is this which helps ensure that the discount market responds quickly to hints by the authorities. In setting restrictions on the extent to which the discount houses can enlarge their assets by borrowing, the Bank classifies their assets by category. Thus, eligible bills with a life of less than three months come within the least risky category, whilst ineligible bills with a life of between three months and a year come within the second category. In the third (and most risky category as far as the bills of exchange are concerned), come some ineligible bills with over a year to run and trade bills (that is, bills of exchange neither drawn on nor accepted by a bank) with a life of over six months.

Discount houses have, over a number of years, sought to extend the range of investments in which they have traded. Among the various securities which can be classified as being traded in the discount market are local authority bills and government bonds of up to five years from maturity. *Local authority* bills are traded in the market and classified by the Bank of England on the same basis as Treasury bills. In reporting its transactions in the money market, the Bank will usually refer to assistance given in both the morning and afternoon. The distinction is made for two reasons. The morning operations are based on preliminary estimates made by the Bank of the shortage of funds in the money market. During the day these preliminary estimates will be adjusted and reflected in the afternoon dealings. Secondly, the morning operations are confined only to help the market cope with fund shortage: in the afternoon the Bank may also offer more bills to the discount houses (and in this case, the commercial banks) if the market has an excessive supply of cash. The daily report may therefore appear as follows:

> The Bank gave assistance in the morning of £71 million, comprising purchases of £7m of Treasury bills in band 1 and, in band 2, £64m of eligible bank bills. All purchases were made at 11% (discount rate p.a.). The afternoon help was made up of bill purchases all at 11% of £205m, comprising £22m of Treasury bills, £23m of local authority bills, £40m of eligible bank bills in band 1; and in band 2, £1m of local authority bills, £104m of eligible bank bills and £15m of Treasury bills.

The involvement of discount houses in government bonds began in the 1930s, during which period there had been a decline in the number of bills of exchange due to the world recession. They still hold short-term government bonds, especially when they believe that interest rates are likely to fall because as interest rates fall, so the price of the bonds will rise and profits will be made from the capital gain. The success and/or failure of the discount houses 'view' on interest rates, as demonstrated in their Gilt portfolio, has been one of the major influences on the performance of each discount house over the past ten years.

Short-term government bonds are also traded by other institutions such as banks and building societies. Stockbrokers and, to a lesser extent, money brokers act as agents and operate in a wide range of money markets ranging from the traditional discount market to the foreign exchange and other sterling deposit markets.

It is not surprising that the markets in which short-term investments are so frequently trading should themselves respond quickly to external events. The changes in the relative importance of Treasury and commercial bills has already been noted. Substantial changes have also occurred in the other money markets.

Parallel Money Markets

Operating alongside the discount market are the 'parallel' money (sterling) markets. Of these, the most important constituent markets trade in *interbank deposits, certificates of deposit* and *local authority deposits*.

The sterling interbank market, as its name suggests, concerns the borrowing or lending between banks of sterling funds. Deposits are usually made on a short-term basis with the majority of deposits being made for maturities of less than three months. The operations carried out by the Bank of England in the discount market will usually affect the rates negotiated in the interbank market. For example, if the Bank injects more cash into the discount market, discount houses may find that they no longer require cash from clearing banks which in turn will place cash on the interbank market. If the amount is sufficiently large, the market rates will fall.

Operations on the interbank market involve a large number of banks and commercial lenders and can at times result in highly volatile rates. For lesser known banks, the volatility is exacerbated since their names may not be acceptable to some market participants or if acceptable, only in limited amounts. All participants operate on a system of limits in which they will restrict the amount of money lent to any other bank. The limits imposed on smaller banks are, of course, more restrictive than those imposed on commercial banks. In addition to the system of limits, rates quoted will also depend on the status of the bank bidding for funds.

Sterling CDs are basically negotiable receipts issued by the banks acknowledging that a specified sum of money has been deposited and will be repaid at a fixed rate of interest on a specified date.

From the depositors' point of view, the issue of a negotiable certificate enables them to realise their cash if required before maturity, since the CD can be sold at a rate that will take into account the time-value of the money on deposit. Depositors will pay a small price for this liquidity but the value of the facility obviously depends to a great extent on how liquid is the secondary market for CDs and the rates of return that can be earned from placing funds in alternative markets.

From the issuing bank's view, they represent an additional and slightly cheaper method of acquiring funds for a fixed term at fixed interest rates. In ensuring a strong secondary market, the discount houses have played an active role in promoting their use; CDs are currently very important in their portfolios.

Unlike the bills traded in the traditional market, CDs are not issued at a discount but are instead issued for a minimum period of three months at face value (for values normally starting from £50,000) with interest payable on maturity. As with other short term markets, the rates of interest quoted are calculated on a simple interest basis (except for periods longer than one year). Thus a 3 month (91 day) CD bought at 12% would be expected to pay $(12 \times 91)/365 = 2.992\%$ interest on maturity.

The further complication exists, however, that although CDs can be issued for periods in excess of one year, the interest payable is still calculated on a simple interest basis. Estimating the return is therefore a slightly laborious task if trading is carried out in the secondary market. For example, if a £1m CD issued for 2 years at 14% was sold after 6 months for a quoted yield of 12%, the price would be calculated in the following way. The interest would be £140,000 payable at the end of the first and second years. At the end of the first year the value would therefore be

$$P_1 \quad = \quad \frac{£1m}{(1 + i)} \quad + \quad \frac{£0.14m}{(1 + i)} \quad + \quad £0.14m$$

where i = the market yield (0.12 here), and six months earlier,

$$P_{0.5} \quad = \quad \frac{P_1}{(1 + it)} \qquad \text{where } t = 182/365$$

Thus

$$P_{0.5} \quad = \quad \left(\frac{1.14}{1.12} + 0.14\right) \bigg/ \left(1 + \left(\frac{182}{365}\right) \times 0.12\right)$$

Price = £1.0925m

Although CDs can be, and are, issued for terms of one, two, three or more years, the secondary market for such long-term securities is very much thinner than that for shorter maturities. In response to this market constraint, issuing banks and depositors sometimes agree on *roll over* terms whereby, say, a six month CD will automatically be replaced by another CD at the time of maturity at a specified rate. In this case, the issuing bank can rely on having the use of the money deposited for twelve months while the depositor will have the liquidity derived from receiving two CDs: the first of six months duration, maturing in six months time, the second also of six months duration, running from six months to twelve months ahead. In this example, the issuing bank has agreed on a forward rate for the second six month period. In principle, it is straightforward to compare the cost of a six month CD (with a six month roll over), with the cost of a twelve month CD. In practice, the comparison depends on the rate of interest which will prevail in six months' time and professional judgement will be required in allowing for the small, but possibly significant, variations. The development of the trading in forward CDs has received more attention recently with the setting up in 1982 of a London market for 'financial futures'.

The remaining parallel sterling market which will be briefly mentioned here is that for local authority short-term finance. Bills issued by local authorities and traded in the discount market are small in relation to the general deposits business carried out for periods varying from overnight to several years. These deposits are, however, not traded in a secondary market, and only come within the area of parallel money markets because lenders are likely to consider the rates offered in the local authority market as an alternative to the interbank market.

As in the other markets, the technical aspects of the trading lead to anomalies from which traders can profit. One such opportunity is the activity of 'round-tripping'. If the market rates are appropriate, a commercial firm may typically create an acceptance credit which will immediately be accepted by a bank and discounted for cash (i.e. sold). The company then places the cash in the interbank market at a marginally higher rate. Similar round trips can be made by companies which have previously arranged with banks the right to overdraw their accounts. Usually these overdraft facilities will be charged at a rate of interest that will be linked to the current short-term rates. But it is possible that, for a large reputable company, the overdraft rate is below the rate currently quoted for CDs or trade bills. Thus the company can borrow from the bank by using the overdraft facility and buy short-term money market securities with the funds borrowed. As with other money market arbitrages, large sums of money have to be traded in order to make small profits: such operations contribute to the effectiveness of the market in transmitting changes in one market to other associated markets.

The scale of arbitrage deals is difficult to estimate. More to the point, the existence of arbitrages cannot be assessed from the published reports of the rates ruling in the respective markets. In *Financial Statistics,* for example, interbank sterling market rates may be reported 11–$11\frac{1}{8}$% overnight and $10\frac{29}{32}$% three months, with sterling CDs (three months) at $11\frac{1}{16}$%. But the interbank rates are, for the overnight rate, the range of lowest bid and highest offer rates over the day. By contrast, the CD rate is the mean of the lowest bid and highest offer rate at 10.30 a.m. In practice, rates for overnight money on the interbank market can be very volatile and crucially depend on the help given by the Bank of England in the discount market.

Besides the intermarket arbitrage trading, which essentially consists of simultaneously trading in more than one market, arbitrage can occur over time: the forward market also operates in interbank deposits. Complicated arbitrage activity can involve both CDs, interbank forward deposits or foreign exchange transactions. Technically, the market refers to forward transactions (i.e. ones involving delivery of securities at a later date) as occurring in the 'forward forward' market. These transactions have been greatly facilitated by the establishment of a market in which standard contracts are traded. Thus the development of a Financial Futures Market is of considerable interest to arbitrageurs. The development will be discussed in Chapter 14.

International Money Markets

The international markets for short-term financial instruments possess similar characteristics to the domestic money markets. Generally, the international markets with which this section is concerned are called 'euro-markets' and involve currency held on deposit at a bank outside the country of origin. Historically, the market traded *euro-dollars* in London; and to a lesser extent other centres such as Paris, Frankfurt, Luxembourg, Singapore and Hong Kong, also operate in sterling, Deutschmarks, Swiss and Belgian francs. New York also is a major centre in which trading takes place with US banks accepting deposits on behalf of their offshore branches and arbitraging between the euro-dollar and the domestic dollar markets. Euro-dollar transactions are also settled via New York.

Euro-markets deal in a wide range of instruments, varying in maturity from overnight deposits to long-term *euro-bonds* which may be issued for up to fifteen years but more usually between five and ten years. In the short-term markets, however, there are close parallels with the domestic operations.

The *euro-dollar certificate of deposit* is thus similar to its domestic UK and US counterparts. They are usually issued in 1 million units and vary in maturity from three months to five years. They are issued by US and other banks, clearing banks and branches of banks located in a number of countries including Canada, Britain and Japan. In some cases, small banks buy CDs from other banks on the understanding that the CD will not be traded. The effect of this agreement is that the liquidity of the small bank will appear, from inspection of the balance sheet of the bank, to be more liquid than it truly is. During times in which borrowing rates fluctuate considerably, the appearance of liquidity may substantially affect the credit rating of the small banks. A second effect of this type of agreement is that the secondary market for euro-dollar certificates of deposit may be thinner in proportion to the volume of CDs outstanding than its domestic counterpart.

In pricing euro-dollar CDs, calculations should take into account the convention that interest is accrued in a 360 day year. Thus, a 10% \$CD issued for 180 days would pay interest of 5% on the par value of the CD, whereas a domestic sterling CD would pay interest of $10 \times 180/365 =$

4.93% on par. In analysing arbitrage operations between domestic and euro-currency money markets, these differences in convention can be confusing to the novice!

Parallel to the euro-CD market is the *interbank euro-market* in which a bank will trade deposits for fixed terms at rates inversely related to the bank's size and status. The rate charged may be fixed relative to LIBOR (London Interbank Offer Rate) with large banks paying rates below LIBOR and lending their borrowed funds to smaller banks at a profit of $\frac{1}{32}$% or more. Alternatively the rate may be fixed in absolute terms. Smaller banks may also pass the funds on to other euro-banks, or may lend the money to corporate customers paying 1% or more above LIBOR. Reports of the interbank activity (and in fact of most other euro-market lending) will usually refer to LIBOR, which is merely the arithmetic mean of the rates on £10m 3-month deposits offered at 11 a.m. by 'reference' banks (typically National Westminster Bank, Bank of Tokyo, Deutsche Bank, Banque Nationale de Paris, and Morgan Guaranty Trust).

Since almost all of the short- to medium-term loans in the euro-currency market are determined on the basis of floating or prespecified rates (in relation to LIBOR), a widely accepted and reported rate has obvious market advantages.

The existence of the euro-money markets has had an enormous impact on the efficiency of currency and domestic money markets. These arbitrage questions are often of bewildering complexity. The introduction of markets in which interests in *future* euro-CDs can be traded in both the US and the UK further enhances the opportunity for the arbitrageur.

The international money markets came into existence for a number of reasons, the main one being the desire of international investors and multinational corporations to find ways around controls on international capital movements imposed by domestic governments (particularly the US government) and to circumvent various restrictions on the issuance of securities. The international markets are essentially unregulated markets. (As in other financial markets, distinctions over maturity are important, but what the euro-money and euro-bond markets have in common is the way they operate outside national frontiers and are therefore largely free of national regulation.) There is little doubt that these markets will continue to adapt and change, to develop new techniques and instruments in response to changes in the financial, the trading and (especially) the regulatory environments.

Summary

The short-term money markets are strictly wholesale markets in which large amounts of money are traded on small margins of profit. Since they involve only professional market participants, details of their operations are more difficult to ascertain. Nonetheless, the pricing of assets within the markets can be analysed by referring to the general principles of discounting introduced in this and earlier chapters.

Further Reading

1. *Bank of England Quarterly Bulletin,* 'The Role of the Bank of England in the Money Market' pp.86–94 (March 1982). The Bank of England publishes regular commentaries on the operation of the money market and almost every issue of *Quarterly Bulletin* has some comment of interest. This article provides some detail on the historical development of the role of the Bank of England as well as an explanation of the changes in the procedures that were made in the early 1980s.
2. G. Dufey and I.H. Giddy, *The International Money Market* (Prentice-Hall, 1978). The authors take an analytical look at the eurocurrency markets. The book is clearly structured and provides a comprehensive discussion of the growth and the current practices in the international money markets.
3. Marcia Stigum, *The Money Market: Myth, Reality and Practice* (Dow Jones Irwin, 1978). A large book written in an informal style. It covers many of the world's money markets and discusses the US institutional issues informatively.
4. E.R. Shaw, *The London Money Market,* 3rd edn (Heinemann, 1981). This book covers in considerable detail the operation of the London money markets, including the parallel and euro-dollar markets.

Discussion Questions

6.1   Briefly describe the functions of discount houses. If they did not exist, how do you think the task of controlling the supply of money would be affected?

6.2   Explain how the Bank of England can affect the short-term rates of interest (a) by buying or selling Treasury bills and (b) by buying and selling commercial bills.

6.3   What risks are faced by the discount houses? How do these risks differ from any other financial institution borrowing and lending in different markets (e.g. banks or building societies)?

6.4   Discuss the advantages and disadvantages to (a) the borrower and (b) the lender, of a loan made for a long period of time at a rate of interest that fluctuates in response to changes in the short-term rate of interest (LIBOR).

Problems

6.5   Referring to Table 6.1, estimate (a) the rate of return that would be earned by an investor buying Treasury bills at the minimum accepted bid and (b) the price corresponding to the average discount.

6.6   If the market (simple) rate of interest is 9%, estimate the value (a) today (b) 6 months from today and (c) 1 year from today, of £1,000 due in three months' time.

6.7   Which of the following investments offers the higher rate of return?
   (a)   91 day bill at 12% discount rate
   (b)   91 day CD at $12\frac{3}{8}$% interest rate
   (c)   365 day bill at 12% discount rate
   (d)   365 day CD at $12\frac{3}{8}$% interest rate

6.8   An investor buys a one year 10% $CD which he sells after 180 days. What will be his return on the transaction if interest rates have remained unchanged over the intervening period? (Assume an initial investment of $10,000.) What would be the price of the CD at the time he sold if interest rates had unexpectedly fallen to 9.5%?

Chapter Seven

The UK Securities Market

In Chapter 3 we discussed some principal characteristics of financial markets and institutions, identifying criteria for the evaluation of their efficiency. In this chapter, we develop this analysis in the context of the Stock Exchange and related markets for securities.

From the discussion it will be seen that securities markets, like their short-term counterparts dealt with in Chapter 6, have expanded and adapted to external conditions; new marketss have been established within recent years and more radical changes have also been proposed. Some of the reasons for these proposals will become clear in the course of this chapter. Others will be further discussed in Chapter 14.

Types of Trading System

Even within the market for financial securities there is a wide range of trading arrangements. In the spirit of Chapter 3, we first discuss the main types of trading system before looking more closely at the efficiency of the markets and their regulation.

Two tasks have to be undertaken when trading securities: locating an investor with whom to make the transaction, and negotiating a price at which the transaction will be completed.

Institutional arrangements for facilitating these tasks differ for historical, sometimes apparently accidental, reasons. The differences, however, are not constant and in common with other types of financial institutions, trading markets change in response to economic forces. Perhaps the most obvious change has been the increase in the use of computer/electronic information transmission. Market prices of shares and bonds are now recorded and transmitted electronically from the Stock Exchange, so institutional investors and market analysts can immediately observe on visual display units in their own offices current security prices revealed by transactions in the market.

Markets may be situated in a central geographical location or may alternatively exist only by virtue of multiple communication links between participants. In the securities markets there has been a traditional emphasis on a physical market place (Stock Exchange) but in recent years, there has been a considerable number of transactions carried 'off the market' simply on the basis of telephone calls.

Where the number of investors is large it rapidly becomes impracticable for potential investors either to congregate or even to communicate with a significant proportion of other potential traders, and it makes sense for intermediaries to set up as *wholesalers* or *brokers*. *Wholesalers* make their living by taking the orders of small operators and putting them together into large deals. *Brokers* act as agents for client investors. The role of brokers is to specialise in searching — perhaps by knowing the likely buyers or sellers of a particular security or by incurring the high fixed costs involved in buying access to the electronic-based market information. In order to offer an economically viable service these middlemen have either to achieve economies by frequent dealing in the securities or to offer special skills and information about the market.

The financial markets have become increasingly dominated by large institutional investors who are potentially capable of acquiring most of the research skills presently offered by the broker. In addition, institutional investors may be very active in buying and selling securities. It is not surprising, therefore, that the institutionalisation of the investment markets has been accompanied by criticism of trading arrangements that have their origins in the historical relationships of individual (personal) investors and corporate brokers.

As an alternative or in addition to brokers, some markets operate on a *dealer* basis, with dealers carrying out a broking role and also acting as principal market makers, participating in a transaction by selling or buying securities for their own account. A dealer-based market will therefore be characterised by a number of firms offering to buy or sell specified securities at quoted prices.

The roles of broker and dealer can be combined so an investor requiring, say, to buy securities may approach brokers/dealers who may either buy the securities on the investor's behalf from another dealer or sell the securities from their own holdings.

A variant of the dealer-based market can be found in the market for financial futures which operates on the basis of open auction. This system can be observed in most securities markets outside the UK. In large markets such as the New York Stock Exchange, a specific 'trading post' is allocated for groups of securities. At each trading post, a *specialist* has the responsibility of maintaining an orderly market by dealing on his own account and will also accept orders from brokers. These orders may be 'market orders' (i.e. orders to buy or sell at the best prices available) or 'limit orders' (orders to deal in securities if the market price falls below or rises above a specified price). In the New York Stock Exchange these orders are held and recorded by the specialist and it is in this context that the term 'market depth' (introduced in Chapter 3) can be best understood. In dealer-based markets, on the other hand, there may be no record of conditional orders which remain to be executed so the 'depth' of the market may not be easy to assess. In this type of market, the interests of the investor are best served by publicising the prices at which transactions are made. Only by this device can investors be assured that they have had a 'fair' deal.

In smaller markets, a 'call-over' system is used, in which securities are called at specific times of the day. Brokers bid or offer for the securities and the calling price will then be adjusted if new prices are agreed by the brokers' transactions. This system operates in the French Bourse and other small exchanges in Europe.

The breadth of the market depends on the number of different types of investor buying and selling securities. One major characteristic of securities trading in the UK is the relative increase in the importance of a small number of institutional investors and the relative decrease in direct participation by individual investors. One might therefore infer that the UK markets were becoming less broad with a consequential increase in volatility. However, despite a number of studies the evidence is not yet clear and any observed increase in volatility can plausibly be explained by economic events rather than the trend towards institutional dominance.

Types of Securities Traded

Although there is much emphasis on long-term characteristics of securities traded in the Capital Markets, the distinction between a capital market security and a money market instrument (discussed in Chapter 6) is not always clear. The most well known long-term security is the *ordinary share* which will usually be irredeemable and which will offer the investor a variable cash income (dividend) in addition to the possibility of a capital gain or loss on selling. The valuation of ordinary shares will be discussed in Chapter 9.

Another long-term security (discussed in Chapter 8) is the corporate or government *bond*. In this case, the security will usually be issued only for a specified period and will therefore be traded on the securities market only for a predetermined period. As the time of redemption approaches, the bond will tend to behave more like a short-term money market instrument (and will often be bought by investors who would otherwise trade in the money markets). Thus the borderline between the money market and securities markets will be blurred when considering short-term bonds.

In Chapter 9 we also discuss a number of securities which largely depend for their value on either the present or expected future price of an ordinary share. These securities include *warrants, options* and *convertibles* and are sometimes described as 'contingent claims'. Although they do not constitute a large part by value of the securities market, they fulfil an important role in making the markets more 'complete', and allowing investors to adjust the risk of their portfolios, by buying or selling contingent securities. This concept of completeness is important in analysing market efficiency. Basically if a market is complete, investors can construct portfolios that will deliver a required cash flow for every conceivable circumstance. In an *incomplete* market therefore, investors would find it impossible to protect themselves against foreseeable events (e.g. hyper-inflation or a dramatic fall in the price of oil).

Of the securities mentioned above, ordinary shares, bonds, warrants and convertibles are all issued first by debtor institutions (e.g. companies) and are subsequently traded on the secondary market by transferring ownership from one investor to another. However, *traded options* (and financial futures) are securities which are effectively issued by one investor directly on the secondary market. Traded options must therefore be distinguished from the *share options* given by companies to selected employees (or directors of the company), which are rights to buy shares from the company at a specific price. These share options, if exercised, result in an increase in the total marketable stock of shares. By contrast, traded options, if exercised, only lead to a change in ownership of shares in the secondary market.

Characteristics of Long-term Markets

Of the capital markets, the *Stock Exchange* is by far the most important. This market has traditionally operated as a dealer/broker based system with separation between the firms associated with each function. Normally *jobbers* act as dealers quoting bid and offer prices on shares that they are prepared to deal in; *brokers* act as agents for investors by transacting securities with the jobbers on their clients' behalf. Whilst the brokers are paid in the form of commission on each transaction made, the jobbers have to rely on the profit made in selling stock at a price higher than that at which they bought. Of course, in order to make a profit, jobbers have to avoid holding either too much stock or selling more stock than they possess. Accordingly, they adjust their bid (buying price) and offer (selling price) to anticipate the reactions of investors. Most obviously this will occur when, say, unexpectedly large profits are announced by a company: jobbers will tend to raise their quotation to avoid having to sell abnormally large amounts of shares to investors who now assess the share as being 'cheap' in relation to the previously quoted price. Similarly, it is common for jobbers to mark down their prices for a wide range of shares on the receipt of news which is expected to depress the profitability of British companies. In reporting prices of shares, newspapers such as the *Financial Times* and the *Times,* publish an average of the bid and offer prices of jobbers at the close of business. The Stock Exchange Daily List provides the closing bid and offer prices whilst various companies report these prices throughout the day by computer-linked terminals.

This marking up or down of prices by jobbers will go some way to maintain their profitability but if it is insufficient, the jobbers will have to ensure a larger profit by widening the spread of 'turn' between the bid and the offer. In practice, jobbers quoting the same share sometimes agree among themselves to maintain a minimum bid–offer spread. Although deals may actually be struck at the prices above the bid (or below the offer), the jobber will usually demand more details of the intended transaction before agreeing to more generous terms. Even this type of restraint on competitive prices has not prevented severe financial problems for small jobbing firms; these have responded by merging with other firms with a consequential loss of competition. It is not surprising therefore that the numbers of jobbing firms have dramatically declined from a hundred in 1960 to only seventeen in 1984. The Stock Exchange argues that there has been little change in the degree of competition because the merging firms have not usually been dealing in the same shares.

Accompanying the relative increase of institutional investing has been a rise in the number of share transactions arranged directly by stock brokers. Since brokers may be trading on behalf of several large institutions it will sometimes happen that one client wishes to sell a large block of shares which another client is willing to buy. Since all trading between members of the Stock Exchange has to be via a jobber, the broker arranges with the jobber to 'put through' this transaction for a lower margin than might normally be quoted in the market. In some cases, jobbers faced with a large stock of shares will approach brokers known to be especially close to institutional investors and ask if any of their institutional clients are interested in buying.

As will be discussed in Chapter 14, the separation of jobbing and broking capacities is not envisaged to continue for many years to come.

Single capacity can be useful in protecting the interests of individual investors. If the competing jobbers are sufficiently numerous, the forces of competition will, by minimising the effective bid–offer price spread, benefit all investors wishing to buy or sell securities. With combined or dual capacity, the market dealer can potentially act against the interests of his clients because he may be arranging for one client to buy from another at prices set at the dealer's discretion. Thus if a 'large' client is buying from a smaller investor, the dealer might be tempted to effect the transaction at a lower price than might be offered by another dealer.

Dual capacity is therefore likely to work optimally in active markets involving well-informed investors who can query any transaction that seems out-of-step with the prices reported by other dealers. To protect the interests of smaller investors, the operation of dual capacity has to be carefully monitored to ensure that dealers/market-makers are acting equitably with respect to their clients. The Stock Exchange has always argued that single capacity is the best method of protecting individual investors and the forecasted end of single capacity emphasises the power of the institutional investors in influencing the future development of the Stock Exchange.

In this area we should also mention the practice of 'dawn raiding' whereby an institutional investor will direct a stockbroking firm to buy a large block of shares in a company. In some cases, this may amount to a transaction worth millions of pounds. The broker will contact the market, other brokers and other institutional investors in a sudden burst of buying at prices often considerably above the quoted market price. By the time that this information has reached other investors, the transaction will be complete and the news will only inform the majority of investors that they have missed an opportunity to sell their shares at an unexpectedly high price. Because of the sense of unfairness about these types of deals, the Council for the Securities Industry has tried to discourage dawn raids by insisting that if investors acquire more than 5% of the shares in a company in any one raid, and thereby hold more than 15% of the shares, they should ensure that other shareholders receive a similar offer.

The importance of the institutional investors to the Stock Exchange has lead some observers to conclude that large companies with large numbers of shares available for trading are more favourably evaluated than small companies. From time to time critics of the City have suggested that small companies find it hard to raise capital by issuing shares partly because of this problem and partly because of the high fixed costs of obtaining a full 'listing' on the Stock Exchange,

In practice, independently of the Stock Exchange, a number of banks and other financial institutions have supplied capital to smaller firms by buying shares and subsequently acting as dealer/brokers in the shares. Amongst these types of informal markets, the most widely advertised are those made by Granville and Co. and by Harvard Securities. The combination of this type of competition and the criticisms mentioned above encouraged the Stock Exchange to create a separate market for smaller companies in 1980—the Unlisted Securities Market (USM).

The USM operates on the same principles as the main listed market but imposes less stringent regulations on companies wishing to have their shares traded. For example, whilst the listed market requires at least 25% of a company's shares to be offered in the primary issue before the shares can be listed, the USM requires only 10%. In practice, companies wishing to have their shares traded have sometimes entered the USM by placing shares with institutional shareholders (arranged by a stockbroker or issuing house). In these circumstances the Stock Exchange requires that 25% of the shares placed must be 'made available' or offered to the public so that a sufficiently wide spread of shareholdings will be achieved.

The emphasis in establishing the USM has been on encouraging small companies to have their shares traded preparatory to a full listing. It is not surprising to find that most of the companies are relatively young. Investment in newly established companies is usually recognised to be more risky, and studies reveal that investment in shares quoted on the USM has tended to be riskier than in equivalent companies quoted on the listed market. This may arise because there has been a preponderance of oil companies and innovatory enterprises (including dance studios and biotechnological companies) brought to the USM, but may also be influenced by the lesser amount of corporate financial disclosure required by the USM.

Yet another market organised by the Stock Exchange is the informal arrangements for trading shares in companies which are quoted neither on the listed market nor on the USM. The trading is allowed under Rules 534 and 535 of the Stock Exchange which refer to (1) securities listed on overseas securities markets (Rule 534(4)(a)), and (2) securities not listed on any exchange (Rule 535(2)). Under this latter rule for example, shares of the following companies were reported to have changed hands during one week in October 1984: Central ITV, Norton Villiers Triumph, Rangers Football Club and Sinclair Research. Under 534(4)(a), in the same week, the shares of over 150 different companies were traded including well known names such as Casio Computer and Texas Instruments. Rule 535(3) allows trading in the shares of companies engaged solely in mineral or oil exploration. In the case of Rule 534(4)(a) the Stock Exchange will always encourage companies to move to the USM or to the listed market if the trading is frequent. It is for this reason that many large firms quoted and traded primarily in the United States also appear in the listed sections of the Stock Exchange.

Government bonds may be bought and sold on the Stock Exchange in a similar way to shares, but investors may also buy and sell through the National Savings Stock Register. This arrangement holds for about fifty government bonds including some index linked stock (e.g. 2% Index Linked Treasury Stock 1988) and irredeemable bonds such as $2\frac{1}{2}$% Consols. Investors can therefore buy and sell these bonds without approaching a stockbroker; the transaction is arranged simply by sending an application form (available from Post Offices) to the Bonds and Stock Office. The register acts as a type of agent-broker but requires that all stock sold to the register must initially have been bought from the register.

Allocative Efficiency of the Stock Market

In Chapter 3 we briefly discussed the implications of *allocative efficiency* and commented that secondary securities markets do not strictly 'allocate' finance to companies. There are, however, three ways in which the secondary market can influence the use made of finance supplied in the primary market.

The first is the demand by investors in the secondary market for up-to-date information from companies. For any one company, new issues are generally few and far between; but in order to make even infrequent use of the primary market, a firm must continue to be listed on the secondary market, and to do this it must provide financial information. In this respect, Stock Exchange regulations go some considerable way beyond the accounting disclosures to shareholders required under the Companies Acts; more to the point, these disclosures are widely disseminated and the subject of much public discussion and comment.

Investment analysts will be continously monitoring the performance and financial results of companies and will also directly question the management of companies. In London, for example, the Society of Investment Analysts regularly holds meetings at which the Chairman or Managing Director discusses the company's performance.

The second (and related) way the secondary markets can influence the use of resources is in the feeding back of information to the management of the company. In the Stock Exchange, for example, firms of brokers employ a number of analysts whose job it is to analyse and appraise the shares of large and medium sized companies in each sector. In the process of carrying out research, the analysts will often find out a great deal about how effective is the management of the company. In circulating the results of their research, analysts can substantially influence the share price. Thus to managers, the behaviour of the share price can indicate an evaluation of the company's performance. Companies may thus react to a sustained fall in their share price by appointing new management or changing their managerial policies to forestall criticism by their shareholders. In addition, managers receive direct feedback from the comments of analysts at the Society's meetings (see previous paragraph).

These communications, although influential, cannot always serve to correct inadequate managerial performance. A third and more dramatic effect occurs in the case of a takeover bid. Takeovers occur for a variety of reasons: a company may wish to establish stronger control of a product market by taking over a competitor; another company may wish to diversify or to buy a 'ready made' investment in an expanding industrial market. Typically a bid may come after some informal approach by the directors of one company to another; but sometimes if a company is felt to be performing badly because of its management, a bid may arrive suddenly with no warning.

The bidder will often advertise in the newspapers and circulate its bid to each shareholder. Invariably the bid will be for a higher price than that currently reported on the Stock Exchange. The justification for many of these surprise bids is that the bidding company will be able to achieve higher profits than the existing management. The claim is usually disputed by the existing management who may similarly circulate to their shareholders forecasts of improved profits anticipated if the bid is *not* accepted. In either event, the takeover or the threat of takeover, the use made by companies of financial resources can be directly affected by the activity in the secondary market.

Allocative efficiency is difficult to assess and there have been few studies which have succeeded in analysing whether takeovers succeed in increasing the allocative efficiency of the market. We conclude only that the *threat* of takeover could reasonably be expected to have some effect on a company's management.

Operational Efficiency of the Stock Market

In applying the concept of operational efficiency to the Stock Exchange we note that many of the preconditions for efficiency are present. There are, for example, many buyers and sellers, at least for the major companies quoted. The transaction costs are relatively low, although it has been argued that the pressure from institutional investors has caused transaction costs to rise, at least as indicated by the bid–offer spread by jobbers.

It is easy to trade in shares, even with quite small amounts of capital. This is facilitated by the accounting system for share transactions. The Stock Exchange year is divided into two or three week periods or 'accounts'. Shares bought within one account are delivered on the second Monday after the end of the account (usually a Friday). Payment for the shares has to be made before or on the same day. Thus it is possible for an investor to buy shares in a company in one week and sell them at a higher price the following week without paying any cash. Of course, in accepting their clients' orders, stockbrokers will try to ensure that their credit is good for the amount of money at risk but the effective cost of trading or speculating in the short-term can be very low. It is therefore likely that if investors are looking out for possible anomalies between shares in, say, the same industry, trading can quickly and easily cause prices to shift back into line.

Another precondition of operational efficiency is the rapid dissemination of information. We have already noted that analysts spend considerable time researching into companies' prospects. They also spend time disseminating the results of their research. An investment analyst will probably produce a 'circular' or special note about a company which he or she is recommending. They will also telephone their potential clients to suggest that more shares should be bought in the company. If the information is recognised as being good, analysts hope that the clients will pay for it by placing business (i.e. orders to buy or sell) with the stockbroking firm. There are therefore considerable incentives to the analyst to find information that will cause a revision in investors' expectations and to disseminate this information as quickly as possible.

Information-processing Efficiency

In the light of the discussion above, it is natural to consider the efficiency with which prices in the market reflect available information. Although there have been many studies on the subject concerned with the American securities markets, the UK stock exchange has been less comprehensively studied. In both countries, studies have sometimes revealed small anomalies but broadly have indicated that the markets react quickly to information as it becomes available.

The concept of efficiency often strikes newcomers to the market as being implausible partly because newspapers and other media recount with enthusiasm of the investment coups of financial entrepreneurs, buying shares in little known companies shortly before some momentous news is announced. "How can the market be efficient", the reader might ask, "when I have read of the millions made by shrewd investors?"

Whilst it is true that an individual investor may from time to time be in a position to benefit from specialist knowledge of a firm's prospects, the case for market information-processing efficiency must turn on the behaviour of the prices in the stock market as a whole. Although there are over two thousand companies registered in the UK with ordinary shares listed on the Stock Exchange, the shares of fewer than 40 companies account for nearly 45% of the value of the shares listed. In fact, of the companies in the oil sector (which sector accounts for over 10% of the market's value) two companies — BP and Shell Transport and Trading—account for almost 10% of all UK listed shares.

Because of the importance of large companies in the Stock Exchange, any remarks on efficiency must take into account the possibility of mispricing of companies such as J. Sainsbury, Beecham, Marks and Spencer, ICI or Barclays Bank. But, as mentioned above, these large companies will be closely followed by investment analysts whose livelihood depends on their skill in evaluating the companies. The pricing of the shares will depend on the activity of the analysts and the institutional investors who will also be trying to out-perform their competitors. Arguing that the shares of large companies are persistently mispriced implies a sceptical if not cynical view of the efficiency of professional investors and their advisors and should provide opportunity for considerable profits (net of costs). An explanation is required as to why such opportunities are not traded away.

With smaller companies, some individuals may be more knowledgeable about the future prospects than analysts covering several industrial sectors. There are just two points which should be borne in mind before inferring that the shares of smaller companies are priced with inefficient use of information. Firstly, the interpretation of future profitability has to be made in the market framework. It is not enough for investors to know that the profits of a company are going to rise; they must also assess how the profits of other similar firms are going to behave. It may well be that in forecasting large increases in profits of the main companies in one sector, 'the market' has also up-rated its expectations for other (smaller) companies in the same sector.

Thus, the report of large profits can lead to increased, decreased or even unchanged share prices, depending on whether the reported profit is higher, lower or the same as that expected by the market as a whole. The interpretation of information requires much more skill than at first appears!

Secondly, individual investors believing that a small company is mispriced may find that, in trying to capitalise on their knowledge, the share price quickly adjusts on trading even modest numbers of shares. Thus observed mispricing does not necessarily imply that large profits can be made from trading.

Having suggested that theory and evidence indicate the UK Stock Exchange is by and large informationally efficient, we would not wish to leave the impression that this inference is undisputed. Many analysts and managers of institutional funds argue that some sectors are less efficient than others, or that the market over emphasises short-term considerations. In the case of property companies, for example, the assets of the firms are usually regularly and independently valued, yet the value of the shares held in these companies can be as much as twenty or thirty per cent under the reported values of their underlying property assets. These 'discounts' can fluctuate considerably from one month to the next and can vary dramatically between apparently similar companies. If the sector were informationally efficient one might expect the two valuations to be consistent. Although there are a number of factors which might go some way to explaining *some* of the differences, a plausible explanation of the discrepancy is still awaited.

Regulation of the Securities Markets

There has traditionally been a strong reliance on self-regulation in the securities markets, but over the last few years external agencies have increasingly intervened. Future developments, to be discussed in Chapter 14, also promise more active and forceful intervention and/or compulsion. However, for some time there have been official bodies including the police, the Department of Trade, the Director of Public Prosecutions, and the Bank of England which have effectively stepped in from time to time to supervise market operations.

Legislation has included controls on the advertising of securities and the handling of money invested by companies on behalf of their clients (The Prevention of Fraud Investments Act, 1958) and on the investment policies of certain fiduciary institutions (The Trustee Investments Act, 1961). More stringent legislation applies to banks and other deposit-taking institutions (The Banking Act, 1979). The Companies Act (1980) covers a number of activities associated with securities including, particularly, the problem of *insider dealing.*

The problem of insider dealing arises at its simplest when an employee of a company sells confidential information to an investor. In more complicated cases, any individual who is professionally related to a company may be able to use some confidential information to make profits from speculating in the shares of the company. Whilst it is not difficult to prohibit this type of activitiy, it becomes very difficult to distinguish between a professional analyst honestly researching into a company's prospects and illegally acquiring confidential information from employees of the company. Part V of the Companies Act (1980) concerns this complicated problem.

Apart from official bodies and legislation, there are a number of organisations which employ non-statutory methods of regulation that affect the securities markets, e.g. the Stock Exchange, the Council for the Securities Industry and various professional associations such as the Association of Investment Trust Companies. Of these the most important is the Council for the Securities Industry which was founded in 1978 by financial and investment institutions in combination with the Bank of England.

The Council oversees a number of operations including the Takeover Panel which investigates takeover bids on the Stock Exchange and issues the City Code on Takeovers and Mergers. Although there have been proposals that the Council should be greatly strengthened, at present it operates almost entirely by persuasion and institutional regulation. It is argued that this method is most efficient when the markets and institutions are concentrated. In other countries, the equivalent body (e.g. the USA's Securities and Exchange Commission) has to cover the dealing and trading practices in a wide range of financial/investment markets located in many different parts of the country, and in these circumstances it may be beneficial if the authority has official status and the possession of significant powers to enforce compliance with regulations.

The role of the Bank of England is likely to grow in importance. In July 1983 it was announced that the Stock Exchange had agreed to abandon fixed price commissions and that the Bank of England would be formally involved in monitoring the operations of the Stock Exchange. The change in the commission structure is likely to have a profound effect on the organisation and structure of the UK securities markets and will be discussed in more detail in Chapter 14.

Summary

The Stock Exchange is the major market for securities in the UK and any discussion of securities markets must therefore largely be concerned with its operation. In this chapter we have tried to generalise the discussion to some extent to reflect the changes that have suddenly affected the capital markets and institutions. We have also used the concepts of efficiency to examine the operations of the securities markets and their regulation.

Further Reading

1. P.H. Richards (ed.), *UK and European Share Price Behaviour: The Evidence* (Kogan Page, 1979) provides an authoritative selection of empirical studies on the efficiency of the UK Stock Market. Although the articles included are not all accessible to the non-mathematician, the linking commentaries are clear and contain some useful discussion.
2. L.G. Chan and R.C. Stapleton, 'Performance in USM, a Preliminary Analysis', *Investment Analyst* No.65 (July 1982, pp.11–13).
   D.H. Roden, 'The Measurement of Performance in the USM', *Investment Analyst* No.68 (April 1983, pp. 22–24). These two articles provide insights into the difficulty of making comparisons between the USM and other securities markets.
3. R.G. Winfield and S.J. Curry, *Success in Investment*, (John Murray Publishers Ltd., 1981). Primarily designed for students in professional courses, contains good descriptions of institutional arrangements for trading of securities.
4. G.J.J. Dennis, 'The Current and Future Role of Stockbrokers', *The Investment Analyst* No. 62 (October 1981, pp. 3–12). The Post Office Staff Superannuation Fund's director of securities investment reflects on the problems facing stockbrokers.
5. J. Dundas Hamilton, *Stockbroking Today*, 2nd edn (Macmillan, 1979). An authoritative account of stockbroking in the context of the London Stock Exchange. Also contains brief descriptions of the trading systems to be found in other parts of the world.

Discussion Questions

7.1 Why do traditional accounts of the jobbing system emphasise that jobbers should not know at the time they state their bid and offer prices whether brokers wish to buy or sell securities?

7.2. Do you think that financial journalists should be able to trade in securities about which they are writing? What safeguards or restraints would you propose?

7.3. 'Asset stripping' is a term used to describe the taking-over of a firm and the selling of its fixed assets to realise cash. Discuss the contribution to allocational efficiency arising from this type of activity.

7.4. 'Sell in May and go away' is an old adage of the Stock Exchange. What does it imply about the efficiency of the Stock Exchange? How would you tell whether it was profitable advice?

7.5. In estimating the return obtained from holding a share for a day, the capital gain can be taken to be the difference between the buying and selling price. Would this correspond to the bid offer spread quoted by the jobber? How would these prices relate to the share prices published in newspapers such as the *Financial Times*?

Chapter Eight

Bonds and Their Valuation

Issuers of Bonds

Bond issues can be usefully categorised by reference to the currency in which the bonds are denominated. In this discussion, we are concentrating on the sterling denominated bonds bought by investors in the United Kingdom. This category includes issues by the government, local authorities, companies and various overseas institutions such as the European Investment Bank or the Province of Nova Scotia, which for one reason or another have decided to issue bonds in London.

The British government is the major issuer of sterling bonds. Although the government borrows from different sources and uses a wide range of financial instruments, the sale of government securities represents a major source of finance. In 1983/84, for example, net sales of government securities accounted for over 80% of the central government borrowing requirement. These funds raised by issuing securities may be used for very different purposes including road expenditure, building and for lending to nationalised industry or local authorities. In many cases new issues are made to replace loans that are to be redeemed. In other cases, the government merely guarantees bonds issued by nationalised industries. Because the effective security to lenders is the same for guaranteed loans and 'pure' government issues, the term 'gilt edged' is used to include bonds issued by the government and by the nationalised industries. One such bond is the 3% British Transport issue which is redeemable between 1978 and 1988.

Sometimes, as in the case of the 3% British Transport bond, gilt edged bonds are redeemable at the borrower's option over a period of time. This feature provides some flexibility to the Bank of England and Treasury who act as investment managers on behalf of the public sector. Because of the upward trend in the number and value of gilt edged stocks issued, the redemption of one issue usually implies a replacement issue of stock at terms which will reflect the market conditions at the time of issue. The ability to delay or advance the redemption and issue of bonds can be very useful to the government.

A way in which cash flows can be phased to help investors is the requirement for less than full payment at the time of issue. For example, in September 1982 the government issued a stock called 'Exchequer 10%, 1988' for which investors had to pay only £20 on application, a further £40 on the 1st November 1982, and a final £37 in December. This stock was issued by tender, that is, investors had to specify the price at which they would be willing to buy the bonds. In the event the issue was successful and because there were applications for more than the amount of stock offered, those investors who had offered prices at the minimum issue price of £97 did not receive the full amount of bonds for which they had applied. Issues by tender are further discussed in Chapter 9.

Besides the variation in issuing and redemption conditions, the government also offered bonds with variable rates of interest linked to the average Treasury bill rate. A more important recent innovation has been index-linked government stocks which were first introduced in 1981 and for which both the interest and the maturity value depend on the level of the Index of Retail Prices eight months before payment. If these bonds are held until they are redeemed, investors can be sure of receiving a return which will more than compensate them for any changes in retail prices. They are therefore especially popular with long-term investors, such as pension funds, who need to secure real returns with the minimum of risk.

Local authorities and public boards (such as the Clyde Port Authority and the Water Boards) also issue bonds which are traded in London. Local authorities have the option to borrow specified quotas of funds from the government's Public Works Loan Board, but do from time to time decide to make direct issues on the market. During the late 1970s a large part of the local authority net borrowings were at variable interest rates, but in 1981 both Leeds and Swansea issued fixed interest bonds (offering interest payments of 13½% and 13¾% respectively) redeemable in the year 2006. A variation in the type of bond issued by local authorities is the 'drop-lock' stock of which one example listed on the Stock Exchange was issued in 1981 by Birmingham. Usually drop-lock stocks have variable interest payments which are linked to short-term interest rates but which remain locked at a predetermined rate if interest rates fall below a minimum level. In the case of the stock issued by Birmingham, the drop-lock feature only existed for a year since the stock was automatically converted in 1982 into a 13½% fixed interest bond redeemable in 1989.

British companies have in recent years issued very little fixed interest debt, although there have been some limited issues of convertible debt (in which the debt can be converted into ordinary shares at some later date).

Convertible debt appears attractive to companies who expect profits to increase in the short or medium term. The argument advanced is that interest payments offered on convertible debt are lower than for fixed interest debt and that market conditions would not currently support an issue of more ordinary shares. For investors, convertible debt is a compromise between the high initial yield of fixed interest payments and the uncertainty involved in holding risky ordinary shares. The valuation of convertible debt is further considered in the next chapter.

Companies may issue bonds either in the form of loan stock or debentures. Both types of bond involve the appointment of a trustee who checks that the borrowing company is carrying out the terms of the contract. Often in the case of debentures, the loan is 'secured' by specific assets such as land or buildings so investors may be reasonably confident, in the event of default, that they will be compensated for losses. Debentures are therefore more secure than loan stock because the debenture holders have the right to enforce their security (by the use of a receiver seizing and selling the specified assets).

Since 1981 foreign companies and institutions have again issued sterling bonds which are traded in London. These bonds are called 'bulldog' bonds and are issued by governments (e.g. Denmark, Sweden and Australia), companies (e.g. Inco Limited) and institutions such as the European Investment Bank. The reasons why foreign institutions wish to raise money by issuing bonds are various; in the case of a company, the proceeds might be used for building and buying equipment for a factory in the UK. In other cases the issuer believes that sterling is going to decline in value and that therefore the 'high' nominal interest rate will be much less important to borrowers making profits in foreign currency, since the loan repayments will be cheaper in real terms.

Another type of bond traded in London is the 'euro-bond'. The *euro-bond market* developed rapidly in the 1960s, largely based on loans denominated in dollars. The distinguishing characteristic of euro-bonds is that they are not subject to the tax and other regulations of the country in whose currency they are issued. So, for example, in London, issues have been made of bonds denominated in US Dollars, Dutch Guilders and Swiss Francs. The range of currencies is extended by the issuing of multi-currency bonds. These bonds can either be issued to give investors a choice of currencies in which to receive interest and redemption payments, or can be denominated in artificial 'packages' such as the European Currency Units.

Most issuers of international bonds have been large international companies, public sector institutions or governments. As with other types of bonds, there is wide variation in the terms of issue and the ways in which interest and repayment are determined: there are fixed interest, variable interest, drop-lock and convertible bonds.

Characteristics of Traded Bonds

Whilst investors are accustomed to hearing of large profits (and losses) being made from investment in shares, investment in bonds is regarded as being safer. This is far from a true picture of fixed-rate bonds, especially in periods during which interest rates shift rapidly. In 1982, for example, bond prices for some government securities rose by more than 30%. With corporate and foreign bonds there is also the possibility of loss from borrower's failure to pay interest or to repay the loan when due.

The problems of assessing the risk of making losses on bond investment because of fluctuating interest rates will be discussed in the following sections. In this section we will look at the characteristics of bonds which have to be assessed in estimating the possibility of default, that is, the failure on the borrower's part to pay either interest or capital to the investor.

Loan stockholders and ordinary creditors will be repaid after debenture holders but before ordinary shareholders. If companies have issued more than one loan stock, the priority of payment *between* loan stock investors will be made known at the time of issue.

Assessing the risks of corporate bonds is a complicated process. It is not surprising that professional investors and investment advisors have tried to find ways of simplifying the problem. In the United States, where bonds are a more important source of corporate finance than in Britain there are a number of specialist firms which produce 'ratings' of bond issues. By far the most popular of these rating services are Moody's and Standard and Poor's. Moody's rate issues from an Aaa (best quality) to a C (indicating extremely poor prospects), whilst Standard and Poor's service uses AAA for the highest grade and D for the lowest quality in which the issue is already in default.

In London, a somewhat less used system was designed in 1973 and approved by the Society of Investment Analysts and the Institute of Actuaries. Basically, there are two aspects which determine the rating — the company and the issue. The company is rated according to its size, the relative amount of debt it uses for financing its operations and the proportion of its profits required to pay interest. The issue is rated according to the security, its priority (in the event of default) and the borrowing limits which are fixed for other issues which might subsequently be made. The ratings are made available to investors by stockbrokers who specialise in analysing corporate bond markets. Unlike in the US, ratings are calculated simply by a mechanical application of well defined criteria. Highest quality is rated as AA whilst lowest is EE; note that a rating of EA is quite possible for a well secured debenture issued by a very risky company.

In the international bond markets there is as yet no universally recognised rating service and the difficulty of estimating the complicated risks of international bonds is a factor inhibiting the participation of a wider range of investors in this type of market. Both Moody's and Standard and Poor's rank some bonds by the type of issuer, which in the case of 'official' bond issues includes an assessment of the political stability of the government. The coverage of the service is, however, more limited than that provided by their US domestic rating operation, though it is expanding.

Maturity, Tax and Coupon

Table 8.1 is an extract of the information on gilt-edged securities published daily in the *Financial Times*. There are five categories: 'shorts', bonds with less than five years to redemption; 'mediums', five to fifteen years; 'longs', over fifteen years; undated; index-linked bonds.

Table 8.1 Government Bond Prices and Yield, 29 October 1984

BRITISH FUNDS

1984 High	1984 Low	Stock	Price £	+ or –	Yield Int.	Yield Red.
		"Shorts" (Lives up to Five Years)				
105 3/8	101 1/16	Treas. 15pc 1985	**101 1/4**	......	14.81	10.41
102 3/4	100	Exch. 12pc Cnv. '85	**100 11/16**	+ 1/16	11.92	10.17
96 3/16	93 5/16	Treas 3pc 1985	**96 3/16** xd	+ 1/16	3.12	10.29
102 5/8	99 1/2	Treas 11 1/2pc 1985	**100 5/8**	+ 1/16	11.43	10.44
99 3/4	96 9/16	Treas 8 3/4pcCnv '85	**98 9/16**	+ 1/16	8.88	10.51
104 3/16	99 7/8	Exch. 12 1/4pc 1985	**101 5/8** xd	+ 1/16	12.05	10.64
103 13/16	99 1/16	Exch. 11 3/4pc '86	**101 1/16**	+ 1/16	11.63	10.77
102 5/16	96 1/16	Treas. 10pcCnv 1986	**99 1/16**	+ 1/16	10.09	10.70
91 11/16	88 1/4	Treas 3pc 1986	**91 5/8** xd	+ 1/16	3.27	8.92
102	96 3/4	Exch. 10 1/2pc Cv '86	**99 5/8** xd	......	10.54	10.82
104 3/16	99 1/16	Treas 12pc 1986	**101 9/16**	+ 1/8	11.82	10.88
98 3/4	93 1/2	Treas 8 1/2pc 1984-86‡‡	**96 7/16**	+ 1/16	8.81	10.82
108 13/16	102 7/16	Exch. 14pc 1986	**105 1/16**	+ 1/16	13.33	11.10
87 1/4	85	Exch. 2 1/2pc 1986	**87 3/16** xd	......	2.87	9.50
107 11/16	100 13/16	Exch. 13 1/4pc 1987	**103 11/16**	+ 1/16	12.78	11.26
100 7/8	94 1/2	Treas 10 1/4pcCv '87	**98 1/16**	+ 1/8	10.45	11.18
86 1/8	83 1/8	Exch 2 1/2pc 1987	**85 5/8**	+ 1/8	2.92	9.53
101 3/16	94 1/2	Exch. 10 1/2pc 1987	**98 1/2**	+ 1/16	10.66	11.21
92 11/16	87	Funding 6 1/2pc '85-87‡‡	**90 11/16** xd	+ 3/16	7.17	10.86
99 5/8	92 7/8	Treas. 10pc 1987	**96 7/8**	+ 1/16	10.32	11.39
85	81 9/16	Treas 3pc 1987	**83 3/8**	......	3.60	10.17
105	97 1/4	Treas. 12pc 1987	**101 11/16** xd	+ 1/16	11.80	11.32
94 7/8	87 9/16	Treas 7 3/4pc 1985-88‡‡	**91 3/16**	+ 1/16	8.50	11.02
100 3/4	92 11/16	Exch 10 1/2pc '88	**97 7/16** xd	+ 1/16	10.78	11.42
98 7/16	89 15/16	Treas 9 3/4pc Cv '88	**94 3/4**	– 1/16	10.28	11.54
82	77	Transport 3pc '78-88	**78 3/16**	+ 1/8	3.84	10.28
96 15/16	88 5/16	Treas. 9 1/2pc '88	**93 11/16**	+ 1/16	10.14	11.52
106 3/4	94 11/16	Treas 11 1/2pc 1989	**99 13/16**	+ 1/16	11.52	11.52
95 9/16	87 11/16	Treas 9 1/2pc Cnv. '89	**93 7/8**	+ 3/16	10.12	11.29
96 3/8	90 11/16	Treas 10 1/2pc 1989	**96 5/16**	+ 1/16	10.90	11.44
100 3/16	88 7/8	Exch.10pc 1989	**94 3/8**	+ 1/16	10.60	11.55
98 1/4	94 3/4	Exch 11pc 1989	**97 3/4**	+ 1/8	11.25	11.58
85 1/8	77 1/2	Treas 5pc 1986-89	**80**	+ 1/8	6.25	10.24
		Five to Fifteen Years				
112 1/4	100 1/8	Treas 13pc 1990‡‡	**109 1/2**	– 1/8	12.30	11.48
110 7/8	100 3/4	Exch. 12 1/2pc 1990	**105**	– 1/8	12.05	11.56
93 1/4	84 7/8	Treas 8 1/4pc 1987-90‡‡	**92**	+ 1/8	9.28	10.93
98 15/16	90 5/8	Treas. 10pcCv 1990	**94**	+ 1/8	10.65	11.44
107	94 3/4	Treas 11 3/4pc 1991	**104 1/4**	......	11.67	11.57
84 1/8	75 5/8	Funding 5 3/4pc '87-91‡‡	**80 1/8**	+ 1/4	7.22	10.11
105 3/4	93 7/8	Exch. 11pc 1991	**98 1/4**	+ 1/4	11.21	11.40
112 5/8	98 7/8	Treas 12 3/4pc 1992‡‡	**109 1/4**	......	12.06	11.53
100 5/8	86	Treas 10pc 1992	**95 1/4**	+ 1/4	10.71	10.34
97 1/8	94 1/16	Treas 10 1/2pc Cv 1992	**97 1/8**	......	10.97	11.34
111 1/8	95 1/8	Exch. 12 1/4pc '92	**105 5/8**	......	11.85	11.56
117 1/2	106 1/8	Exch 13 1/2pc 1992	**111**	......	12.32	11.60
113 3/8	98 1/8	Treas 12 1/2pc 1993‡‡	**109 1/8**	......	11.86	11.48
78 3/4	71 1/8	Funding 6pc 1993‡‡	**76 1/4**	+ 1/8	7.95	10.26
121 3/4	106 3/4	Treas 13 3/4pc 1993‡‡	**111 3/8** xd	+ 1/8	12.25	11.54
126 3/4	108 1/4	Treas 14 1/2pc 1994‡‡	**119 3/4**	......	12.35	11.42
120 5/8	106	Exch 13 1/2pc 1994	**111 1/4**	......	12.15	11.54
114 1/8	96 3/4	Exch. 12 1/2pc 1994	**108 1/8**	......	11.82	11.49
94 1/2	82 7/8	Treas 9pc 1994‡‡	**87 1/4** xd	......	10.26	11.05
109 1/4	94 7/8	Treas 12pc 1995	**106 1/8**	......	11.66	11.48
64 1/4	58 3/4	Gas 3pc '90-95	**62 1/2** xd	......	4.80	8.46
99 1/8	86	Exch. 10 1/4pc 1995	**96 1/8**	+ 1/8	10.99	11.34
117 7/8	102 5/8	Treas 12 3/4pc 1995‡‡	**108** xd	+ 1/8	11.74	11.38
122 5/8	106 7/8	Treas. 14pc '96	**119**	+ 1/8	12.16	11.53
94 3/8	83 1/2	Treas 9pc 1992-96‡‡	**88 1/4**	+ 1/8	10.33	11.01
134 7/8	118 1/4	Treas 15 1/4pc 1996‡‡	**123 3/4** xd	+ 1/4	12.31	11.47
122 1/8	106 1/2	Exch 13 1/4pc 1996‡‡	**112** xd	+ 1/4	11.77	11.29
69 1/2	63 1/4	Redemption 3pc 1986-96	**67 1/2**	......	4.46	7.12
120	104 1/2	Treas 13 1/4pc 1997‡‡	**116 1/2**	......	11.74	11.27
104 1/2	87 3/8	Exch 10 1/2pc 1997	**97 3/4**	+ 1/8	10.97	11.13
92 1/2	77 1/2	Treas 8 3/4pc 1997‡‡	**86 1/4**	+ 3/8	10.31	10.97
134 5/8	118 1/8	Exch. 15pc 1997	**123 1/2**	+ 1/4	12.16	11.49
95 1/2	84 1/2	Exch. 9 3/4pc 1998	**94 1/8**	+ 1/8	10.67	10.99
78	68	Treas 6 3/4pc 1995-98‡‡	**72 3/8** xd	+ 1/4	9.32	10.66
138 5/8	123 7/8	Treas. 15 1/2pc '98‡‡	**129 5/8**	+ 1/8	12.08	11.38
115	100 1/8	Exch. 12pc 1998	**105 1/2** xd	+ 1/8	11.30	11.13
96	83 7/8	Treas 9 1/2pc 1999‡‡	**93 1/8**	......	10.52	10.83
116 3/4	104	Exch. 12 1/4pc 1999	**109 1/2**	+ 1/8	11.31	11.08
104 1/2	91	Treas. 10 1/2pc 1999	**96 3/8** xd	+ 1/4	10.83	10.93
		Over Fifteen Years				
102 1/2	89 1/4	Convers'n 10 1/4pc 1999	**94 1/2** xd	+ 1/4	10.77	10.92
121 1/2	106 3/8	Treas. 13pc 2000	**118 1/2**	+ 1/8	11.34	11.01
128 1/2	112 3/8	Treas. 14pc '98-01	**117 3/4** xd	......	11.80	11.30
113 1/8	98 5/8	Exch. 12pc '99-02	**110**	+ 1/8	11.25	11.04
98 7/8	90	Conv. 10pc 2002	**96**	+ 1/8	10.47	10.57
126 3/4	110 3/4	Treas. 13 3/4pc 2000-03	**123 3/4**	+ 1/8	11.45	11.02
114 7/8	101 1/2	Treas. 11 1/2pc 2001-04	**107 1/8**	+ 1/8	10.87	10.74
50	43 3/4	Funding 3 1/2pc '99-04	**48 1/4**	......	7.41	9.46
123 5/8	107 3/4	Treas. 12 1/2pc 2003-05	**114** xd	+ 1/8	10.89	10.68
87 1/8	76 7/8	Treas. 8pc 2002-06‡‡	**81 1/2**	+ 1/4	9.88	10.19
115 5/8	100	Treas. 11 3/4pc 2003-07	**112**	+ 1/8	10.80	10.63
132 1/8	117 5/8	Treas. 13 1/2pc '04-08	**124 1/8**	+ 1/8	10.99	10.68
64 7/8	56 1/8	Treas. 5 1/2pc 2008-12‡‡	**60 1/2**	+ 1/8	9.22	9.70
84 1/8	72 3/4	Treas. 7 3/4pc 2012-15‡‡	**81 1/8**	+ 1/4	9.80	9.97
124 1/2	108 7/8	Exch. 12pc '13-'17	**121**	......	10.31	10.22
		Undated				
40 7/8	35 7/8	Consols 4pc	**39 7/8**	......	10.29	—
37 3/8	32 1/2	War Loan 3 1/2pc‡‡	**34 3/4** xd	+ 1/8	9.98	—
44 7/8	40 1/2	Conv. 3 1/2pc '61 Aft.	**41 3/4**	......	8.44	—
31 5/8	27 3/4	Treas. 3pc '66 Aft.	**29 1/2**	+ 3/8	10.24	—
25 3/4	22 3/4	Consols 2 1/2pc	**24 5/8**	+ 1/4	10.22	—
26	23	Treas. 2 1/2pc	**24 5/8**	......	10.23	—
		Index-Linked (b)			(1)	(2)
108)	101	Treas. 2pc '88 (297.1)	**106 7/8**	......	3.70	4.65
94 1/2	85	Do. 2pc '90 (333.9)	**92 3/4**	......	3.76	4.39
108 5/8	98 3/4	Do. 2pc '96 (267.9)	**108 1/4**	......	3.43	3.73
99	88 5/8	Do. 2 1/2pc '01 (308.8)	**98 1/4**	......	3.23	3.50
99 1/4	87 7/8	Do. 2 1/2pc '03 (310.7)	**97** xd	......	3.23	3.44
102	90 1/4	Do. 2pc '06 (274.1)	**101 1/2**	......	3.13	3.31
99 3/4	87 3/8	Do. 2 1/2pc '09 (310.7)	**97 3/8** xd	– 1/8	3.04	3.22
104 1/4	91 5/8	Do. 2 1/2pc '11 (294.1)	**103 1/2**	......	3.04	3.20
95 1/2	82 1/2	Do. 2 1/2pc '16 (322.0)	**94 5/8**	......	2.98	3.13
93 1/4	81 3/8	Do. 2 1/2pc '20 (327.3)	**92 3/8**	......	2.96	3.10

Prospective real redemption rate on projected inflation of (1) 10% and (2) 5%. (b) Figures in parentheses show RPI base month for indexing, ie 8 months prior to issue. RPI for Feb., 1984: 344.0 and for September, 1984: 355.5.

Securities are classified as *short* if they are likely to be redeemed within five years. Within this category, there is a range of securities which differ in their maturity and in the rate of interest paid. In late 1984, the terms ranged from an Exchequer 2½% bond redeemable in 1987 to a Treasury 15% bond redeemable in 1985.

The interest payment (or coupon) differs for two reasons. First, the market rates of interest change so that the government may at one time be able to borrow at 8% and another at 12%. As described earlier, bonds may be redeemed to take advantage of these fluctuations. Secondly, there are tax implications whereby the profit made by buying and selling a bond at a higher price (the capital gain) may be liable to tax at a different rate than the rate charged on income received in the form of interest. In the case of government securities, there is no tax paid on any capital gains made if the stock is held for more than one year, whilst income received by government bond investors by way of interest payments is liable to income tax only for some investors, e.g. charities are not so liable. As will be seen in the next section, the effect of tax alone can make the analysis of bond investment a complicated and technical problem. But the principle is simple enough: many investors pay different rates of tax on their income and capital gains and the actual rates vary between different groups of investors. The effect is to encourage investors to look for particular combinations of income and capital gain that will maximise their returns net of tax.

A complicating issue in looking at 'shorts' is that the price quoted in the financial pages of newspapers does not indicate the effective cost of the bond to an investor. In the case of an investor buying, say, Exchequer $11\frac{3}{4}$%, 1986 at £$101\frac{1}{16}$, the price[1] would be increased to include the part of the interest which had built up between the last interest payment and the date on which the stock is paid for. In the case of Exchequer $11\frac{3}{4}$%, 1986, interest is paid on 25 August and 25 February, so that an investor who bought the stock for settlement on 1 November would have to pay £$101\frac{1}{16}$ and a further 68/365 of £11.75 or £103.25 in total. (There are 68 days between 25 August and 1 November.) Correspondingly, when the stock is quoted 'ex dividend' the buyer effectively pays less than the quoted price because the seller has to refund the amount of interest that accrues between purchase and the next payment of interest. With gilts with longer than five years to maturity the price quoted is inclusive of this accrued interest.

The effects of these UK conventions can be seen during the period in which the stocks become quoted ex dividend, from the following hypothetical example:

| | | | *Quoted prices* | |
	Interest paid	*Date ex dividend*	*14 April*	*16 April*
Short gilt 12%	22 May, 22 Nov.	15 April	100	100
Long gilt 12%	22 May, 22 Nov.	15 April	104.73	98.85

---

[1] In the market, bond prices are often given in per cent. Thus the price of the Treasury bond would be described as £104%. This convention is used for all stock which are priced in units of £100 but traded in multiples of one penny.

In the case of the short gilt, the buyer on the 14 April will have to pay an additional £4.73 to the seller, representing accrued interest from the previous interest payment (144 days have elapsed since the previous interest payment on 22 November). In the case of the long gilt the price includes the accrued interest. On 16 April, the buyer of the short gilt is credited with 35/365 of the coupon. (Payment is made on the day after the transaction and there are 35 days between 16 April and 22 May.) Taking these adjustments into account, the prices of the stocks can be seen to coincide as far as the buyer and seller are concerned, even though the quoted prices differ.

Undated stocks are curious investment instruments in that, as their name suggests, no date is fixed for their redemption although typically the government can redeem them at three months' notice. These issues typically offer low interest payments of between £2.50 and £4.00 per £100 nominal value. Needless to say, these bonds are worth far less than their nominal values; but as interest rates rise and fall over time their prices fluctuate. Thus investors can still expect to make profits from capital gains on the sale of irredeemable bonds as well as from the receipt of interest payments.

It has already been noted that the tax regulations are complex in their effect, and professional tax and investment consultants can substantially improve the performance of a gilt portfolio by careful investment transactions. The exploitation of these effects is eased by the fact that for non-convertible bonds, transaction costs are low because no Stamp Duty is payable. Furthermore, for gilts, commission charged by stockbrokers is considerably lower than for other securities. In the circumstances, it is not surprising that the volume of trading in government stocks is very large. Over the last few years, for example, the value of transactions in government bonds has been about five times larger than the value of ordinary shares traded, even though the number of transactions in gilts has been less than a quarter of the number of transactions in equities. This difference clearly reflects the tendency of investors to trade large blocks of government bonds in order to make small per unit gains from relative changes in prices and tax liability. (The average value of a transaction in fixed interest stocks was over £180,000 in 1983 compared with less than £12,000 for an ordinary share transaction.)

As explained in the last section, the interest paid on government bonds has historically been fixed in money terms, but for some issues varies according to changes in the Index of Retail Prices or in short-term interest rates. In the case of fixed interest bonds, the interest payment is expressed as a percentage of the nominal price of the stock (£100). So a 12% bond will pay £6 half yearly. This payment is referred to as the *coupon*. In fact, investors will normally receive a direct payment of less than this because interest on most government stocks is paid after the deduction of tax at the standard rate for income. Investors who are not liable to tax then have to claim the tax back from Inland Revenue. However, for bonds marked with the symbol ++ in the *Financial Times*, interest is paid gross to overseas investors who satisfy the Inland Revenue as to their status so that they do not have to go through the formalities of claiming back the tax.

Running and Redemption Yields

Differences in coupons can result in different bond prices. For example, if one bond pays £6 each half year and another of the same maturity pays only £2, other things being equal, it would be surprising if they traded at the same price in the market. Moreover, equality of coupons does not mean that the bonds will have the same prices. Tax implications can influence the market valuation of a bond. These complications apart, there are two statistics which are calculated for all bonds. These are the *running yield* (or interest yield) and the *redemption yield;* they appear in the financial columns of newspapers which publish Stock Exchange prices.

The running yield is calculated simply by dividing the coupon amount by the bond price, net of accrued interest. The running yield indicates in a rough and ready way the relative importance of the coupon payments in the return but no account is taken of the delay before the interest payments are received. From an investor's point of view, receiving the payments in two or more instalments will increase the value of the bond because the cash receipts are thus accelerated. The calculation of the running yield will depend on whether or not the bond is short. For short bonds, the running yield is given simply by dividing the annual coupon by the quoted (clean) price of the bond.

For longer term bonds, the price of the bond must first be adjusted to remove the effect of the accrued interest. Thus if interest on a 12% ten-year bond is paid on 10 May and 10 November, the adjustment for 15 July will be 66/365 of the annual interest payment. The running yield (y) will then be given by,

$$y = 12/[P - (66/365)12]$$

P being the quoted price of the bond.

The redemption yield indicates the return which an investor will earn from his investment if the bond is held until redemption. It includes both the return from receiving interest and the capital gain or loss on redemption. Although redemption yields are normally calculated by ignoring the effect of taxation, analysts often estimate the net of tax redemption yield from the point of view of a particular investor. As can be seen from Table 8.1, there have been large differences between the running and redemption yields. In the case of the short-term Treasury 3%, 1987, the gross (i.e. pre-tax) running yield was only 3.60%, whilst the gross redemption yield was 10.17%. The yields on this bond were relatively low because most of the return was then expected to come from the capital gain (being the difference between the current price of £$83\frac{3}{8}$ and the maturity value of £100) in the course of its remaining life.

The calculation of these yields can best be explained from an investor's viewpoint. We will start by considering a very simple example of a bond, on which interest is paid every six months and on which the interest has been paid the day before the investor pays for the bond. In this way we will defer some of the more complicated factors of the calculation, i.e. the consideration of accrued interest. Consider an investor who is analysing a bond which pays £6.00 per half year and will be redeemed in two years' time. The value of this bond will be given by

$$P_t \quad = \quad 6a_{\overline{4}|\,i} \quad + \quad 100\,(1 + i)^{-4}$$

where i is the investor's opportunity cost of capital per half year. If i is given, there is no difficulty in estimating P_t. But suppose the bond is quoted on the Stock Exchange at £95. What is the interest rate that will be earned if the bond is held until it is redeemed? There is no simple way of calculating the answer to this question. Trial and error must be used; calculators that have the redemption yield programmes included as functions are also available. The method which will be used here is 'interpolation', that is, by finding a weighted average of two rates that have been selected to produce valuations that are respectively larger and smaller than the quoted price.

Rate	Value
0.06	100.00
i?	95.00 (the quoted price)
0.08	93.37

From these calculations we can estimate i by the following expression,

$$\frac{i - 0.06}{0.08 - 0.06} \quad = \quad \frac{95 - 100}{93.37 - 100}$$

therefore $i = 0.07508$, or approximately 7.5%. We can also represent this calculation in the form of a diagram (Figure 8.1).

To check the approximation, the estimated yield should be substituted in the valuation formula,

$$P_t \quad = \quad 6a_{\overline{4}|\,0.075} \quad + \quad 100\,(1.075)^{-4} = 94.976$$

which approximates very closely to the market price of 95. In this example, therefore, the running yield would be taken as 12/95 or 12.63% and the redemption yield would be 7.5% per half year or an effective annual rate $(1.075)^2 - 1 = 15.56\%$ or 15% nominal. In practice, the redemption yields are usually quoted in nominal terms.

In general, of course, the redemption yield will be calculated on dates which do not coincide with interest payments, and the calculation has to be adjusted to reflect the accrued interest and the delay in the time before the

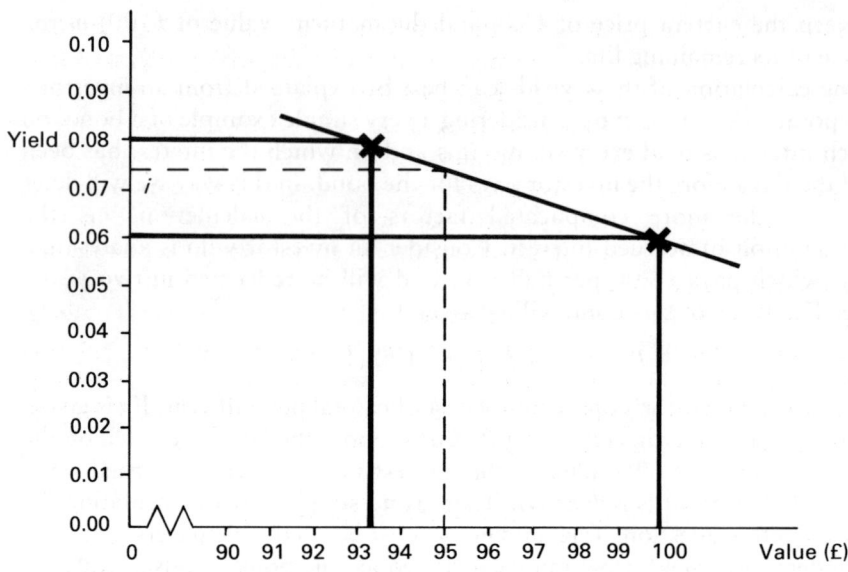

Figure 8.1   Interpolation of Redemption Yield.

next interest payment is due. This complication is dealt with in the Appendix to this chapter.

To calculate the redemption yield for an investor paying tax at 30% on interest income, the conventional method is to deduct from the interest received the rate of tax and to treat the tax as being payable at the same time as the interest is due. In this example, this would reduce the £6 to £4.2 and the redemption yield would then be calculated using the method as demonstrated.

Although the redemption yield is widely quoted, it is not an altogether satisfactory indicator. It shows the highest rate of interest that could be paid by the investor on a loan to finance the investment without making a loss. It can be also thought of as the average return on the investment if all intermediate cash flows are reinvested at the same rate throughout the life of the investment. It is in this latter aspect that the weakness of the redemption yield can be seen because, as Table 8.1 shows, the redemption yield of bonds that differ only in maturity can be markedly different. For example, the Treasury $11\frac{3}{4}\%$, 1991, stock had a redemption yield of 11.57% whilst the Treasury $11\frac{3}{4}\%$, 2003–07, stock had a redemption yield of 10.63%. The redemption yield can be thought of as a kind of average of the rates of interest over the remaining life of the bond. Thus the differences might at first suggest that the bond with the highest redemption yield would be the most profitable investment. However, as we shall show later, this interpretation is too simple. As the preceding discussion may have suggested, some differences in redemption yields arise from the effect of tax;

but some residual part stems from the inherent weakness of the redemption yield as an indicator of the investment return. The disturbing effects of tax can be clearly seen in Table 8.1 by comparing the redemption yields on Treasury $13\frac{3}{4}$%, 2000–03 and Funding $3\frac{1}{2}$%, 1999–2004. The redemption yield on the first was 11.02% compared with 9.46% on the second. The $3\frac{1}{2}$% stock was attractive to investors paying tax at high marginal rates, and their attention caused the price to rise with a consequent fall in the redemption yield, because they could realise their income in capital gains subject to lower tax rates.

Despite these shortcomings, redemption yields remain popular (albeit crude) indicators, which are widely referred to in commentaries on the behaviour of bond prices over time. They are also used to indicate the 'view of the market' with regard to bonds of different maturities, and it is this aspect to which we now turn.

Term Structure of Interest Rates

In the previous section we showed that different tax rates on capital gains and interest distorted the prices of bonds. In order to minimise this distortion, one way of analysing the effect of maturity on the redemption yield would be to limit the analysis to bonds on which returns would be earned only from a change in the price; that is, bonds for which the coupon is zero. In addition, we will assume in this section that all returns are based on annual compounding.

Suppose an investor examined a series of bonds and found that one bond was redeemable in one year's time with a redemption yield of 10%, and another was to be redeemed in two years' time with a redemption yield of 12%. Under what circumstances would the two-year bond be a better investment?

To answer this question we need additional information, such as the length of time for which the investor wishes to invest funds and the investor's attitude to risk. Let us assume that the investor wishes to invest funds for two years and that the objective is to maximise returns over the period. Is this information sufficient to decide which bond to buy? Again, the answer is no, because if the investor buys a one year bond, then in one year's time the bond will be redeemed and cash will be available for investment in another bond that will mature at the end of the second year. The investor needs to know the return that will be earned on that part of the investment. If he has £1000 invested in the one year bond, then at the end of the first year he will receive £1100 which he will re-invest. If one-year rates are then 15%, he will finish up with £1265. If, on the other hand, he invests in the two-year bond, he will realise £1000 $(1.12)^2$ or £1254 at the end of the second year.

Alternatively, if one-year rates of interest are 12% at the end of the first year, the re-investment of the proceeds from the one-year bond will only amount to £1232 by the end of the second year. From this example it will be appreciated that the optimal investment policy will depend on the interest rates expected to be ruling at the start of the second year; if interest rates are below 14% the two-year bond will realise a higher overall return.

This example can be extended to include a large number of investors all considering the same problem. If we observe market prices when all investors have made their decisions, we may assume that the effect of their actions gives rise to what we might call a 'market view'. On average, therefore, if we observe two-year bonds trading to give a redemption yield of 12% and one-year bonds at 10%, then on average investors expect that rates of interest in the second year will be 14%. Another way of expressing this is that the expected returns over two years will be the same regardless of the specific bond in which the funds are invested.

In a crude way, therefore, the observation of a redemption yield of 10% on a one-year bond and 12% on a two-year bond *implies* an expected one-year rate of about 14% in one year's time. This can be generalised. From a series of redemption yields, one can derive a series of short-term expected or implied interest rates linking up each bond of different maturity. These implied rates were in Chapter 5 referred to as implied 'forward' rates.

The implied single period forward rate for year n is given by

$$F_n = \frac{(1 + i_n)^n}{(1 + i_{n-1})^{n-1}} - 1$$

where i_n = the redemption yield on an n-year bond.

In this example, $n = 2$, $i_2 = 0.12$ and $_1 = 0.10$, so

$$F_2 = \frac{(1 + 0.12)^2}{(1 + 0.10)} - 1 = 0.1404 \simeq 14\%$$

In other words, the investor buying one-year bonds would expect to receive an average of 12% annually — 10% per cent in the first year and an *implied* rate of 14% in the second. This illustrates the comment made earlier in the chapter that a redemption yield represented a type of average return over the life of the bond.

It would be possible to derive a series of implied forward rates if we had redemption yields for a number of bonds that differed *only* in maturity. Suppose, for example, that we observed redemption yields as follows:

Maturity	1 yr	2 yr	3 yr	4 yr	5 yr	6 yr	7 yr	8 yr
Redemption	10	12	13	13.73	13.78	13.48	13	12.6

The implied forward rate for the second year has already been shown to be 14%; likewise, the forward rate of the third year can be calculated by,

$$F_3 = \frac{(1 + 0.13)^3}{(1 + 0.12)^2} - 1 = 0.15 = 15\%$$

Remember that the expected returns will be the same regardless of the specific bonds in which funds are invested. We can check this calculation by estimating the position if we invest in three one-year bonds. The final wealth would be $(1.10)(1.14)(1.15) = 1.44$, whereas the final wealth from the three-year bond would be $(1.13)^3 = 1.44$. Final wealth is constant regardless of the bonds, therefore the returns are the same.

By similar calculations, the complete set of one year forward rates is found to be 10%, 14%, 15%, 16%, 14%, 12%, 10% and 10% respectively.

Notice the relationship between the forward rates and the redemption yields: if the forward rate is above the redemption yield, the redemption yield will be rising, and if the forward rate is below the redemption yield, the redemption yield will be falling as maturity increases. Correspondingly, if the redemption yields rise with increasing maturity, the short-term forward rates are above today's short-term rate. Observers of the bond market might infer that the market 'expects' that short-term rates will rise in the future. This interpretation was made on the basis of some restrictive assumptions about the behaviour of investors. Nevertheless, it helps us to understand why, for example, redemption yields of long maturities do not fluctuate as much as shorter-term yields. Referring to the series of forward rates above, suppose investors revised their beliefs about the one-year forward rate in the eighth year to 20% from 10%. Because the redemption yield for an 8-year bond is the same as the yield on a 7-year bond, followed by the implied one year forward rate, it follows that

$$(1 + i_8)^8 = (1 + 0.13)^7 (1 + 0.20)$$
$$\text{or } i_8 = 0.1385$$

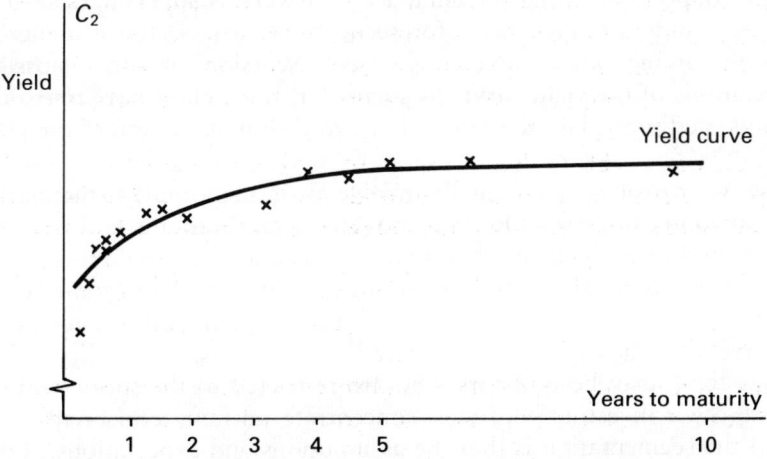

Figure 8.2   Term Structure of Interest Rates.

The redemption yield on the 8-year bond would therefore be 13.85% rather than the 12.6% shown above. The redemption yield has changed by less than 2%, compared with the difference of 10% in the forward rates. For longer terms, the redemption yields will change even less significantly; so it is common to find that if the series of redemption yields are graphed against the maturity, this 'yield curve' becomes flat as the maturity increases over about ten or fifteen years. See Figure 8.2.

In the shorter term, the shape of the yield curve can change sharply. Over the last fifty years or so, the 'normal' shape of the yield curve was upward sloping over the one-to-ten-year maturity range and almost flat thereafter; there have been other shapes that have been observed. In July 1973 the curve was upward sloping under four years and almost flat thereafter. A similar pattern could be observed in January 1979, while in August 1984 the yield curve sloped upwards for maturities less than six years, and downwards for greater maturities.

Hypotheses on the Behaviour of Interest Rates

The explanation of the yield curve given above is referred to as the *'expectations hypothesis'* of the term structure of interest rates. The principal shortcoming of the expectations hypothesis is that the forward rates derived from the redemption yields often do not bear a close relationship to the short-term rates subsequently observed in the market. In the example, this is equivalent to finding that the short-term rates for the second, third and fourth years turn out to be, say, 10%, 9% and 9% instead of the implied forward rates of 14%, 15% and 16% respectively. This finding is, by itself, insufficient evidence that the expectations hypothesis is invalid. There are several reasons, including the effect of tax bias arising from the coupon effect, that preclude easy answers. Also, changes such as oil crises could not have been foreseen. Nevertheless, the evidence is sufficiently ambiguous to encourage the discussion of other possible interpretations of the yield curve. In particular, researchers have remarked upon and tried to explain the 'normal' upward-sloping pattern of the yield curve.

These other explanations usually involve an assumption that the market is segmented in some way. One way in which segmentation could arise is if some institutions decided, as a matter of policy, that they would invest only in short-term bonds. This kind of restraint seems to operate to some degree in practice. When the Bank of England publishes a graph of its version of the yield curve, it explicitly divides the curve into two parts.

Just as there may be investors who are restricted to the short term, so there are other investors who may concentrate on long-term bonds. The effect of the segmentation is that the assumptions and expectations of one set of investors may be inconsistent with the other. Put simply, the long-term investors may be expecting the short-term rate to rise while the short-term investors may expect it to fall.

If there are restrictions on the dealing between different segments of the market, there is no particular reason why the assumptions should ever be consistent between long-term investors and short-term ones. Thus the persistent upward slope of the yield curve may simply represent the competition amongst buyers of bonds to hold short-term instruments. This competitive pressure, unless satisfied by borrowers, would make itself evident through a consequent rise in the price of short bonds and the associated fall in yield. Since there may be little switching (by borrowers) from long to short-term instruments, the pattern of the yield curve could be derived from the *segmentation hypothesis*.

Another reason that has been suggested for the upward sloping yield curve is risk aversion on the part of the investors. In these circumstances, investors will want additional reward for investing in long-term securities and will therefore demand a greater yield. Their preference for 'liquidity' will thus lead to a risk premium for long-term securities, and short-term bonds will thus normally trade at lower redemption yields than long-term bonds — the *liquidity preference* hypothesis.

Bond Clientele

It has already been suggested that some investors may limit their bond purchases to specific maturity ranges. In this section we consider the effect of maturity and tax liability on bond investment.

Since pension funds and charities do not pay tax on their investment income, we would expect their investment policy to take this tax advantage into account. However, there are other factors that also influence investment policy and which make the position more complicated. For example, pension funds and life assurance companies both have very long term liabilities and, in order to reduce their risks, will try to match their long-term liabilities with long-term assets such as long-term fixed interest stock or equities. But the supply of fixed interest stock is dominated by the public sector; the Stock Exchange estimated at the end of March 1984 that the market value of government securities was £107 billion compared with a value of £7.3 billion for debt of UK companies.[2] For company securities, the market is dominated by the investing institutions; pension funds and insurance companies held (at the end of March 1983) in aggregate more than 56% of the fixed interest stock. They also hold 85% of the long-term (over 15 years to redemption) government securities.

For the short-term government securities (i.e. those maturing in less than 5 years), other investors are more important; banks hold more than 18% and building societies hold 27%. Individual investors have the alternative

---

[2]   These and the following statistics are drawn from various issues of both the *Stock Exchange Fact Book* and the *Bank of England Quarterly Bulletin*.

outlet of non-marketable securities such as National Savings Certificates, Save As You Earn schemes and Premium Bonds, so their involvement in the marketable securities markets is less than one might expect from a consideration of the tax and term implications of marketable debt.

Some idea of the clientele effect can be gained from a consideration of the relative weights that various types of investors hold in the different maturities of government securities.

Table 8.2

Holdings of Government Securities by Investors Expressed as Percentages as at 31 March 1983

Investor	Shorts (under 5 yrs)	Mediums (5 – 15 yr)	Long and irredeemable (over 15 yr)	Total
Banks	76	22	1	100
*Insurance Companies (General)	34	54	7	100
Insurance Companies (Long term)	7	44	49	100
Pension Funds	3	27	70	100
Investment/ Unit Trusts	16	44	40	100
Individuals	26	51	23	100
Building Societies	73	26	1	100

* Insurance Companies' statistics as at end of 1983.
Sources:　*Bank of England Quarterly Bulletin*, December 1983.
　　　　　British Business, 7 September 1984.

The difference between the insurance companies and the pension funds may partly be explained by the range of activities undertaken by insurance companies. For general insurance companies carrying out business such as household and motor insurance, funds may be available for investment for up to three or four years, and therfore the insurance companies tend to invest these funds more heavily in short-term government securities. Banks are clearly biased towards the short-term market whilst the investment and unit trusts, who are investing on behalf of their individual share or unit holders, are apparently reproducing the type of investment that individual investors are making on their own account.

Summary

This chapter has covered a good deal of ground in discussing bonds. The valuation of bonds involves institutional and quantitative information. The interpretation of running and redemption yields is by no means a simple task. Some insight is gained by analysing not just one but the whole series of yields in the form of a yield curve.

The term structure of interest rates so revealed has various interpretations which have been briefly discussed in the final parts of the chapter.

Further Reading

1. Factual information on the bond market may best be gleaned from the regular commentaries in the *Bank of England Quarterly Bulletin* and from the annual surveys of new capital issues which appear in the *Midland Bank Review* (Spring issues).
2. T.G. Goff, *Theory and Practice of Investment*, 3rd edn (Heinemann, 1980). Chapters 3, 9 and 10 provide some institutional-based discussion of the tax effects of bond investment. The book is aimed at bankers taking the Investment paper in the Institute of Bankers examination and tends to be light on arithmetical calculations.
3. M.E. Polakoff and T.A. Durkin (eds), *Financial Institutions and Markets,* 2nd edn (Houghton-Mifflin, 1981). Chapter 23, written by A.M. Wojnilower, contains a readable explanation of the term structure of interest rates, albeit concerned with the US market.
4. The *Bank of England Quarterly Bulletin* also contains illustrations of the yield curve for government stocks in its *Financial Review*. The method of fitting the yield curve was first described in the December 1972 and September 1973 issues but has since been modified several times. (For latest information see the June 1982 issue, pp. 226–231 'Yield Curves for Gilt-edged Stock: An Improved Model'.)
5. J. Rutterford, *Introduction to Stock Exchange Investments* (Macmillan, 1983) provides a clear introduction to bond calculations with a UK emphasis. The book contains a very useful explanation of the indexed gilts and their valuatons.
6. P. Phillips, *Inside the Gilt-Edge Market* (Woodhead-Faulkner, 1984) provides a first rate discussion of the analysis and operations of gilt-edged securities. The mathematical treatment is not consistent with the terminology used in our text but overall the book by Phillips provides very useful information on both the market and the analytical techniques used.

Discussion Questions

8.1   It is sometimes suggested that the term structure of interest rates is directly related to the state of the economy. In recessions, for example, the yield curve may be steeply sloping if the recession is expected to be temporary. What shape would you associate with (a) economic recovery, and (b) the 'top' of an economic boom?

8.2   What difference might you expect if an accurate and widely accepted bond rating service were to be established in the international bond markets? Consider, in particular, the effects on (a) the rates of interest payable, and (b) the behaviour of bond prices.

8.3   Explain the relative bond holdings by maturity of the personal sector shown in Table 8.2. In what other ways do individuals borrow or lend money at fixed rates of interest? Do you think the personal sector tends in aggregate to lend/borrow for short/long periods of time?

8.4   Compare the benefits and risks of investing in (a) short term, (b) long term, and (c) indexed gilt-edged securities.

Problems

8.5   An investor is considering (on 1 November 1984) applying for a 10-year government bond for which he has to pay £20 immediately, a further £40 on 1 January 1985, and a balance of £36 on 1 March 1985. What price will the bond have to trade for on 2 March 1985 if he is to earn a return of 12% on his investment?

8.6   The following are redemption yields for bonds maturing in 1, 2, 3, 4 and 5 years, respectively: 8%, 8.5%, 9.33%, 11.9% and 11.7%. Estimate the implied one-year forward rates. Comment on your results and suggest an appropriate investment policy to profit from any market anomalies.

8.7   Estimate the gross redemption yield as at 5 March for a 13% corporate bond which will be redeemed in the following year on 4 September with interest payments made on 4 March and 4 September. The price on the 5 March was £94. Estimate the redemption yield for an investor subject to a 30% capital gains tax and income tax at 65%.

8.8   When was interest last paid on Exchequer 10½%, 1997 if the price on 5 December was £99 and the running yield was 10.95%?

Appendix

Calculation of Redemption Yields

In this chapter we simplified the calculation by assuming away the need to adjust the accrued interest. In general, of course, there will usually be accrued interest which is either included in the price (for long-dated stock) or will require an adjustment to the quoted price (as in the case for shorts). The following example illustrates the method.

Consider an investor who wishes to buy, on 27 January 1983, 14% Exchequer Stock, priced at £103¼ and with interest payments due on 22 May and 22 November, redemption due 22 May 1984.

To estimate the redemption yield we carry out the following steps:

1. *Adjust the price to include the effect of accrued interest.*
   In this case the adjusted price will be

$$P_0 \ = \ 103.25 \ + \ \frac{\text{days between 22/11/82 and 28/1/83}}{365} \ \times \ 14$$

$$P_0 \ = \ £105.82$$

2. *Take as first focal date, the next date on which interest is payable and specify the valuation of the remaining cash flows in half-yearly periods.*
   In the example, the interest is next payable on the 22 May 1983. The valuation at that time will be

$$V_1 \ = \ 7 \ + \ \frac{7}{1 + i} \ + \ \frac{7}{(1 + i)^2} \ + \ \frac{100}{(1 + i)^2}$$

   In general terms this would be expressed as

$$V_1 \ = \ \tfrac{1}{2}C(1 + a_{\overline{n}|i}) \ + \ 100(1 + i)^{-n}$$

   where C = coupon, and n = the number of periods (usually six monthly periods) between the next interest payment date and redemption.

3. *Discount the valuation expressed in step (2) to the appropriate date.*

$$V_0 \ = \ V_1(1 + i)^{-t}$$

   where t = the number of days between 'tomorrow' and the next interest payment date $\div$ the number of days between interest payment dates.
   In the example $t \ = \ 114/181$ or 0.630

$$V_0 \ = \ (7(1 + a_{\overline{2}|i}) + 100(1 + i)^{-2})(1 + i)^{-0.63}$$

4. *Equate this valuation to the adjusted price P_0 and by interpolation find i.*

$$P_0 \ = \ 105.82$$
$$V_0 \ = \ 105.825 \text{ using } 0.05624$$

5. *The annual (nominal) redemption yield is then $200i\%$.*
   Thus in this example, the redemption yield is 11.248%.

Chapter Nine

Shares and Related Securities

The Stock Exchange exists to provide a market place for securities. In the previous chapter we discussed the characteristics and valuation of bonds. This chapter is devoted to the analysis of ordinary shares in UK firms which account for most of the transactions (by number) on the Stock Exchange and which were valued at more than £172 billion in March 1984. After first discussing the methods by which shares are issued, we look at the characteristics and valuation of shares. Finally we discuss some of the share-related securities which are traded on the Stock Exchange.

Issue of Shares

The issue of ordinary shares for cash has two effects. The first and most obvious effect is the receipt of cash by the company concerned; a second effect is that the purchasers of the ordinary shares become part-owners of the company. In looking at the issuing process, these two effects can help to explain why one particular method of issue is chosen against another.

The most obvious case (and the most prevalent) occurs when an existing public company with shares already listed on the Stock Exchange wishes to raise additional funds, perhaps for new investment projects or, as frequently may be the case, to replace some of its existing finance (fixed interest debt which is due to mature or bank loans, for example). In this instance there will already be shareholders in the company and many of them may be willing to buy additional shares. Institutional shareholders, for example, might be willing to buy a large number of shares in a small or medium-sized company but be unable to buy shares in the open market without causing the market price to rise. To such institutions, *rights issues* offer a good opportunity of substantially increasing their shareholding. Furthermore, Stock Exchange regulations normally require companies with shares already quoted on the Stock Exchange to offer additional shares first to existing shareholders or to have the approval of shareholders in offering the shares to other investors.

Issues of additional shares to existing shareholders usually take the form of sending a *prospectus* with details of the offer (including the purpose of the issue and the number of shares for sale) to each shareholder. The new shares will generally be offered to the shareholders at a price below the current market price of the existing shares. Shareholders will thus have the right to buy additional shares at a price which appears cheap. This type of issue is referred to as a 'rights issue' and shareholders can realise the profit from the issue by exercising their right to buy the new shares and selling the shares in the market as soon as possible. Alternatively, the shareholder may sell the rights without themselves actually buying the shares offered. In this case the rights will be bought by another investor who wishes to increase his shareholding in the company in question. Investors will offer a price for the rights which, together with the cost of buying the shares at the rights price, will approximate the cost of buying shares in the open market.

Rights issues are of major importance to companies raising new finance. In 1984, for example, Charterhouse Petroleum raised over £40 million, whilst Exco International raised over £72 million.

It should be noted that the pricing of a rights issue does not directly determine the profit made by existing shareholders who exercise their rights. This statement might seem surprising at first but a simple example can readily demonstrate it to be correct. Consider a company with issued capital of one million ordinary shares, quoted in the market at 100p per share. The total value of the equity will be £1million. If the company wishes to raise an additional £200,000 it may do so by offering, say, one million shares at 20p each or half a million shares at 40p each. In either case, the company will acquire £200,000 which we assume will be expected to increase the value of its total equity by the same amount. The price of each share *after* the rights issue has been made will therefore depend on the number of shares in existence. In the first case, there will be a total of two million shares so the price of each share will be £1.2million ÷ 2 million = 60p. In the second case, the price of each share will be £1.2million ÷ 1.5 million = 80p per share.

Shareholders exercising their rights will have spent 20p for each share originally held. In the first case, after the issue, they will hold twice as many shares, each worth 60p. Their total shareholding will therefore be worth 120p times the number of shares originally owned; but in acquiring this extra holding they have spent 20p (times the number of shares owned before the issue). Thus the net value of their portfolio is 100p times their original investment — which is exactly the same as the original value. (It is easy to show that the same effect will hold in the second case; the value of the portfolio will remain unchanged. See Table 9.1.)

This analysis is too simple to explain the changes in companies' share prices before and after rights issues. In practice, the announcement of a rights issue may signal a profitable opportunity which may cause investors to bid up the price of the traded shares. On the other hand, it is possible for the company's share price to fall between the day on which the offer is announced and the day on which the offer must be accepted. The fall could occur for a variety of reasons — perhaps the prices of most company shares have fallen. If this fall occurs, shareholders are unlikely to take advantage of the offer to buy additional shares in this particular company at a price

Table 9.1   Analysis of Rights Issues

	Pre-issue			Issue				Post-issue	
(1) Number of shares	(2) Market price	(3)=(1)×(2) Market capitalisation	(4) Number of shares offered	(5) Price	(6) Value	(7)=(6)+(3) Total value		(8)=(1)+(4) Number of shares	(9)=(7)÷(8) Market price
(A) 1m	100p	£1m	1m (1 for 1)	20p	£0.2m	£1.2m		2m	60p
(B) 1m	100p	£1m	0.5 (1 for 2)	40p	£0.2m	£1.2m		1.5m	80p

Case (A)   Owner of 1 share (value 100p) will spend 20p and (after issue) will hold a portfolio of 2 shares, each worth 60p = 120p, therefore no change in shareholder's wealth.

Case (B)   Owner of 2 shares (value 200p) will spend 40p and (after issue) will hold a portfolio of 3 shares each worth 80p = 240p, therefore no change in shareholder's wealth.

higher than that at which the shares are trading in the market. To avoid this problem, the price of rights issues can be set at a price which is greatly below the current market price. A very low price might, however, be interpreted by investors as signalling a lack of confidence on the part of the issuing company. Usually, therefore, the issuer will arrange for institutions to *underwrite* the issue. The underwriting institutions, which will usually include the major institutional investors, agree to buy the issue if existing shareholders fail to accept the offer. This transaction is effectively a type of insurance for which a commission is paid to the underwriters.

For companies wishing to raise finance by selling ordinary shares to the public, there are two main methods of issuing: *offers for sale* and *sale by tender*. An offer for sale is arranged by a specialist *issuing house* (or stockbrokers or banks acting in the same capacity). The issuing house will take the shares and advertise them for sale in newspapers at a fixed price. The prospectus will contain a considerable amount of information about the history of the company and its present financial position as well as some estimates or forecasts of its future profitability. The information supplied is largely determined by the Stock Exchange rules which specify the conditions under which new issues can subsequently be traded (listed) on the Stock Exchange. (As discussed in earlier chapters, the existence of an efficient secondary market greatly enhances the attractiveness of new shares for investors who may subsequently wish to revise their portfolios.)

If the offer price is set too high, there will obviously be insufficient applications and the issuing house will be left with a supply of unsold shares. As with the case of the rights issue, this problem is avoided by appointing underwriters who take on this risk associated with new issues. If the offer price is too low, the issuing house will find an excessive number of applications and will have to devise some equitable method of allocating the shares amongst applicants. Often there are advantages in trying to achieve a widely distributed share ownership, so the issuing house may discriminate in the allocation of shares in favour of individual investors; but in some cases a ballot will be held. For an issue which arouses a great deal of interest on behalf of investors, professional investors will try to overcome the bias against institutional applications by submitting multiple applications, each for small numbers of shares. It is therefore not unusual to hear of 'sackfulls' of applications arriving on the closing date. If an issue is heavily over-subscribed the price of the shares when traded on the Stock Exchange for the first time after the offer will be considerably higher than the offer price. The possibility of a price increase following an offer for sale consequently encourages investors to apply for shares, intending to sell them after issue. This behaviour (professionally termed 'stagging') can magnify the apparent popularity of share issues as indicated by the degree of over-subscription.

Setting the offer price for new issues is thus considerably more difficult than setting the price of a rights issue. In a period during which share prices have fluctuated substantially, the problem can lead to massive over-subscriptions which attract criticism of this method of issue. An extreme example of the problem was the issue in February 1983 of the ordinary shares of Superdrug Stores, a discount retail store group: 8.8 million of the shares had been offered at 175p, and the offer was oversubscribed 95 times! In the circumstances it was not surprising that at the end of the first day's trading after the issue, the share price had risen to 270p, an increase of 54%. The existence of stagging on this issue was indicated by the report that about 60% of the shares had changed hands on the first day's trading, with prices opening at 295p and fluctuating up to a maximum of 300p. Despite this fluster of speculation, two months later, the share price had fallen slightly to 263p, during which time, the Financial Times All Share Index had risen by 10%. Other issues which aroused criticism of the fixed price method were the sale on behalf of the government of shares in Amersham International and in Associated British Ports. In both cases, the issues were heavily over-subscribed and the share prices at the end of the first day of trading were between 20 and 35% higher than their offer prices.

To deal with this criticism, issuers sometimes arrange to offer shares for *sale by tender*. Investors, in applying for shares, have to specify the price at which they will be prepared to buy their specified quantity of shares. The issuing house will then rank the applications in order of price and allocate all the shares to the higher ranked offers at the *striking price*, i.e. at the price of the lowest acceptable application which, taken with the bids at higher prices, will account for the stock of shares on offer. Some guidance of a minimum price will be given in the prospectus and if insufficient tenders are made, the surplus shares will be sold to the underwriting institutions at the specified price.

The efficiency of this method is questioned by some critics *precisely* because it rarely leads to volatile changes in the price of shares in the period following the issue. The argument is made that offers by tender fail to attract sufficient interest from professional traders and that the issue price is consequently lower than the price that could be set if the shares were sold by offer at a fixed price. It is difficult to draw any conclusions from this argument since it is usually conducted on the basis of anecdotal evidence of particular issues. One cited example was the offer by tender used in selling the shares of Britoil in November 1982. In this case, no new funds were raised, the issue being carried out solely to change the ownership of the equity. Partly because of a number of events that occurred in the interval between arranging the sale and the day on which applications were finally accepted, the minimum acceptable price was too high and there were insufficient applications. Consequently, the underwriting institutions had to buy most of the shares on issue. When the share was subsequently traded on the Stock Exchange, the price was effectively about 20% less than the minimum tender price.

Three other methods of issuing shares should briefly be mentioned — *placing, introduction* and *capitalisation* issues. Of these, only placing (usually) represents the raising of additional finance for the company on whose behalf the shares are issued. It is used mainly with corporate debt but also with small issues when the issue cost of a full offer for sale would be relatively high.

In placing a share issue, the issuing institution will sell shares to a number of institutional (and sometimes to individual) investors besides supplying the stock market jobbers with a supply in order to facilitate the market-making process. The Stock Exchange regulates such placings, ensuring that information about the issue is publicised so that investors not participating in the placing can assess the value of the shares once they are traded in the market.

An introduction is usually appropriate for foreign registered companies wishing to have their shares listed on the UK Stock Exchange. Introductions involve no issue of new shares but shares will be sold to jobbers, for market-making purposes (as with the placing method).[1] In some cases, an introduction will be made for a company with a number of existing shareholders who may then sell part or all of their holdings. In both instances, the issue has the effect of changing the composition of the shareholders (even if only marginally).

Capitalisation issues create more shares but without any cash passing to the company from this issue. The procedure creates more shares by transforming some part of the profits retained from previous years' operations. In other words, capitalisation is essentially a bookkeeping operation. The balance sheet entries for retained earnings will thus fall by the nominal value of the shares created which will appear in the balance sheet as an increase in the issued capital of the company. Consequently, the company will distribute these additional shares to its shareholders in proportion to the number of shares held.

The effect of capitalisation issues is that more shares are owned (and presumably traded). The total value of the company is nominally unchanged, so the price of the shares should adjust accordingly, e.g. if the number of shares is doubled, the price of each share should halve. In practice, this does not often occur, mainly because of the same kind of signalling effect observed with rights issues. Capitalisation issues seem to be made during a period in which the company is making superior profits, and *after* the issue the company may expect to increase the total amount of dividends paid to shareholders. Obviously, if a company doubles the number of shares and maintains the dividend payment per share, the shareholders will receive double the amount of cash anticipated. If they believe that the company will be able to maintain this increased dividend in subsequent years, the share price will reflect these increased expectations and may consequently fall very little, stay the same or even increase. Reasons for capitalisation issues range from the belief that high-priced shares are unpopular with individual investors to providing a technical method of increasing shareholders' income during periods in which incomes and dividends are controlled by a government prices and incomes policy. Instead of making a capitalisation issue, companies can increase the number

---

[1] Shares in foreign companies may of course be traded on the Stock Exchange under Rule 534(4)(a) (see Chapter 7). There may also be investors in London who own and are trading in foreign securities who may be instrumental in supplying shares to the market.

of shares by splitting each share. Thus a share split may involve replacing each £1 share by four shares each with a nominal value of 25p.

Characteristics of Traded Shares

Since ordinary shareholders own a company, the returns from owning shares might be expected to relate to the profits made by the company. Unlike bonds, ordinary shares do not promise a fixed payment to shareholders, and investors should be aware that in holding ordinary shares, the income received in the form of dividends may fall and even disappear if the company becomes unprofitable. Dividends may also be cut to ensure that the company has sufficient funds to maintain an investment programme that will benefit shareholders in the longer term.

From this, it will be recognised that shareholders will need to consider the likelihood of dividends rising or falling before they buy shares in a company. If investors generally forecast a large and sustained increase in dividends, the price of the shares may rise in response to the increased demand. If expectations of future dividend are revised downwards, the price of the share may be similarly affected. The implication seems clear: prices of shares will fluctuate in response to expectations of future dividends and underlying profitability.

Despite the diversity of information that investors might find useful in forming expectations, it is evident that some benchmarks would generally be looked for.

One such might be an indication of the share price movements to be expected. Both *The Times* and *Financial Times* publish information each day about a large number of shares traded on the Stock Exchange. As an indication of the fluctuations in share prices both newspapers publish the highest and lowest prices quoted in the previous twelve months. Also as an indication of the return to shareholders in the form of dividends, the *dividend yield* is presented. This is similar to the running yield discussed in the previous chapter. Dividends, like interest, are usually paid semi-annually on a net-of-tax-basis. The first payment, which is termed the *interim dividend*, is fixed by the directors of the company, and will usually be less than the *final dividend*, which has to be agreed by the shareholders. Hence, in dividing the grossed-up dividend (i.e. the sum of the net-of-tax dividend and the tax deducted) by the current share price, a simple interest basis is implicit in the calculation. Furthermore, because the fluctuations in share prices will usually cause the reported dividend yield to change substantially over time, no adjustment is made for the accrued dividend effect.

The usefulness of the dividend yield is limited because it does not take into account changes in the dividends that have yet to be announced. Dividend yields for similar companies pursuing identical dividend policies, can still differ markedly because the dividends may be announced and paid at different times of the year. The published yields take this problem into account to a limited extent by indicating changes in, say, interim dividends or using published forecasts where appropriate. Professional investment analysts will usually prefer to make an explicit forecast of the dividends that will be paid over the following twelve months, thus making the analogy between dividends and running yields closer (although at a cost of uncertainty caused by the introduction of subjective estimates).

As a complement to the dividend yield, the *earnings yield* or its reciprocal — the *price earnings* (P/E) ratio — is also widely reported. The importance of this measure stems from the recognition that if the company can profitably employ shareholders' funds, money could be retained in the firm to the benefit of the owners, rather than paid out in the form of dividends. Following this line of thinking, shareholders might therefore look to the total profits earned, rather than to the dividends received, as a measure of the benefits from holding the shares: high profits may coincide with low dividends if profits are re-invested. Shareholders may then look forward to receiving increased dividends sometime in the future. Thus the shares of two companies, with differing dividend policies but with similar investment programmes, might be expected to trade at similar earnings yields but with different dividend yields.

The earnings yield is calculated by dividing the profits after tax by the number of shares, and expressing the result as a percentage of the current share price. Adjustments are often made for such factors as the effect of dividend policy on the company's tax charge, the impact of overseas tax and so on.

The interpretation of the earnings yield is difficult for the same reasons which we discussed when interpreting dividend yields. If calculated on an historical earnings basis, two companies may differ in reporting dates and the reported earnings will refer to different periods. The earnings yield will be low (and the P/E ratio will be correspondingly high) if shareholders expect future earnings to increase steadily over a number of years. This characteristic is considered further in the next section, which deals with the ways in which shares may be valued.

Methods of Valuing Shares

In discussing methods of share valuation, we have to be careful to distinguish between the formal mathematical models and the activity of share analysts. In discussing the models we are not arguing that analysts will explicitly use one or other of the approaches. We are asserting that the models illuminate the results, i.e. the prices in the market. The most important way in which professional analysts value shares is by *fundamental analysis* of the companies and their management. In carrying out such exercises, there is wide variation in the factors considered by different analysts. It is still possible, nevertheless, to refer to fundamental analysis as being one general approach to share valuation.

The main emphasis in analysing a company's previous performance is to assess how successful the management of the company has been in running and developing the company. The task of forecasting the future profitability of the company involves forecasting the conditions in which the company will be operating in distant years, and assessing the skill with which the management of the company will handle the problems that are likely to arise. Fundamental analysts, therefore, naturally emphasise the quality of the management in keeping the company 'on course'. Given an assessment of the management and of the future economic environment (the competitive structure of the industry, the economic and political changes, etc), analysts will then form estimates of the future profits that each firm will subsequently report. The term 'earnings quality' is sometimes used to describe the behaviour of a company's profits through time: profits which increase at a reasonably predictable rate and which produce no unpleasant surprises to analysts engaged in forecasting are of high quality.

Fundamental analysis, therefore, proceeds to derive a share valuation from multiplying the forecasted profits per share by a forecasted P/E ratio.

$$\text{'Fundamental' price} \quad = \quad \text{P/E} \times \hat{E}$$

where P/E = Price/earnings ratio, and $\hat{E}$ = Forecasted earnings per share.

The ratio is chosen by reference to the *capitalisation rate* used by the market for the shares of other similar companies. Thus if profits are expected to grow faster than other similar companies, the P/E ratio will be adjusted upwards, whereas if profits are expected to be more variable or less certain, the P/E ratio will be lower. Since even the P/E ratios of firms within the same industry can vary widely, the selection of the appropriate number can be crucial to the share valuation. Investors have to take into account not only their own estimates of the future profitability of the company, but also the views of other investors which will be reflected in the share price after the profits are reported.

The need to assess the P/E ratio has encouraged some researchers to use a more formal method of arriving at P/E based valuations. In a simple model, the P/E ratios of different companies, together with indicators of financial performance and profitability will be used in a statistical analysis. The aim of such exercises is to find a number of variables that will explain the behaviour of P/E ratios sufficiently well for forecasting purposes. In addition, there have been attempts to find statistical models that will forecast the share prices directly, but this has presented researchers with severe problems at both a practical and theoretical level. In practical terms, the useful variables that explain share prices in one period are not the same as those which are useful in another period. It is difficult to identify any variables which are consistently useful.

An alternative method of generating models of P/E ratios and share valuation is by means of *discounting techniques*. The fundamental analyst stresses the importance of earnings and P/E ratios. In this section, we will use discounting models in conjunction with the dividend component of earnings.

The valuation of a share is assumed to depend on the receipt of future dividends and the price of the share when sold. The value of a share at time $t=0$ will therefore be given by

$$P_0 = \frac{D_1}{1+i} + \frac{D_2}{(1+i)^2} + \frac{D_3}{(1+i)^3} + \dots + \frac{D_n}{(1+i)^n} + \frac{P_n}{(1+i)^n} \quad (9.1)$$

where D_t = annual dividend; i = the appropriate discount rate; n = number of years between now and the date at which the share is sold.

It is assumed that the share is being valued twelve months before the total dividend is paid; in other words, the first dividend is received at the end of the first period.

By making various assumptions, simple formulae can be derived. The simplest assumption is that dividends are constant. In this case, the valuation can be expressed in terms of the annuity formula, introduced in Chapter 5.

$$P_0 = D_1 a_{\overline{n}|i} + P_T (1 + i)^{-n} \quad (9.2)$$

If it is further assumed that the buyer of the share at time T will also use the same valuation model, and if the dividend flows are perpetual, the valuation will simplify to

$$P_0 = \frac{D_1}{i} \quad (9.3)$$

More interesting is a model which assumes some systematic growth in dividends over time. Suppose dividends are expected to grow at an annual rate of $100g\%$. In this case we have the general formula:

$$P_0 = \frac{D_1}{1+i} + \frac{D_1(1+g)}{(1+i)^2} + \dots + \frac{D_1(1+g)^{n-1}}{(1+i)^n} + \frac{P_n}{(1+i)^n} \quad (9.4)$$

If n is very large then the last term $P_n/(1 + i)^n$ will be insignificant and the valuation can be re-expressed in the form:

$$P_0 = \frac{D_1}{1+i} \left[1 + \frac{1+g}{1+i} + \frac{1+g^2}{1+i} + \dots + \frac{1+g^{n-1}}{1+i} \right] \quad (9.5)$$

The first n terms inside the parenthesis will be recognised as a geometric progression which has the form

$$\left[1 + x + x^2 + \dots x^{n-1} \right]$$

with the solution

$$(1-x^n)/(1-x)$$

In this example we are assuming that n is indefinitely large so x^{n-1} can be ignored as long as x is smaller than 1. (This is equivalent to the condition that g will be less than i.) Thus we can substitute for x, the term $(1+g)/(1+i)$ and, after some manipulation, produce:

$$P_0 = \frac{D_1}{i-g}$$

(9.6)

This growth formula is an over-simplified yet useful model which can be used as a basis for comparing firms which differ in dividend policy but which are expected to have comparable profitability. The assumptions are: (a) constant growth in dividends; (b) constant interest rate; (c) g is less than i; (d) either the share is held for an indefinitely large period or sold to another investor with the same expectations and valuation.

Expression (9.6) can be rewritten in the form:

$$i = \frac{D_1}{P_0} + g$$

(9.7)

clearly indicating the split between yield and the capital growth effect.

There have been numerous variations on this type of model: the growth rate may be assumed to fall or rise over time; a high rate of growth may be fixed for a specified number of years, after which it may quickly revert to 'normal' growth or gradually decline over a period of time. Researchers have sometimes specified growth rates that differ for three or four different periods in the drive to produce more 'realistic' models.

The difficulty with all of these dividend discounting models is that there are usually too many unobserved values to be included. Consequently the valuation can turn on decisions which may embody very arbitrary assumptions; for example, in using a model that requires the specification of two periods of 'superior' growth, the occasion will be rare when the investor can determine whether the profitable investment opportunities will be maintained two, five or even ten years ahead. In view of these difficulties, the models are rarely of practical use, other than as indicators which may alert the investment analyst that shares of similar companies may reflect very different expectations. Further discussion of discounting approaches is deferred to Appendix A to this chapter.

Share Price Behaviour

Although we have commented on the lack of information about the method of valuation actually employed by analysts, we do know that profits are of prime importance. We can observe that the share price is particularly volatile around the date at which the profits of the respective company are announced. We also note that in reporting changes in share prices, newspapers, television and radio reports often refer to the market's reaction to 'disappointing' profits or to forecasts of profits expected to be announced within the immediate future.

The market's reaction to earnings announcements is a topic which is of great relevance to the assessment of market efficiency. In a very efficient market, the release of the profits figures should not have any predictable effect on the share price. On the day of the announcement the market price should, therefore, rise (in which case commentators will say the market was pleased with the unexpectedly good results) or fall with equal probability. In the event of a fall, reporters will refer to the market's disappointment. What we cannot know, of course, is the profits forecasted by the market *before* the announcement! Market efficiency implies only that it should on average be equal to the actual announcement — in effect this means that it is equally likely to be too high as too low.

Academic researchers have spent considerable time in examining the reaction of share prices to the release of specific announcements. Usually the studies have traced the behaviour of share prices before and after the announcement. After controlling for other sources of disturbance, the overwhelming evidence suggests that the market reacts to important announcements in advance, e.g. for companies reporting high profits, the share price will increase before the announcement, as investors trade on the basis of their expectations.

This discussion of share price reactions raises the related issue of the behaviour of share prices over time. We have suggested that prices are more variable around the time at which announcements are made. What may not be so obvious is that prices will *usually* be variable over time. If investors are continuously monitoring the news, a large proportion of the reported events *may* be interpreted to have implications for shares. For example, a change in government policy may imply heavier taxes on consumers with a drop in consumer expenditure. But less consumer expenditure means less income for retailing and consumer good manufacturing. Investment analysts would thus examine the sensitivity of company profits to the changes in tax, perhaps recommending investors to sell those companies most seriously affected. The consequent effect is that share prices for specific companies might fall as market forces interact.

Since many news items are of potential significance share prices are observed to change almost continuously. Most research studies of share prices have found that over time, they move in what seems to be 'random walks' and it is now recognised that this randomness in share price behaviour is one indication that the market is operating efficiently.

Portfolio Models

The analysis of stock markets became a popular topic for research in the US in the 1960s and 1970s, and resulted in a rather different approach being taken by academics and professional researchers to the valuation of shares. To a lesser extent, this change also affected the UK stock market, albeit at a later date. The more recent approaches have been stimulated by the growth in importance of the institutional investors. The emphasis is changed to the *analysis* of numbers of shares together in a *portfolio* and starts by explicit consideration of the portfolio for which investment decisions are made.

For institutional investors, with large portfolios containing perhaps hundreds of different shares, the profitability of investment in one company is likely to have a negligible effect on the return obtained from the whole portfolio. On the other hand, at times when the stock market as a whole becomes more optimistic (with investors revising upwards their expectations of profits and dividends), most shares in the market may rise in response to the more favourable sentiment. For an institution, therefore, achieving a satisfactory return during such a period will depend more on being fully invested in shares than on the selection of a few companies which are expected to perform particularly well. In other periods, disasters may easily affect one industry or sector and leave a large portfolio relatively unaffected as long as the portfolio is well diversified.

The realisation that *diversification* is of crucial importance in determining portfolio performance has had the effect of concentrating investors' attention on distinguishing market effects from individual firm effects. Thus, the forecasting of future dividends is not, for a single company, as important as answering a series of questions of the type 'What will happen to the share price and dividends if the market as a whole rises (or falls) by, say, 10% or 20%? In statistical terms, this involves investigating the covariability of share prices with the market index. By considering these questions, the investor can construct portfolios that behave in a way which is *systematically* related to the changes in the market as a whole. Risk-averse investors will aim for a portfolio which is more stable than the market; more adventurous investors will construct a portfolio which magnifies market movements. In some cases, institutions have produced portfolios that try to match as closely as possible the movements in an index of the stock market. These so-called *index funds* have been used by institutional investors involved in managing pension funds. Index funds aim to achieve 'average' performance in that if successful they will yield a return that never differs much from the return that would be earned from the market as a whole.

The related concept of a market model (discussed in Appendix B to this chapter) is developed from these elementary ideas of the importance of the market as a whole. At this stage we only wish to point out that portfolio theory and other related models have been rigorously developed from a statistical and mathematical approach, and readers wishing to further their interest in portfolio modelling are advised to pursue their study in one of the texts suggested at the end of this chapter.

Share Clientele

In discussing bonds, the tax and maturity effects were suggested as being important for determining the type of investor holding a particular bond. Thus a bank would tend to hold short-term bonds whilst a pension fund might hold long-term (high coupon) bonds. There are some parallels in the market for ordinary shares since profits earned by capital gains are leniently treated in comparison to the receipt of income in the form of dividends. Thus, personal investors paying high marginal rates of income tax might be expected to prefer low dividend paying shares if proportionately high capital gains are expected. Correspondingly, institutional investors such as pension funds who are exempt both capital gains and income tax, might prefer the shares of companies paying relatively high dividends. Although there are arguments in favour of this type of portfolio clientele effect, the inherent variability of share prices precludes wholesale commitment to a tax-based investment policy; generally the arguments in favour of diversification outweigh those based on tax clientele.

Other aspects do bear on *share clientele*. Institutional investors wishing to buy large quantities of shares will tend to concentrate on large firms because the shares will tend to be traded more efficiently and frequently. Thus the shares of large companies tend to be held by large institutions; in turn many investing institutions such as unit trusts (who invest on behalf of individual investors) tend to hold a 'core' portfolio which year by year changes relatively slowly. In the 1970s, for example, the most popular institutional shares were Shell Transport, BP, ICI and Imperial Group. Individual investors, on the other hand, not only invest in both large and small companies, but also for different motives perhaps by taking advantage of their special interest or experience. Individual investors also invest heavily in local companies or in companies with household names for quality consumer goods. Since individual investors tend not to revise their portfolios as often as institutional investors, the shares of smaller companies tend not to be traded as regularly as those of large companies. In some cases, this leads observers of the market to conclude that shares of small companies are less efficiently priced than those of larger companies, or that there is a two-tier market consisting of large companies with shares traded by institutions in the first tier and small companies with shares held mainly by individuals in the second tier. To the extent that these tiers exist, it is reasonable to refer to a clientele effect for ordinary shares.

Other Equity Based Securities

In the stock market, the behaviour of ordinary share prices also influences the value of three other types of security traded: *warrants, options* and *convertible stock*. These securities have several features in common; they carry the right for the holder to buy a specified number of ordinary shares in a company at a specified price, and the conversion is usually constrained either to specified dates or to a period. In the case of traded options, the period will initially be confined to three, six or nine months; convertibles, on the other hand, may be converted into ordinary shares ten or even twenty years after issue.

Convertible stocks are issued by companies raising finance. They offer the investor a fixed rate of interest and the right to convert the bonds into ordinary shares. Since they combine elements of bond and equity characteristics, they are complicated instruments to evaluate. As bonds, they may be viewed as a low-coupon fixed interest stock, and consequently most investors will calculate a running or redemption yield. The redemption yield calculation is not straightforward since it involves the assumption of the term to maturity which is often unknown, depending as it does on the date of conversion into the ordinary share. Also, as the redemption value will depend on the price of the ordinary shares at the time of conversion, the redemption yield necessitates assumptions about the share price behaviour in the future.

In addition to this bond-based valuation, the analyst will take into account the current value of the stock when converted into ordinary shares on the appropriate terms. Thus Hanson Trust 9¾% Convertible quoted at £369.5 in October 1984 was estimated to have a running yield of 2.6%. At a time when other fixed interest bonds were giving a running yield of more than 11%, the price clearly was higher than one would expect if the convertible was valued as a simple fixed interest bond. Effectively, each £100 nominal of the stock was convertible into 160.7 shares (which were currently quoted at 242p). Thus the value of the convertible *if converted* was 369.5 ÷ 160.7 or 230p per share. Convertibles are attractive to investors because if the ordinary share price falls, the convertible will be 'cushioned' by the bond-based valuation, yet if the ordinary share price rises the convertible will also tend to rise.

Warrants, which are usually issued by companies at the same time as issuing loan stock, are also designed to present the investor with an incentive to buy fixed interest stock. A warrant entitles the holder to buy an ordinary share at a specified price. A portfolio consisting of a warrant and a fixed interest bond should effectively provide the same return as that obtained from a convertible stock. The portfolio will increase in value as the price of the company's ordinary shares rises, whilst the payment of interest on the bond provides income in the form of cash before conversion.

In the case of convertible stock and warrants, the financial structure on the issuing company will be affected by the investors' decision to exercise their rights. Convertible stocks will involve the company replacing debt financing by equity. Warrants imply the issue of additional equity. The third type of security dealt with in this discussion, although similar in some respects to the other two, is not issued by a company raising finance and does not affect the financial structure of the company if the option is exercised. The most important securities related to ordinary shares are *options*; these are traded in increasing numbers on the Stock Exchange. There are two types of options: *call options* which give the holder the right to buy a share at a specified *exercise price*, and *put options* which give the holder the right to sell a share. Call options in ordinary shares have been traded on the UK Stock Exchange since 1978 (although jobbers have been prepared to offer options on a less formal basis for many years) and provide a cheap method of speculating on the future price movements of a share.

For example, a call option (expiring in three months) in Marks and Spencer shares might be quoted at 34p for an exercise price of 180p when the ordinary shares were listed at 200p. An investor buying the option would hope that the ordinary shares would rise in price. If shortly before the option expires, the share price has increased, to say, 220p, the investor can exercise his option by paying an additional 180p. He has thus acquired the ordinary share for an effective price of 214p (180+34) and can immediately realise a 6p profit by selling the ordinary shares for 220p.

In practice, option holders can realise their profits by selling the option in the traded option market. Since there will always be the alternative method of exercising the option, prices of options will tend to converge to their 'fundamental' price. In the above example, we would expect the call option to sell shortly before expiry at about 40p and thus the investor can realise the 6p gain either by selling the option on the market or by exercising it as described above. The investor has therefore 'geared up' the 10% gain in the underlying share (220−200)/200 to more than 17% gain in the option (40−34)/34. Of course, if at expiry of the option, the share price has fallen below the exercise price, the option will be worthless. (No investor would want an option to buy a share at an exercise price of 180p if the share price was currently 150p and the option was due to expire at the end of the day.) The gearing effect of the option will therefore magnify the effect of share price movements both upwards and downwards.

In a simple form, the valuation of call options can be carried out by discounting the expected value of the option on maturity, thus:

$$C_t = (S_T - E)(1 + i)^{-q} \qquad (9.8)$$

where C_t = the value of the option at time t
S_t = the value of the underlying share at t
T = expiry date (assumed also to be the exercise date)
E = exercise price (i.e. the price which has to be paid by the holder of the option at the time of exercising the option)
i = the appropriate discount rate
q = $(T-t)/365$ time to expiry date

This formula, however, suffers from the difficulty of estimating S_T, the share price at the time of exercising the option. If we assume that no dividends are paid on the share and that it appreciates at an effective rate of $100i\%$ per year, we can rewrite (9.8) in the form

$$C_t = S_t - E (1 + i)^{-q} \qquad (9.9)$$

Although this formula avoids the problem of estimating a future share price, it still requires the choice of a discount rate that must reflect the risk of the share being below the exercise price at expiration of the option. Fortunately this difficulty can be overcome.

If the investor buys a put option at the same time as a call option, the risk of the share price falling has been covered, so eliminating the risk of the portfolio.

With such a portfolio, the discount rate will reflect only the cost-of-waiting, i.e. the riskless rate of interest. Thus the value of the call option will be given by:

$$C_t = P_t + S_t - E (1 + i)^{-q} \qquad (9.10)$$

where P_t = the price of a put option at time t (i.e. downside insurance), and i = the riskless rate of interest.

This expression in one form or another is known as the Put–Call Parity Theorem; it provides a useful check on the call option price *if* there are put options traded in the market. It does not, however, show whether *both* put and call options are over- or under-priced. For this purpose more complicated models are required.

Numerous academic and professional researchers in the US have analysed the behaviour of option prices, and various competing models have been developed. The formulation of the most recent models has reached a stage in which considerable mathematical skill is required for their comprehension. Despite their complexity, option pricing models have become widely adopted by professional investors and several stockbrokers in the UK circulate clients with estimated values based on one or more of the option pricing models. There are various ways in which the option pricing models have been adapted, but amongst the more important are the allowance for dividend payments, the variation in interest rates and adjustments for share price behaviour.

Summary

The behaviour of ordinary share prices has attracted the interest of many researchers. This chapter has reviewed some of the ways in which shares have been valued and prices analysed. In addition, we have also discussed the main methods by which shares come onto the Stock Exchange. Finally we have examined other securities, such as warrants and options, which depend for their value on the current and future values of ordinary shares.

Further Reading

1. F.K. Reilly, *Investment Analysis and Portfolio Management* (Dryden Press, 1979) presents a useful discussion of fundamental analysis of share prices in a US context. The presentation is conventional but emphasises the relationship between the profitability of the firm and the economic environment.
2. W.F. Sharpe, *Investments,* 2nd edn (Prentice-Hall, 1982) discusses the portfolio aspects more authoritatively and is particularly useful for the discussion of option pricing. Overall, readers will find it more difficult than Reilly's text.
3. For a readable account of market models and their application to the Stock Exchange, see R. Hagin, *The Dow Jones–Irwin Guide to Modern Portfolio Theory* (Irwin, 1979). This text is aimed at a US professional readership but UK readers will find much of interest in its discussion.
4. A number of models of share valuation based on the growth of dividends and earnings were reviewed by P.F. Wendt, 'Current Growth Stock Valuation Methods', *Financial Analysts' Journal* (March/April 1965, pp.91–103).
5. A recent book on the UK scene is J. Rutterford, *Introduction to Stock Exchange Investment* (Macmillan, 1983). It provides a first class introduction to investment principles with a clear discussion of modern portfolio theory.

Problems

9.1   A shareholder is holding 1000 shares (price 200p) when the company unexpectedly announces a rights issue (at 140p) on the basis of 1 new share for every existing 5 shares held. What would you expect the market price of the shares to be after the rights issue has been made? For how much could the rights of the shareholder be sold?

9.2   An investor is analysing a share, currently priced at 55p. The dividend (of 4p) is payable within the next few days. The following dividend is forecast to be 5p, and thereafter she expects that dividends will grow by 10% a year. What return will she earn on the share if she buys the share now and holds it indefinitely?

9.3   All companies in the same sector are expected to yield the same return to shareholders, and the dividends on Beemrup (Printing) are expected to grow at 5% per year. What growth rate of dividends is expected on (a) English Print, (b) McDonalds (Printing)?

	Price	Forecast dividends (p) 12 months time
Beemrup	128	4
English Print	35	1
McDonalds	180	8

9.4   Using the information in 9.3, calculate the share prices of the three companies in twelve months' time, immediately after the dividends have been paid.

9.5   The dividends and profits of a bio-technological company have been growing steadily at 22% per year over the life of the firm. If a shareholder expects to earn 20% from his investment, value the share if dividends are currently 50p. Comment on your calculations.

9.6   The price of shares in Fluidonics is 500p and the P/E ratio is forecast to be 20 (for the next reported earnings at the end of the current year). Fluidonics have regularly paid out 30% of their profits in dividends, but unexpectedly announce that they are changing their dividend policy. In future their pay-out ratio will be 50%. The share price falls to 192p. Estimate the return expected from holding the shares and the expected return on investment. (Assume both are constant.) Refer to Appendix A.

9.7   A 5% convertible bond is quoted at 90 (ex div). The conversion terms provide for £100 nominal to be converted into 50 ordinary shares in two years' time. What will be the redemption yield on the convertible if the expected share price at the date of conversion is 300p? (Assume annual payments of interest.)

9.8   Shares in P & O were quoted at the beginning of February 1983 at 121p. Call options were available (exercise price = 100p), expiring at the end of February, May and August at 22p, 25p and 26p, respectively. If the expected return on both the shares and options is assumed to be constant over the whole period, which option is the best investment? (Ignore the effect of dividends.)

9.9   If the call options (exercise price = 90p, expiration end October) of Courtaulds are priced at 8p, and the share price is quoted at 88p at the beginning of May, what would be the value of the corresponding put option if the risk free rate was 12% per year? (Ignore the effects of dividends.)

Appendix A
Discounted Earnings Models

In this chapter, we have briefly described the simple dividend growth model

$$P_0 \;=\; \frac{D_1}{i - g} \tag{9A.1}$$

where D_1 = the estimated dividend, payable at the end of the current year; i = the discount rate, and $100g\%$ = the percentage annual growth in dividends. In this appendix we look at a valuation model based on dividend policy and earnings per share.

The model owes its derivation to the observation that firms *tend* to pay out dividends as a stable proportion of their profits, taking one year with another. Thus if profits per share are E_1, dividends paid may be written $(1 - b)E_1$, where b is the proportion retained in the business for re-investment. Earnings per share are assumed to be net of depreciation, interest and tax and are assumed to be maintainable at this level in perpetuity. It follows that the firm will, after the end of year, be able to maintain its profits of E in perpetuity but also will be able to earn *additional* profits from its re-invested funds.

If the firm is assumed to earn $100R\%$ from the re-invested profits, the profits will be:

in the second year: $E_1 + RbE_1$, or $E_1(1 + Rb)$

in the third year: $E_1 + RbE_1 + Rb(E_1 + RbE_1)$
or $E_1(1 + Rb)^2$

and so on. Thus the earnings in the nth year will be given by

$$E_1(1 + Rb)^{n-1}$$

of which $(1 - b)$ will be paid out in dividends. The present value of the dividends will be given by

$$P_0 \;=\; \frac{(1 - b)E_1}{(1 + i)}\left[1 + \frac{1 + Rb}{1 + i} + \left(\frac{1 + Rb}{1 + i}\right)^2 + \ldots + \left(\frac{1 + Rb}{1 + i}\right)^{n-1}\right] \tag{9A.2}$$

The terms in the square parentheses again have the same form as

$$\left[1 + x + x^2 + \ldots + x^{n-1}\right] \tag{9A.3}$$

which we have already identified in the chapter as a geometric progression with sum equal to $(1 - x^n)/(1 - x)$. As n becomes very large, the nth term becomes insignificantly small as long as x is less than 1. In this case, the same condition requires Rb to be less than i. Thus

$$P_0 \;=\; \frac{(1 - b)E_1}{(1 + i)}\left[1 - \left(\frac{1}{\dfrac{1 + Rb}{1 + i}}\right)\right] \tag{9A.4}$$

which can be expressed as

$$P_0 = \frac{(1-b)E_1}{i - Rb} \tag{9A.5}$$

It will be noted if $g = Rb$, this expression reduces to (9A.1), since $(1-b)E_1$ is by definition the same value as D_1. Thus Rb can be interpreted as the growth rate of dividends (or earnings, since earnings are a constant multiple of dividends) or alternatively as the product of the proportion of earnings retained times the (marginal) return on investment.

From this discussion it will be recognised that

$$E_1 = E_0 (1 + Rb)$$

so

$$\frac{P_0}{E_0} = \frac{(1-b)(1+Rb)}{i - Rb} \tag{9A.6}$$

This expression provides a basis for evaluating the P/E ratio based on historic (current) earnings. Reverting to equation (9A.5) for ease of discussion, it will be expected that for a higher value of R (the return earned by the firm on its re-invested funds), the greater the P/E ratio. Similarly, the greater the value of Rb (the growth rate), the higher will be the P/E ratio. Caution should be taken, however, in accepting these tentative inferences, because the variables are not independent. At higher estimated growth rates, for example, investors might employ a higher discount rate to allow for increased risk. Thus the P/E ratio might fall if both i and Rb increased. Similarly, a company which retained most of its profits ($b \rightarrow 1$) would tend to be assessed as a risky company because of the higher growth rates implied. Finally, we should re-emphasise that the model requires a constant earnings growth rate, a constant return on re-invested earnings, a constant proportion of retained earnings and a constant discount rate. It will be recognised therefore that the model is illuminating in its general form rather than useful for prediction.

Appendix B
Market Models

In our discussion on portfolio-based approaches to share evaluation, we referred to the construction of portfolios which behaved systematically in relation to the market as a whole. The purpose of this appendix is briefly to explain one method of analysing portfolios by this type of approach.

The assumption is made that since shares seem to be influenced by 'market sentiment', the returns on shares are *linearly related* to a market index:

$$r_{jt} = \alpha_j + \beta_j r_{mt} + e_{jt} \tag{9A.7}$$

where r_{jt} = the rate of return on share j in time period t

$\quad r_{mt}$ = the rate of return on the market index in time period t

$\quad \alpha_j, \beta_j$ = constants over time for share j

$\quad e_{jt}$ = error term

In combining two shares, say j and k, equally in a portfolio, we would expect the portfolio to earn a return that would consist of $\frac{1}{2} r_{jt}$ and $\frac{1}{2} r_{kt}$. It would follow from (9A.7) that the portfolio return would be given by

$$r_{pt} = \tfrac{1}{2} (\alpha_j + \beta_j r_{mt} + e_{jt}) + \tfrac{1}{2} (\alpha_k + \beta_k r_{mt} + e_{kt}) \tag{9A.8}$$

Since the α's and β's are constant, we can rewrite this as

$$r_{pt} = \tfrac{1}{2} (\alpha_j + \alpha_k) + \tfrac{1}{2} (\beta_j + \beta_k) r_{mt} + \tfrac{1}{2} (e_{jt} + e_{kt})$$

or letting $\bar{\alpha}$ = the average of α_j and α_k, and $\bar{\beta}$ = the average of β_j and β_k

$$r_{pt} = \bar{\alpha} + \bar{\beta} r_{mt} + \tfrac{1}{2} (e_{jt} + e_{kt}) \tag{9A.9}$$

In considering this expression for the portfolio return, the variability or uncertainty depends on the behaviour of e_{jt} and e_{kt}. If, for example, the companies j and k are in the same industry, then it is quite possible that in any period, if e_{jt} is positive, e_{kt} will also be positive. On the other hand, if j and k were in different industries, e_{jt} might equally be positive or negative for any observed e_{kt}. In this latter case, the average variation in e_{jt} and e_{kt} would tend to be less than the average variation in e_{jt} alone.

In increasing the size of the portfolio by adding more shares, the influence of the error terms e would become less and less important and the relationship would become more and more like the following:

$$r_{pt} = \bar{\alpha}_p + \bar{\beta}_p r_{mt} \tag{9A.10}$$

In (9A.10) the portfolio returns depend on only the two constants ($\bar{\alpha}_p$ and $\bar{\beta}_p$) and the return from the market index. The importance of the relationship is if a portfolio is constructed with many shares (in different industries) with, say, high values of the constant β_j, the portfolio will tend to magnify movements in the market index. Professional investors would call this an aggressive portfolio, and would consider that it represents a high-risk investment strategy. In other words, the value of β_p, being the average of all the individual β_j's, will determine the risk of the portfolio.

This has become widely recognised in the security markets. A share j with a high β_j is described as having a high *beta factor*. Portfolios can be evaluated by reference to the beta factor and the values of the beta factor for most shares regularly traded on the Stock Exchange are available from published sources. Finally, the analyst evaluating individual shares can concentrate on assessing the α_j value (or alpha) for each company. Unlike the beta factor, the alpha is difficult to estimate and will require close study of the characteristics of the individual firm and its management.

Part Three

FINANCIAL INSTITUTIONS

Chapter Ten

The Impact of Institutional Investors

Intermediaries exist in order to exploit economies in the financing process. Their specialised knowledge and skills in catering for the needs of surplus and deficit units complement the workings of the financial markets. If it were possible to bring borrowers and lenders together at zero cost then it is hard to see what demand there would be for the services of middlemen. But financial transacting is not a costless activity, and there is a considerable demand for intermediation. The structure of transaction costs has changed greatly over the years, bringing with it new forms of intermediation and the decline of old forms. These changes in transaction costs came about in a variety of ways: through technological advances; as a direct consequence of changes in taxation; from variations in the regulatory environment; because of shifts in trade and in propensities to borrow and lend; and by chance.

The purpose of the present chapter is to examine some of the major ways in which intermediaries have come into existence and the impacts they have had on the financial system. Later chapters consider the workings of these institutions in greater detail.

Development of Financial Institutions

We have seen in earlier chapters how financial intermediaries serve to reduce the costs of financial transactions. As Europe's economies expanded, trade became more important. Precious metals provided a means of payment in the form of bullion or minted coins, but problems arose when the quantity and quality of such metals were inadequate to meet the needs of trade. Banking has its origins in the need to economise in hard currency: the traders who frequented the great medieval fairs developed means not only of offsetting mercantile debts, but also of assigning these debts by means of the bill of exchange. By the mid-fourteenth century the Venetian money-changers had developed into recognised keepers of deposits, while a little later they were settling the debts of their customers by book transfers of credit. These practices became commonplace in England with the expansion of trade in the latter part of the Tudor period. In the reigns of Elizabeth and James I certain English businessmen became recognised as money-lenders, money-changers, bullion-merchants, exchange specialists, and financial middlemen. Out of these activities, particularly those of the goldsmiths, the trade of banking emerged.

Rapid growth in trade, industry and colonialisation created a big demand for capital. The banks became the specialists who mobilised capital for trade and for the Exchequer. The growth of banking was rapid, but in times of absolute monarchism the establishment of a large joint-stock banking corporation was too risky to contemplate. (Charles I commandeered the bullion deposited by London merchants for safe custody in the Mint and released it only on receiving payment of £40,000 ransom!). With the accession of William II, though, this kind of risk disappeared. The Bank of England was created in 1694. In return for a £1,200,000 loan to the government to finance the war with France, the Bank received certain benefits, including the right to issue notes; other banks were forced to operate as private partnerships which restriction, together with poor communications, limited banking largely to London. The needs of trade and the industrial revolution soon began to create a demand for banking facilities outside of London, so an act was passed in 1826 permitting joint-stock banking with right of note issue. By 1836 a hundred joint-stocks had been established.

By the mid-nineteenth century London had become the leading centre of European commerce. Like Amsterdam in the previous century, but in contrast with earlier commercial centres (e.g. Antwerp and Lyons), London was not only a centre of shipping and trade finance but also for the provision of long-term capital. London's swift rise to pre-eminence owed much to the way the Napoleonic wars had concentrated the world's trade in the British Empire and made Britain the country where capital might be invested safely. London's gain was Amsterdam's loss.

By the nineteenth century, Britain had become a major exporter and London was finding the short-term finance for this activity and providing a system for settling international payments. A good deal of this trade credit was provided by London's merchant banks and private banking companies. By the turn of the century, London was financing the bulk of the world's trade. Merchant banks (or acceptance houses) 'accepted', i.e. guaranteed, bills of exchange drawn on them by clients needing credit. No other centre was equiped for the financing of foreign trade to the same extent as London.

As the name implies, merchant banking has its origins in merchanting. For example, Barings were in wool and Morgans in cotton. Success in trade gave them the ability to back others. Often their name was enough to guarantee success.

In addition to financing trade (by accepting bills of exchange) the merchant banks risked their own money by providing long-term adventure capital for the development of industry and foreign lands. Later, they introduced foreign government and industrial loans on the London capital market. Vast sums were raised in this fashion to finance railways (especially), mines, plantations, harbours and utilities throughout the Empire, in the Americas and in Europe.

The development of London as a financial centre had much to do with its prosperity as a port (at the centre of a thriving Empire). The world's leading freight market, the Baltic Exchange, was based in London, naturally enough, given that Britain had built and operated the world's largest merchant fleet. Shipowners seeking a cargo and shippers and merchants wanting to shift cargoes found it convenient to meet at the Baltic Exchange to do business. The proximity of excellent sources of trade credit, venture capital and a marine insurance market was (and still is) a great convenience.

Insurance is a complicated and highly specialised trade. Knowledge and reputations acquired in marine insurance were readily adapted to other kinds of insurable risks. There are great economies of scale in the writing of contracts, in the procurement of business and in the carrying of risks in the insurance business. The prompt and large payments following the San Francisco earthquakes and fire consolidated London's reputation in this field.

London's role as the world's leading international insurance centre had a profound influence on its capital markets. Insurance companies receive large sums in premium income, much of it from abroad, which has to be invested. In the case of life assurance, the income is in contractual form on a predictable, continuing basis, so investment can be in long-term assets. In the nineteenth century, insurance companies were major holders of railway stock and the better class of foreign issues, but the overwhelming majority of stock exchange securities were held by the personal sector. Since the Second World War insurance (and pension) funds have been net acquirers of ordinary shares, because of the dramatic growth in the use of contractual saving by the personal sector (see below).

The Industrial Revolution created the conditions in which there was a role for a new type of financial intermediary, the building society, which would satisfy two needs: provide a safe harbour for the savings of the new urban workers and make funds available for the financing of house purchases, the demand for the latter being acute in the new cities. In contrast to the banks and insurance companies, the building society movement did not commence life in the capital but rather in the Midlands and the north. The movement came into being at a time when banking firms were thin on the ground outside London and were largely concerned with the issuance of notes. Banks and building societies have competed ever since for deposits, competition for which has become acute in recent years.

The history of the development of Britain's financial institutions is a long and fascinating one and justice cannot be done to the subject in the space of a few paragraphs. What is important for our purpose is to note the way in which intermediaries have come into being in order to smooth the flow of savings. Shifts in population and trade provided the conditions in which specialist intermediaries could operate (e.g. building societies and merchant banks). The proximity of different financial services, e.g. shipping exchanges, sources of trade credit, and marine insurance, have reaped economies of scale.

Advances in technology have played an important part as well. It is difficult to imagine that the great increases in international investment in the nineteenth century would have taken place on such a large scale if communications had not greatly improved — faster ships, the invention of the telegraph — and risks commensurately decreased. The massive expansion of retail banking in recent times is due in great measure to the economies of operation made possible by computerisation. Improvements in technology explain in part the growth of *all* forms of intermediation because it allows intermediaries to narrow the spread between their borrowing and lending rates.

Rapid changes are taking place at the present time, the most important of which are discussed in Chapter 14. As far as financial intermediation is concerned, the most important developments have been: the internationalisation of financial operations generated by the rapid increases in flows of funds across national frontiers associated with the growth of international trade and the greater use by companies and governments of international credit and capital markets; rapidly accelerating concentration and conglomeration of financial intermediaries and providers of financial services (mergers between banks and leasing companies, between building societies, and between members of the securities industry; and entry by financial firms into other types of financial activities, e.g. banks entering underwriting, jobbing and brokerage).

The role of government should not be overlooked. Fear that the sovereign would expropriate the deposits of a large joint-stock banking corporation long acted as a brake on the development of the banking system. For a more positive example we need look no further than the role of the early merchant bankers in securing large loans for the Crown. The impact of government has been enormous in recent times, and it is to this subject that we now turn our attention.

Taxation and Government Policy

Arguably, taxation is nowadays the major factor influencing the development of intermediaries. As noted in Chapter 1, the system of taxation is not neutral in its impact: the flow of savings has been directed into certain forms of investment at the expense of others. Two major tax-induced distortions are to be found in the areas of (a) contractual savings schemes for individuals and (b) corporation financing.

The tax rules in Britain have encouraged contractual saving, thereby resulting in heavy personal sector investment in owner-occupied housing, in pension funds and in life assurance. These means of investment now account, in aggregate, for about the *whole* of net personal saving in the UK. The funds of building societies, insurance companies and pension funds have been growing very rapidly, in consequence. The personal sector has been a net seller of government and company securities in every year since the Second World War. Insurance companies and pension funds have increased their holdings of these assets, to the point where investing institutions (of which they are by far the most significant component) now hold about half of all government securities and more than half of the ordinary shares in issue.

The tax rules encourage these forms of contractual saving in the following way. Owner-occupied housing is encouraged because interest paid on loans for house purchase attracts tax relief, while the enjoyment of occupancy (measured, say, in rent payments saved) and the capital gains on eventual resale escape tax. Investment in insurance policies was until the 1984 Budget encouraged, firstly, by allowing some tax relief on premiums paid and, secondly, by favourable treatment of the incomes earned by the insurance companies. Savings in the form of pension contributions are exempted from taxation.

Taxation promotes certain forms of company financing at the expense of others. The rapid growth of leasing in recent years was attributable in part to the fact that many companies accumulated large tax losses and leasing was the only way they could obtain tax benefits when acquiring plant and machinery. The leasing company was able to set the costs of acquiring the asset, including loan interest charges, against its rental income for tax assessment purposes whereas the firm wanting to use the equipment had no taxable income against which to offset the equipment costs. The leasing company was therefore able to reduce the total tax bill incurred and to share these tax gains to the mutual benefit of both firms. This arrangement also was changed in the 1984 Budget.

Contractual saving and lease financing are but two examples of intermediation becoming profitable to all the parties concerned because of the system of taxation.

Government has influenced the development of intermediaries in other ways as well. We noted in Chapter 4 how the Bank of England's attempts to control the money supply has had the side-effect of causing a switch in deposits away from banks into building societies. Various governments have also deliberately tried to keep the level of interest rates down in order to lower the cost of mortgage financing.

The PSBR increased enormously in the last decade and this has served to stimulate the growth of non-bank intermediaries. Financial institutions intermediate between the issuers of public debt and surplus units (households), developing and issuing financial instruments appropriate to the needs of the latter (e.g. deferred annuities such as pensions) and using the monies collected to purchase public sector securities.

Governments have done much to try to ensure the smooth functioning of the financial system. These interventions take many forms, but they can be conveniently divided into two classes — support and control. Support for the financial institutions has been made available by the provision of 'lender of last resort' facilities to the banks (via the discount houses); and by the launching of 'lifeboats', i.e. the provision or organisation of financial assistance, when one or more important institutions have foundered (recent examples include building societies and insurance companies). Control is exercised both overtly and covertly. Banks have long been required to operate within 'reserve ratios' set by the Bank of England. (Originally reserve requirements were imposed for the express purpose of ensuring the liquidity of the banking system, but in more recent times the main intention has been to facilitate control of the aggregate volume of money and credit.) Insurance companies are required periodically to estimate the actuarial value of outstanding liabilities and to maintain adequate funds to meet these obligations.

Controls can sometimes damage the ability of institutions to compete. We have already noted the problems that banks claim they face in competing with building societies for deposits. An illustration of the advantages enjoyed by the *absence* of detailed controls is offered by the insurance industry. It has been argued that an important factor in London's success as an international insurance centre is the lack of governmental restrictions on its operations compared to other countries, enabling London insurers to invest funds more or less as they please and to pay claims without delay.

Competition

Although it must be acknowledged that the growth and development of our financial institutions owe much to government actions, sight should not be lost of the fact that market factors have played a large part as well. London's rise to pre-eminence as a financial centre began in times when government was little exercised by problems of monetary management and when taxation amounted to only a small proportion of the nation's income. London's success has been due in no small measure to its ability to economise in operations, thereby keeping the spreads between borrowing and lending rates as narrow as possible.

Competition between institutions is very intense, notwithstanding the generally low-key, restrained manner in which it is carried out. This competition is most evident among the deposit-taking institutions. For example, building societies increased their share of the personal deposit market from 29% in 1968 to 48% in 1983 at the expense of the savings banks, mainly, and also the commercial banks. We have already noted that this change was due, at least in part, to the governmental controls and regulations imposed on the banks but not on building societies. The longer and more convenient opening hours operated by building societies also seems to have played a part. Already one bank (Barclays) has reintroduced Saturday opening in selected branches; other banks may well follow suit.

Apart from their rivalry with the building societies and among themselves, the commercial banks face competition from foreign banks. There are approximately 400 commercial banks in the UK of which about two-thirds are subsidiaries or branches of foreign banks. These foreign banks are overwhelmingly concentrated in London and many of them are principally concerned with foreign currency business. But some of them are very active in wholesale corporate lending and compete vigorously with UK-owned banks in this and other areas of domestic lending. Many banks offer investment management services to pension funds, unit trusts etc, and to wealthy private individuals, and are in strong competition with other financial institutions in this area.

Insurance companies operate in a competitive environment. Apart from competing amongst themselves, British insurance companies have to compete against foreign, notably American, rivals as well. Although the American market is larger (in value terms) than the UK one, a great deal of American business finds its way to London via the reinsurance market. The life assurance companies compete not only among themselves but also with other institutions for savings, some of which also receive favourable tax treatment. Competition amongst life companies is largely concerned with premium rates and the payment of bonuses, which boils down to trying to minimise costs and to improve their long-run investment performance.

Intermediation involves costs. Competition cuts intermediation costs, since the most efficient institutions are able to undercut their less efficient rivals and so attract business from them. Regulation can weaken competition among institutions and hence push up the costs of intermediation. The purpose of the change in the method of monetary control introduced in 1971, known as Competition and Credit Control, was to encourage competition among institutions by abandoning quantitative controls on credit and interest rates; in this respect the new policy was a success. Restrictive agreements also restrain competition, for example the Building Societies Association's recommended rate system and the clearing banks cartel (abandoned in the 1970s).

Impact on the Markets

Intermediaries affect the financial markets in many different ways. Perhaps the most extreme case is to be found in the money markets: these markets consist of little more than the dealings between financial institutions and the government. Another striking example of the impact of the institutions, discussed in Chapter 7, was the existence of an informal private market in the shares of small companies operated by a number of important financial institutions; this development played an important part in the creation of a new organised market, the Unlisted Securities Market. We also mentioned in that chapter the practise of 'dawn raids' by institutional investors, a practice which the Council for the Securities Industry is trying to discourage.

The growth in non-bank intermediation is affecting the financial markets in other, less striking, but even more significant ways. Concern has been expressed about the prospect of share prices and trading becoming dominated by institutional investors. The argument runs as follows. Ideally, a share market should be an 'active' one, exhibiting considerable 'depth' and 'breadth', a state of affairs most likely to be achieved if there are a large number of participants of diverse type (see Chapter 3). It is argued that the growth of institutional share ownership is steadily reducing the number and diversity of participants in the market. Already we have witnessed marked increases in the number of instances of interinstitutional share trades which effectively by-pass the market. Taken together, these changes may well lead to increases in the volatility of share prices, with adverse impacts on assessments of the riskiness of equities. The market mechanism could be damaged further by the preference of institutions for the securities of large companies, thereby bringing about the *de facto* creation of a two-tier market.

There is undoubtedly some truth in these claims, although how far increases in institutional activity are likely to undermine the securities markets is far from clear. Any costs imposed on the functioning of the markets have to be balanced against the gains in reduction of transaction costs made possible by increased intermediation.

Classification of Institutions

There is an enormous range and variety of financial institutions. It is neither possible nor desirable to try to account for them in their full complexity. Something must be discarded; institutions must be grouped together in some manner. A variety of classification schemes are worthy of consideration; the one we have adopted as the basis of organisation of the next three chapters has the following features.

A distinction is drawn between (a) institutions which finance their operations by accepting deposits, (b) those engaged in contractual saving, and (c) other institutions. Bearing in mind the purposes of the present book, this classification scheme has a number of advantages.

Firstly, it recognises that savings are not homogeneous. It is important to distinguish between contractual and non-contractual forms of savings in understanding the growth of non-bank intermediaries in recent years. Contractual saving behaves differently from non-contractual saving. Contractual saving arising from pension schemes is more usefully regarded as a form of remuneration than as saving, and it is unresponsive to changes in interest rates, relative yields, inflation and the like, for the simple reason that it is based on standard contracts specifying the deductions to be made from employees' salaries and contributions required of employers. As we have noted, there are fiscal incentives to contractual saving. Contractual saving grows more than proportionately with increases in income and wealth.

Secondly, deposits are more volatile than pension deductions, insurance premiums and the like. This has a marked influence on the investment policies of deposit-taking institutions and insurance companies. The former's policies are dominated by the need to be in a position to cover unpredictable outflows of deposits; whereas the latter's can be based on the knowledge that outflows are highly predictable (in aggregate). Deposit-taking institutions invest heavily in money market securities, insurance companies and pension funds in equities and other long-term securities. Our classification of institutions thus mirrors the classification of markets we employed in Part Two of the book.

All classification schemes have their deficiencies and ours is no exception. The most important deficiency here is the way it tends to obscure the *degree* of intermediation involved in the savings–investment process. Some institutions intermediate directly between surplus and deficit units; others occupy a more distant position from one or both of these fundamental sectors. (An example of a direct intermediary is a building society which borrows funds, in the form of deposits, from the personal sector and lends them to persons borrowing to finance house purchases. An example of indirect intermediation is to be found in the money markets, where discount houses borrow mainly from banks — which institutions have borrowed in turn from the personal sector — and use the funds to purchase the short-term securities issued by the government, companies, etc; many of these securities are acquired from other investors rather than from the original issuers.) Thus, the deposit-taking institutions consist of direct as well as indirect intermediaries, e.g. retail and wholesale banks.

This latter weakness is not fatal to our purpose, which is to classify institutions by the kinds of financial markets in which they operate rather than illuminate the economics of intermediation.

Conclusion

In this chapter we have briefly recounted the development of the UK financial system. Institutions that exist today are still subject to market pressures and are very responsive to the economic environment. Taxation and government policy are shown to have played a major role in shaping the present structure of financial institutions. We conclude the chapter by reference to our classification of the types of institution. The comparisons within each type are made in the following chapters.

Further Reading

1. R.D. Richards, *The Early History of Banking in England* (Frank Cass & Co.,

1965) provides a fascinating explanation of the development of banking from
pre-Tudor times through to the early nineteenth century.
2. C.K. Cairncross, *Home and Foreign Investment, 1870–1913* (Cambridge
University Press, 1953). A scholary account of Britain's role in financing overseas
development.
3. J.A. Kay and M.A. King, *The British Tax System*, 2nd edn (Oxford University
Press, 1980), especially Chapters 4 and 11–13. Provides a very readable, yet
authoritative, account of the structure of taxes in the UK and the ways in which
taxation impinges on the savings and investment process.
4. *Report of the Committee to Review the Functioning of Financial Institutions*
(Wilson Report), Cmnd. 7937 (HMSO, 1980), Chapters 21 and 25 provide some
details of the main regulatory arrangements concerning the UK financial system.
5. K.W. Wilson, *British Financial Institutions* (Pitman, 1980). Chapters 1, 2 and 7,
in particular, explore in some detail the reasons for the growth in non-bank
intermediaries.
6. T.M. Rybczynski, 'The UK Financial System in Transition', *National
Westminster Bank Quarterly Review* (November 1984), analyses recent changes
in the financial system.

Discussion Questions

10.1 Using a transaction cost framework, explain the rise of London as a financial
centre in the nineteenth century.

10.2 Outline some of the ways in which the tax system affects savings and
investment decisions in the economy.

10.3 How has the increase in the PSBR in the last decade stimulated the growth of
non-bank financial institutions?

10.4 Outline the major ways in which financial institutions are affecting the
workings of financial markets. In what ways do intermediaries (a) encourage
and (b) discourage savings and the use of savings?

Chapter Eleven

Deposit-taking Institutions

This chapter considers the functions and operations of the deposit-taking institutions (DTIs). DTIs consist of those financial intermediaries authorised to borrow funds on a 'time' or 'demand' basis from the public. They include the commercial banks, the savings banks, the building societies, and other institutions such as the credit unions and the discount and finance houses. The Banking Act of 1979 distinguishes between banks and other licensed deposit-taking institutions (LDTs), a convenient distinction for our purposes in this chapter.

We dealt with some of the economy-wide implications of the operations of the banks and LDTs in Chapter 4. This chapter is principally concerned with the lending behaviour of the deposit-taking institutions and the reasons why they operate as they do.

The Deposit Markets

The markets for deposits can be divided into two: retail and wholesale. Some banks operate in both markets, but most DTIs specialise in one or the other. The retail market is provided with funds mainly by the general public, the sums lent usually being small. To gather up these funds, institutions have to maintain extensive branch networks. Deposits are accepted on standard terms. In contrast, the wholesale market is provided with funds by wealthy individuals, large corporations and other financial institutions, the sums lent being large. The interest rates paid for wholesale deposits are negotiated individually. Operations in the wholesale market are a head-office function. The wholesale DTIs are part of the sterling money markets (see Chapter 6).

The retail and wholesale deposit markets behave differently. Generally speaking, depositors in the retail market do not 'shop around' from institution to institution. A customer of a commercial bank will usually have established a connection which goes beyond the immediate transaction. For many, the sum on deposit will be too small to warrant the effort. Transitory differences between institutions in the terms offered will not therefore usually lead to much movement of funds — although large and persistent differences can eventually lead to substantial movements. In the wholesale market, on the other hand, the amount of deposits taken by any institution is greatly affected by the terms it offers. Funds are lent often for very short periods of time (even literally overnight) and on an impersonal basis. The competition is very keen.

DTIs compete for deposits (in both the retail and wholesale markets) not simply to attract as many deposits as possible but in order to finance their investment activities. There is of course no point in attracting funds unless they can be lent at a profit. Lending activity is where institutional specialisation lies; the securing of deposits is a secondary activity. The lending activities of the DTIs are considered shortly.

We explained in Chapter 4 how the banks can add to or subtract from the stock of money. As the acquisition of a financial asset (e.g. by making a loan) results in an increase in bank deposit liabilities, the authorities have placed considerable emphasis on controlling the growth in aggregate amount of bank liabilities. These controls have made it easier for other DTIs (notably the building societies) to make inroads into the retail deposit market. To the extent that these non-bank deposits can be used to make personal and business expenditures, the authorities' M_1 monetary controls have been weakened; this has led, in turn, to increasing official concern over the behaviour of monetary aggregates which contain liabilities other than bank demand deposits, with the inevitable consequence of greater Bank of England surveillance of the operations of the DTIs concerned.

The Banks

The Banking Act of 1979 distinguishes between banks and other LDTs on the basis of the breadth and character of services provided. In order to be recognised as a bank, the Bank of England requires the DTI to have enjoyed a good reputation in the financial community for a reasonable period of time and to provide a wide range of banking services, such as: current and deposit account facilities (or accepting funds in the wholesale money market), loans and overdrafts (or lending in the wholesale money markets), foreign exchange services, the handling of bills of exchange and promissory notes, and financial advice and facilities for the purchase and sale of investments.

Listed banks can be classified in a variety of ways. Perhaps the most obvious distinction to draw is between domestic banks and those which are subsidiaries or branches of foreign banks. Table 11.1 provides data on the relative sizes of the different types of banks.

The retail banks, dominated by the London clearers, account for 21% of all banking liabilities (but about half of all sterling deposit liabilities). The clearers handle most of the country's money transmission business and are therefore at the very centre of the financial system. The foreign banks, on the other hand, deal largely in the wholesale and money markets, accounting for about three-quarters of all foreign currency deposits. Consortium banks are banks owned by other banks (one of which must be an overseas bank) but not controlled by any one of them.

Table 11.1   UK Banking Sector Assets/Liabilities, 16 May 1984

	£m	£m	%
British banks:			
Retail banks	143,504		21.1
Accepting houses	25,473		3.8
Other	87,258		12.8
		256,235	37.7
Overseas banks:			
American banks	106,915		15.7
Japanese banks	133,955		19.7
Other	153,727		22.7
		394,597	58.1
Consortium banks		19,302	2.8
Discount market institutions		6,379	1.0
Bank of England banking department		2,579	0.4
Total		679,092	100.0

Source: *Bank of England Quarterly Bulletin,* June 1984.

The London clearing banks number six in all and consist of the 'big four' (Barclays, Lloyds, Midland, and National Westminster), plus Coutts and Williams & Glyn's. The big four together account for practically all of total clearing liabilities; National Westminster wholly owns Coutts, and Williams & Glyn's is a subsidiary of the Royal Bank of Scotland (itself part-owned by Lloyds). In addition to the London clearing banks there are three Scottish clearing banks (Bank of Scotland, Clydesdale, and Royal Bank of Scotland) and two in Northern Ireland (Northern Bank and Ulster Bank). Although the clearing banks are primarily retail banks, since the early 1970s they have been expanding into the wholesale and international banking fields. They also have extensive hire purchase and leasing interests.

The accepting houses are banks specialising in the wholesale market. There are seventeen such houses, all being members of the Accepting Houses Committee, and their distinctive function is to guarantee repayment of bills of exchange, for which service they charge a commission. Accepting houses are merchant banks, and as such concentrate on the provision of financial advice to and raising finance for the corporate sector.

The discount houses are recognised banks under the 1979 Banking Act, but their specialised role is to ensure the smooth functioning of the secondary money markets, in particular, the market for Treasury bills (see Chapter 6). As such, they provide liquidity to the banking system as a whole.

The Trustee Savings Banks (TSBs) are unincorporated societies, the original principle function of which was to encourage thrift, but now providing a full range of banking services to the personal sector. There are sixteen TSBs each operating within a clearly defined geographical region. Originally they were required to invest their funds with the National Debt Commissioners, and they are still required to do so with part of their funds. Subject to Government prudential controls, these funds are being returned to the TSBs to be invested as they see fit. Lending facilities have been provided to customers since 1976.

The National Savings Bank (NSB) is an institution with a similar purpose to the TSBs, but it remains outside the banking system. The NSB is a public institution which operates through the Post Office branch network. It is essentially a government institution for collecting personal savings to finance the PSBR. It provides demand and time deposit accounts. Unlike other banks, its demand deposits earn interest and this interest is tax free. Overdraft facilities are not provided. Virtually all of the NSB's funds are invested in central government and local authority debt.

Other Licensed Deposit-taking Institutions

The most important of the LDTs are undoubtedly the building societies. The building societies are friendly societies (non-profit making associations) whose primary objectives are to encourage both thrift and home-ownership. The accumulated small savings of depositors are used to grant loans to individuals for house purchase which loans are repaid steadily out of income.

The societies are major rivals of the commercial banks and the savings banks in the retail deposit market, accounting for over half of the personal deposit market. The societies are by far the largest providers of mortgage finance in the UK, although in recent years the commercial banks have moved into this field and are now providing the societies with stiff competition.

The building society movement has grown very rapidly, its assets more than doubling in the second half of the 1970s alone. The societies now account for a greater proportion of total liquid assets of the personal sector than the banks. This rapid growth has been achieved partly by providing incentives for those wishing to borrow from them also to save with them; by opening for longer and more convenient hours than the banks; and by offering attractive rates of interest.

The building society movement has experienced a good deal of rationalisation of operations through mergers, the number of societies having fallen from over two thousand at the turn of the century to about 200 now. The movement's mortgage assets increased a thousandfold in monetary value during this period. The major increase in concentration has come through mergers among the medium-sized societies. The five largest societies account for over half of the movement's total assets. Lending by building societies to house buyers now exceeds lending by the banks to the corporate sector.

The building society movement has clearly changed in the last two decades, the small mutual society having been replaced by huge societies operating nationwide branch networks. In law, building societies are treated differently to other financial institutions, banks in particular, and yet it is difficult to see what justification there is for doing so. They are effectively providing banking facilities, some have even started issuing certificates of deposit (see Chapter 6) to companies and other financial institutions, but they continue to be free of many of the restrictions under which banks operate.

Finance houses traditionally specialised in instalment lending (i.e. hire purchase) to consumers and to business firms to finance the purchase of durable assets. Now they provide personal loans and offer leasing and factoring services to businesses as well. (Leasing has become so important a source of financing to the corporate sector that we return to it again later in this chapter.)

The method by which hire purchase finance is made available is not by direct contact between the borrower and the finance house, as is the case with other financial institutions, but between the buyer and the retailer. The advantage of this arrangement is that it (a) allows the retailer to use the financing dimension as part of his marketing strategy, and (b) reduces search costs for the borrower/customer. Against these savings and economies have to be set the problems of high default rates brought about by the enthusiasm of the retailers to make a sale, often to customers whose credit rating is too low for them to obtain finance from any other source; the interest rates charged for hire purchase are correspondingly high.

The finance houses have been included in this section because their lending activities are highly specialised. It should be noted however that many of the finance houses are subsidiaries of banks, and as such their liabilities are included in the official money supply statistics.

The Operations of DTIs

Few interesting distinctions can be drawn between DTIs in terms of the financing side of their operations. As we have seen, the real differences are in their lending activities. Insights into these activities can be obtained in two ways: (a) by examining their asset portfolios and (b) by considering the services they provide. We shall employ each of these approaches in turn below.

Portfolio Composition

An examination of the balance sheets by different types of DTI reveals some notable differences. In particular:

■ *The commercial banking sector*[1] has about one-third of its sterling funds invested in short-term assets, partly to meet the requirements of the Bank of England, but mainly reflecting managerial judgements of the need for liquidity. The sector's main earning assets consist of loans and advances to customers and these account for about half of all bank assets. In addition, the banks have about 3% of their resources in the form of investments, about half being in public sector securities and the balance in subsidiary companies, etc. The public sector securities are mostly purchased near to maturity and as such provide a supplementary source of liquidity.

■ *Building societies* are heavily invested in mortgages, over 75% of their assets being of this form. The next largest asset is their investment in public sector securities. Less than 10% of their resources are held in the form of short-term assets.

■ *Finance houses'* portfolios mainly consist of loans and advances, the next largest asset being real assets either for own use or for leasing, hiring or renting to customers. Liquid assets account for less than 10% of the total.

■ *The savings banks* are heavily invested in public sector securities, partly for historical reasons. Essentially all of the NSB's assets are held in this form. About a quarter of the portfolios of the TSBs is in short-term assets.

Clearly, there are considerable differences in the investment policies of the various types of DTI. For example, compare the portfolios of banks and building societies. The former hold a large proportion of their assets in liquid form, whereas the latter hold very little, and yet they are keen competitors for funds in the retail deposit market. The reasons for the differences in asset structure are worth exploring.

We can view the managers of both banks and building societes as facing an asset composition (and related financing) problem. The objective of each is to select a portfolio of assets which offers the prospect of highest returns subject to meeting risk and other constraints. Alternatively, they might view their institution in terms of a tank of a liquid assets. Into the tank flow new deposits, repayments of loans (with interest) and the sale-proceeds of investments. Out of the tank flow withdrawals of deposits, new loans and outlays on new investment. The manager has in mind a target level of liquid assets determined by prudential controls and experience with the kinds of borrowing and lending activities in which it specialises.

---

[1] It is not possible to distinguish between the retail and wholesale sectors because the retail banks are heavily involved in wholesale business — surpluses of funds arising from their retail operations commonly being placed in the wholesale market.

Services Provided

It is obvious that in order to survive, an intermediary's lending rate must exceed its borrowing rate by an amount sufficient to cover its operating costs. To do this, it must provide a service. Banks are able to pay zero interest on demand deposits because the payments (and safe custody) service they provide is clearly a very convenient and valuable one. If banks had to pay the same rate of interest on demand deposits as they can earn in the market then they would have to make further charges for the cheque-processing facilities made available to demand-depositors. One of the costs of providing this payments service is the restrictions it imposes on bank portfolio decisions: banks have to maintain a high proportion of funds in liquid assets if the payments system is to work without disruption. The payments service provided by the banks (and to a lesser extent by other DTIs) is of very great importance to the smooth functioning of the economy.

DTIs provide another service, that of investment at low risk. In particular, they guarantee liquidity. The existence of this service, too, is implied in the difference between their borrowing and lending rates. Thus building society depositors can be thought of as investing in a portfolio of property mortgages with the liquidity of their own stake effectively guaranteed. By maintaining a well diversified portfolio of mortgage investments, a building society has a predictable and even flow of cash receipts with which to repay depositors when required. Furthermore, by charging borrowers a variable rate of interest a building society can increase its borrowing rate if necessary to stem any continued draining away of deposits. Though borrowing very short and lending very long, building societies are able to guarantee liquidity without holding a big proportion of funds in low-earning short-term assets.

Each of these models has its strengths and weaknesses. The portfolio selection model is of limited applicability to DTIs, having greater descriptive power in relation to institutions which are more obviously investment vehicles, e.g. unit trusts. But all DTIs do have large funds to invest and are concerned to invest them prudently, so the portfolio (or asset composition) model is not without interest. The service industry model is of particular applicability to banks. Banks provide a range of facilities which can be equivocably described as services.

The operations of the banks warrant special attention because of the way in which they operate over all parts of the economy, attracting funds from whichever sectors have surpluses available and lending them to whichever sectors have a demand for them. We will restrict our attention to the ways in which banks lend to the corporate sector — an aspect of the banks' operations which has aroused a great deal of interest and controversy over the years.

Bank Lending to Industry

The banks are important suppliers of finance to the corporate sector, this source now accounting for between a quarter and a third of new finance raised by industrial and commercial companies. Bank finance takes a variety of forms, such as: ordinary overdrafts (i.e. demand deposits overspent) and term loans (i.e. loans of specified duration, rate of interest and repayment schedule); loans for exports of consumer goods and overseas construction projects secured on insurance policies against non-payment provided by the government's Export Credits Guarantee Department (ECGD); finance provided by Finance for Industry which is in turn funded by the banks.

It has been suggested that the banks in Britain are too restrictive in their lending to industry as compared to their counterparts in Germany and Japan. The British banks have indeed been rather conservative in their lending, preferring short-term self-liquidating loans rather than medium- or long-term ones, and it is possible that this has tended (in the past, at least) to make life difficult for businessmen, particularly those starting up new firms. Part of the problem can undoubtedly be traced to the situation faced by the banks before 1971 whereby all their deposits were repayable either on demand or within seven days. Bankers were understandably reluctant to lend more than a small part of the potentially very volatile deposits on a long-term basis. They sought to lend on a self-liquidating basis, e.g. to finance a firm's seasonal build-up of inventories with the prospect of the loan being paid off out of the proceeds from later sale of the goods; or to carry a farmer through to harvest time.

Banks have shown themselves to be willing to lend more on a longer-term basis in recent years, partly because they are now free of the restrictions concerning the acceptance of deposits, partly in response to criticisms, and perhaps also because of increased demand from the corporate sector for medium- and long-term finance.[2]

Bank finance is not without costs for a company. Obviously, interest is charged, either at a variable rate related to other short-term interest rates or at a fixed rate. A large company of national repute ('blue chip') is usually able to borrow at a more favourable rate than is a smaller firm, partly because larger loans are cheaper per pound borrowed to administer, and also reflecting the lower risk. Small firms can get good rates if they are exporting and can offer the bank the security of an ECGD guarantee. Less obvious but no less real costs to the borrower are any restrictions which the bank places on the firm's operations.

Bank restrictions take a number of forms. A borrower might be required to offer security by lodging deeds of property or stocks and shares with the bank such that the bank either has legal title to the asset or has a first claim on any proceeds from sale or redemption. The cost to the company of this

---

2   In the early days of the Industrial Revolution the demand was not so much for external funds to purchase fixed assets as for finance to meet working capital needs not already covered by trade credit from suppliers. Banks served to fill the gap. See H. Heaton, 'Financing the Industrial Revolution', Chapter 2 in F. Crouzet, ed., *Capital Formation in the Industrial Revolution* (Methuen, 1972).

arrangement is that it loses its freedom to dispose of the asset as and when it pleases, locking it into the investment. In the case of a small company the bank might require the owner-directors to pledge some of their own assets or to provide personal guarantees in the event of the company not having sufficient funds to repay the loan. To do this negates some of the advantages of corporate limited liability, imposing greater personal risks on the owners. Thirdly, the bank might require the firm to operate at or above a certain ratio of current assets to current liabilities, or to maintain compensating cash balances with the bank, at the cost of tying up funds in unwanted assets. Lastly, the bank might require the company to submit detailed financial statements and cash projections on a regular basis.

Restrictions such as these are imposed not without good reason. At the time of seeking a loan, a would-be borrower has a strong incentive to represent the risks as being less than they really are. Afterwards, the borrower might be tempted to apply the funds to purposes other than those set out to the bank in the loan application. The bank can avoid some of these risks by the kinds of restrictions outlined above. In short, the costs of borrowing ('agency costs') are those stemming from the asymmetries of information inherent in external financing.

We have noted that the British banks have been criticised for being too restrictive in their lending to industry. A question of the opposite nature could be asked: Why are the banks such an important source of external finance for the corporate sector when capital markets and other financial institutions exist which could also do the job? In some other countries, of course, the lack of highly developed capital markets of the kind found in the UK (and the USA) compels firms to turn to institutions like the banks. Nevertheless, it cannot be overlooked that in the UK great use is made of the banks by firms, and surprisingly little recourse is had to the equity and debt markets.

The explanation would appear to be the informational advantages the banks enjoy over their competitors. Firstly, banks are known to potential borrowers. Even the smallest firm has to maintain a bank account, and through this means is in regular contact with a potential source of borrowing. These firms might have little or no idea of alternative lenders and are therefore likely to turn first to their bank when looking for external finance. Larger firms seeking larger sums could be expected to look further afield.

Where the banks have a really major advantage over other lenders is not in their visibility to potential borrowers but rather in the information they possess concerning the cash flows of their customers. In the course of handling money transmissions on behalf of customers the banks build up a detailed picture of the way each business manages its finances. This information is of great value when it comes to assessing the customer's creditworthiness. The capital markets and other financial institutions do not have this kind of information immediately to hand. The longer the period of time the customer has maintained an account with the bank, then the better the bank's record of the customer's creditworthiness, a factor which might go some considerable way to explaining why individuals and firms tend not to switch from bank to bank. (To do so might imply an unwillingness to be monitored over a number of years and signal that the customer is a bad risk.) To the extent that banks enjoy informational advantages concerning potential borrowers, they will be able to process loan applications at lower cost, and experience fewer bad debts. Other things being equal, these advantages will enable them to charge lower rates of interest than competitor institutions.

One of the ways in which banks have made more longer-term funds available to the corporate sector is by the provision of lease financing. Leasing has grown rapidly in the UK over the past decade, to the extent that over one-quarter of fixed investment in plant, machinery and motor vehicles is now financed in this manner. The banks are dominant in this field, accounting for three-quarters of assets acquired by members of the Equipment Leasing Association, who in turn account for over 90% of all domestic leasing. In the next section we consider the reasons why leasing is so important a source of company finance and why the banks are so heavily involved.

Leasing

Leasing is an alternative to outright purchase as a means of acquiring the use of an asset. Leases can be separated into two types. 'Operating' leases are of short duration (compared with the economic life of the asset) and can be cancelled at the option of the lessee. Ownership resides with the lessor. An operating lease is essentially the same as an ordinary hire or rental agreement.

In contrast, a 'finance' lease is essentially equivalent to outright purchase of the asset by means of a loan. The asset is selected by the lessee, bought by the lessor and leased to the lessee in return for a series of rental payments over a term which usually approximates its economic life. Provision may be made in the agreement for the lease to continue, at the option of the lessee, into a secondary term at a nominal rental, or for part of the sale-proceeds to be passed on by the lessor to the lessee. As the lessee is in essentially the same position as if the asset had been purchased outright, finance leases are clearly a source of finance.

Why is leasing so popular a means of financing? We pointed out in the previous chapter that prior to the 1984 Budget, finance leasing provided a means by which companies which were not paying taxes could obtain tax benefits. Assuming the lessor was paying taxes, it could claim deductions against taxable income when buying an asset; but as the lessee had no taxable income it would be unable to make these tax deductions if it had purchased the asset outright. The company interested in acquiring the asset would want to lease to the extent that the lessor was willing to pass on some of the benefits. Evidence suggests that the majority of the tax benefits from leasing were being passed on to the lessee. The depression had placed a large number of companies in a non-tax-paying situation, providing ample incentive for finance leasing.

The 1984 Budget reduced the incentives for lease financing. Around half of all manufacturing and distribution companies currently pay no corporation tax.[3] Prior to the Budget, a firm which purchased plant and machinery could set the whole of the outlay against its taxable profits in the year of purchase. If its first-year profits were insufficient to cover the outlay then no tax benefits would be obtained that year (the taxable losses could be carried forward to set against the taxable profits of later years); hence the advantages of leasing. The 1984 Budget altered this state of affairs by phasing out the 100% first-year allowances: reduced to 75% in 1984/85, to 50% in 1985/86, and to 25% thereafter. Firms can charge in subsequent years 25% of the reducing balance of expenditures not already charged. The effect of this budget change will be to slow the rate at which capital expenditures serve to reduce taxable profits, bringing more firms back into a tax-paying position, and therefore reducing the demand for lease financing. The Budget has further reduced the incentives for firms to seek tax-efficient means of financing by reducing the standard rate of corporation tax: previously 52%, corporation tax will be reduced by stages to 35% in 1986/87.

Leasing provides tax advantages which can be shared between lessee and lessor if (and only if) their tax rates differ. To the extent that the 1984 Budget placed more companies in a tax-paying position, and therefore in a comparable tax environment to the leasing companies, the advantages of leasing have diminished. Deveruex and Mayer[4] estimate that although around 50% of companies currently pay no corporation tax, this figure will fall to around 20% in the foreseeable future. This 20% will continue to benefit from lease financing.

Bank involvement in leasing can also be explained by tax considerations. Banks have been making profits and hence paying taxes consistently throughout the past decade, unlike many other business enterprises. They have therefore been well placed to enter the leasing business and share the tax savings on equipment purchases with loss-making companies (and with organisations which are not required to pay corporation tax, such as those in the public sector). In addition, banks have direct access to funds needed to finance the purchase of lease assets, unlike tax-paying companies which might also otherwise consider entering the leasing business. Certain other

---

[3]   See M.P. Devereux and C.P. Mayer, *Corporation Tax: The Impact of the 1984 Budget* (The Institute for Fiscal Studies, 1984).

[4]   See footnote 3.

financial institutions which might otherwise be tempted into lease finance receive favourable tax treatment, e.g. insurance companies and building societies, and have therefore been at a competitive disadvantage to the banks because they were unable to pass on as much tax savings to lessees.

Although the taxation argument has now diminished, companies might still turn to leasing if other sources of finance are hard to come by. In both operating and finance leases legal ownership of the asset resides with the lessor — an attractive arrangement for any lessor especially if the lessee were to default. The lessor could regain control of the asset: loss of ownership is an agency cost to the lessee. The collateral obtained obviates the need for detailed investigation of the financial affairs of each borrower with attendant savings in overhead costs.

A third reason for the popularity of leasing is to be found in the way assets, even business assets, are marketed. As we noted earlier when explaining the operations of finance houses, hire-purchase and leasing finance is arranged at the time of purchase of the asset and obviates the need to search around for a lender. (This argument is likely to be more telling in the case of consumer purchases of durable goods.) Leasing companies can bring overheads and administrative costs down by using simple standard lease contracts, thereby avoiding incurring large investigative and legal costs.

Taxation of DTIs

We noted earlier that the costs of many of the services provided by DTIs are covered not by direct charges to customers but implicitly in the low rate of interest they pay on certain kinds of deposits. A consequence of this non-charging of services is that the magnitude of these services is not properly quantified. Thus the contribution of DTIs to the gross domestic product (i.e. aggregate output of goods and services) is greatly underestimated in the national accounts. More important, the problems of quantifying these services properly has led to banking and financial services being exempted from value-added tax (VAT).

Most goods and services are subject to VAT. A firm pays VAT on the excess of revenues from sales of goods and services over outlays on materials and services purchased. In other words, VAT is charged not on profits but rather on roughly the equivalent of profits plus wages and salaries. In the case of DTIs, the method of charging for services means that VAT collections, if levied, would be zero. It has been suggested that this problem could be solved if the banks and other financial institutions were required to present their accounts differently with a charge for services provided being disclosed therein. (The banks' reported 'bottom line' profit would be unchanged, the increase in income from services provided being exactly offset by increased interest expense on deposits.)

Another area of controversy concerns the way in which the banks are said to benefit from inflation. In times of inflation interest rates increase with the result that banks pay more out in interest to depositors and receive more from lenders. But as demand deposits do not earn interest the effect of increases in interest rates is to increase the profits of the banks. In order to capture some of this 'inflation endownment' a special tax was imposed in 1981 on the banks in the form of a 2½% levy on their sterling non-interest-bearing deposits.

Whether this additional tax is justified or not is moot. The answer depends on how one thinks business enterprises ought to be taxed in times of inflation. All that can be said in our present state of knowledge is that, when due allowance is made for inflation, it is by no means clear that the banks have been more profitable than the corporate sector as a whole — a key assumption underlying the imposition of the special bank levy.[5] As it is, we have already noted that the failure to pay interest on demand deposits is offset by under-charging for the costs of servicing customer transactions; inflation increases not only the level of interest rates but also the costs of providing services.

Summary

This chapter has examined the group of institutions collectively known as the deposit-taking institutions. The special role played by the banks has been noted. Emphasis has been placed on the way these institutions compete for deposits but tend to specialise in their lending activities. Consideration has been given to the functions of these institutions: whether they are best thought of as investment vehicles or as providers of services, and some of the implications of treating them as the latter. Special attention has been devoted to lease finance and taxation issues.

Further Reading

1. K.W. Wilson, *British Financial Institutions* (Pitman, 1983). Chapters 3 and 4 deal at some length with the development and significance of the main classes of deposit-taking institutions.
2. D.P. Whiting, *Elements of Banking*, 2nd edn (MacDonald and Evans, 1979), Chapters 13–15. A professional text for beginning students of banking, these chapters provide some nitty-gritty information about bank lending practices.
3. R. Weston, *Domestic and Multinational Banking* (Croom Helm, 1980). The first part provides a good introduction to the microeconomics of banking.

---

[5]   See J.S.S. Edwards and C.P. Mayer, *Issues in Bank Taxation* (The Institute for Fiscal Studies, 1983), Chapter 3.

4. E.J. Cleary, *The Building Society Movement* (Elek, 1965). Provides a detailed account of the development and impact of building societies.
5. 'The Future of Building Societies: A Central Banker's View', *Bank of England Quarterley Bulletin* (June 1983). A speech by the Governor of the Bank of England on the ways in which building societies have been expanding their operations in recent years and the problems which might ensue.
6. T.M. Clark, *Leasing* (McGraw-Hill, 1978). A very thorough explanation of the leasing industry and the economics of lease financing by the Chairman of the Equipment Leasing Association.
7. J.S.S. Edwards and C.P. Mayer, *Issues in Bank Taxation* (The Institute for Fiscal Studies, 1983). A useful research study into the question of whether or not banks pay their fair share in taxes.

Discussion Questions

11.1 Explain what is meant by the term 'deposit-taking'. What kind of markets for deposits exist and in what respect do they differ?

11.2 In what respect do banks differ from other deposit-taking institutions? Explain the functions the discount houses serve in the financial system.

11.3 What is a building society? Explain why they have been so successful in attracting deposits from the personal sector. Do the banks enjoy any advantages over the building societies in the raising of funds?

11.4 In what respects are the various kinds of deposit-taking institutions similar to and different from other kinds of business enterprises?

11.5 Explain what is meant by the term 'self-liquidating advances' and provide some examples. Describe some of the ways in which the banks have become involved in longer-term lending.

11.6 Explain what is meant by the term 'creditworthiness'. Outline some of the ways in which a lender can try to minimise the risks of loss.

11.7 Describe some of the main sources of finance available to companies. Why are the banks such an important source of finance to the corporate sector?

Chapter Twelve

Insurance Companies and Pension Funds

Insurance companies and pension funds are important in the context of this book not only because of their effects, but also because they provide many problems that can be solved only with the help of financial analysis. Thus the explanation of some of the products offered in the field of insurance are best understood by analysing their characteristics in financial terms. However, in the text we have covered only the simpler cases and policies and have provided in the appendix of this chapter a more technical discussion of the actuarial aspects.

Cash Flow Inputs and Outputs

Insurance is designed to protect a policy holder against the financial loss arising from some specified event. One obvious way of categorising insurance is therefore by the type of event, e.g. personal accident, or fire. More usually, two broad categories are used; *long-term* and *general*. This distinction is made for a variety of reasons but follows directly from legal constraints which require long-term and short-term insurance business to be separated. This legal distinction is not always simple since it has to accommodate those companies which have traditionally carried out both long-term and general insurance business.

The difference has considerable effect on the way in which risk is dealt with. For example, in motor insurance (a class of general insurance) companies have found that the cost of settling claims has tended to rise year by year — partly because of inflation and changes in the type of claim, and partly because of an increase in the frequency of claims. Because of this change, insurance companies have raised their premiums in an effort to ensure that total premiums match total claims. With life insurance policies, however, because the contract is a long-term one, insurance companies are unable to alter the premiums of policies for existing policy holders.

Any decision made on life insurance business may therefore affect the profitability of the company for many years in the future. In reacting to this problem, companies have created long-term policies in which some of the uncertainty in the value of the eventual claim is passed on to the policy holder. Although there is a distinction between general (short-term) and long-term insurance, there is the similarity that both types of insurance involve *risk reduction* through the aggregation of independent events. In general insurance for example, the insurer accepts that of the total number of buildings covered by its policies, some buildings will be damaged each year. By careful analysis of the historical data, the insurance company will arrive at an estimated number of buildings and a consequential figure for the compensation that it will be required to pay. In the long run, therefore, the company fixes its premiums to exceed its estimated claims by an amount sufficient to cover its administration and operating costs (and a required profit margin). Year by year fluctuations in actual losses may, of course, exceed actual premiums but the company expects that a satisfactory profit will be achieved in the long run. The position is complicated by the fact that insurance companies receive the premiums months or even years before they pay out claims. During the intervening period, they will have the use of the premium money which can be invested to earn a return. It is possible therefore that an insurance company would have a very small profit (or even a loss) between its claims and expenses and its premiums but still make a viable return when its investment income is taken into account.

In life business, an insurance company can analyse the incidence of death from its previous policy holders and arrive at an estimate of the likely number of claims to be met in the following years. For example, it will be obvious that the chance of a person aged 82 surviving five years is considerably lower than that of a 25 year old surviving a similar period. Consequently, the estimated claims arising from a group of 82 year olds would be greater than the claims from a group of young people. There is, therefore, a strong emphasis on linking a stastistical analysis of the events with the determination of the premiums at which the insurance contracts are offered.

In the longer-term context, *pensions* can also be represented as a type of insurance policy in that an individual will contribute to a pension scheme and on retirement will start to receive payment or 'benefits'. The benefits will stop when the pensioner dies (unless protection has also been arranged for other surviving dependants). The pension scheme is therefore faced with estimating the cost of providing pensions from the date of retirement until the date of death. It will be seen that this concerns the same central issues as that considered by an insurance company paying out on claims made on a policy holder's life policy (in which benefits are payable on death). In both cases, the company or pension scheme has to estimate the death or survival rate of its policy holders (or pension scheme members). It is logical that insurance companies dealing with life business should have expanded their activities by taking on pension business.

Another similarity between long-term life insurance, pensions and general insurance is the need to minimise risk. One method of doing so is to match the characteristics of assets and liabilities, e.g. life insurance and pension funds invest their assets in long-term investments which match the long-term liabilities represented by the outstanding policies.

General Insurance

The sectors of insurance business are variously classified for statistical purposes. One such classification used by the British Insurance Association is by (a) Fire and Accident, (b) Motor Vehicle, and (c) Marine, Aviation and Transport. Some indication of the relative size of the sectors is given in Table 12.1.

Table 12.1   Premiums Received by British Insurance Companies

	1977		1982	
	£m	%	£m	%
Fire and Accident	3788	58	6605	60
Motor	2180	34	3642	33
Marine, Aviation and Transport	540	8	806	7
Total general	6508	100	11053	100
Total long-term	4278		9465	

Source: *Insurance Facts and Figures,* British Insurance Association, 1983.

There is a variety of institutions in the insurance market besides the insurance companies. The most famous of these is Lloyds insurance market in which clients requiring insurance have to deal with *brokers* who negotiate the best terms for the insurance contract with *underwriters*. The underwriters compete for insurance business on behalf of the members of their *syndicates*. A large insurance contract may involve many syndicates each underwriting a small proportion of the risk, but the premium for the contract will be determined by the *leading underwriter* who first accepts the risk. There are over 400 syndicates with more than 20,000 members, each of whom must be able to demonstrate considerable financial resources before they are accepted as members. (At the end of 1982, the average available personal wealth of the members was over £80,000.) Members receive the profit from the underwriting (and the associated investment income) at the end of a three-year *account.* Thus the surplus from premiums received on policies covering 1980 are finally distributed to members (after paying claims and expenses and reserving for outstanding claims) at the end of 1982. Table 12.2 presents a summarised extract of the 1980 account on closure.

From the table it will be noted that *re-insurance* is an important element in the operations of Lloyds (this also applies to general insurance transacted by companies). In this particular case, the re-insurance premiums are paid in order to close the account — in effect they are valuations of the unsettled claims — the syndicates are *re-insuring* their liabilities.

Table 12.2   Income and Expenditure for the Lloyds Account

	£m
Income	
Premiums	3653
Investment profit	399
Total income	4052
Expenditure	
Re-insurance premiums	2113
Claims	1518
Other expenses	157
Total expenditure	3788
Total profit	264

Source: *Lloyds Global Accounts,* 1982.

More generally, the term is applied whenever one insurer passes on some part of the risk to another insurer. Although re-insurance has the beneficial aspect of spreading the risk it has also been the basis of some institutional problems suffered by Lloyds over the past decade. Because of the freedom with which underwriters have been able to transact re-insurance business with companies registered outside Lloyds and outside the insurance regulations of the UK, some individual underwriters were able to set up re-insurance contracts on terms which were favourable to their own interests. By the summer of 1983, the self-regulatory system of Lloyds had received some harsh criticism and changes were being widely advocated. Indeed the debate on the type and extent of regulation in financial markets recurs during any period in which the markets are seen to be disturbed, whether by economic pressures or sudden development.

The profitability of membership varies considerably from one type of insurance to another, but increasing competition has depressed profits and emphasised the importance of income earned from the short-term investment of premiums. In general liability business, for example, Lloyds underwriters consistently made losses from underwriting in the period 1976 to 1980, and by 1980 an overall loss was made as the underwriting loss of £119 million exceeded the investment income. The impact of this loss however, might not be as dramatic as at first it appears because of the special tax considerations which attract high tax payers to become members of Lloyds (e.g. the facility to carry forward losses to offset against future tax liability on underwriting profits). By contrast, the motor vehicle account earned nearly £39 million underwriting profit from £325 million premiums. The variability of profit between types of business is matched by the various syndicates' results. For the 1980 year one syndicate was reported to have made more than 45% return on its members' capital whilst another made a 30% loss.

Lloyds brokers also compete with insurance broking companies. *Insurance brokers* act as intermediaries between clients and insurers and place the insurance with insurance companies or with Lloyds. The brokers' income is earned in commission and investment income from funds held prior to paying insurers. In addition to advising clients on their insurance business, brokers may also manage insurance on their own account. Other insurance intermediaries include the *insurance agents* who sell insurance, mainly to individuals, on a commission or fee basis for insurance businesses.

Some companies in the general insurance business are classified as composite insurers since they undertake long-term, as well as the shorter-term, business. These *composite insurance* companies which include firms such as Royal, Eagle Star and Commercial Union dominate the insurance company market in the UK, and like Lloyds syndicates have faced increasing competition. In the commercial market this has been exacerbated by the increasing trend of large industrial companies to make their own arrangements for insurance, usually by setting up subsidiary or 'captive' insurance companies. Expansion of overseas insurance companies (and also of insurance markets in the US) has led to the current oversupply of insurers with the inevitable reduction in profits made by insurance companies. In 1982 for example Royal Insurance made a £166 million loss from underwriting, more than compensated by £249 million income from investment and over £10 million from its long-term business.

The important conclusion from these illustrative statistics is that institutions engaged in short-term insurance business are often heavily dependent on their investment activities for their profitability.

Risk Management in General Insurance

In taking on insurance business, insurers have to minimise risks. We noted above that this can be achievd by re-insuring all or part of the contracts with other companies. In other cases, insurers can try to improve the risk either by imposing conditions under which the risk is accepted or by taking on only some types of policy. Insurers will also try to find out all the relevant information in considering a proposal and may, if they think fit, refuse to cover a risk. The difficulty in managing risk in insurance on unusually uncertain events is not helped by the problems of *adverse selection* and *moral hazard*.

Adverse selection arises when one company becomes recognised as offering insurance on 'difficult' proposals (for example, in motor insurance, one company might offer generous terms to a 21 year old driver with a record of previous accidents). The company might be able to expand its business quickly by taking on a large number of inadequately rated risks, but the calculation of the claims from this biased sample of drivers might be very difficult to forecast. Therefore, to minimise risk there is a tendency for an insurance company to avoid this type of client either by refusing the business or by imposing abnormally high premiums.

A second problem with which insurers have to deal is that of moral hazard which arises when the insurance policy is issued. Plainly, from the policy holder's point of view better terms may be gained if less adverse information is available. There is therefore incentive for the applicant to conceal information which might lead to a policy being refused or issued only on punitive terms. This problem is minimised by companies refusing to pay any claims if the full information was not disclosed at the time at which the policy was issued.

In most types of insurance, the insurer will aim merely to provide *indemnity*, i.e. on settlement of a claim, a policy holder should not be in a better financial position than before the incident leading to the claim. This principle could be particularly important in settling fire policies, for example if it was found that a businessman had 'accidentally' set fire to a warehouse full of stock which might in any case have been unsaleable. The insurance company would, on the basis of indemnity, be justified in paying no compensation for the valueless stock. An exception to this principle can be found in the area of household contents insurance, since there has been a tendency for insurers to offer 'good as new' policies. Thus, for example, a stolen secondhand TV will be replaced by a new one.

Life Assurance and Pensions

The long term nature of life and pension business means that substantial funds build up for investment. These are considerably in excess of the funds generated by short-term insurance (see Table 12.3 on p.184).

Whereas general insurers hope that claims will total less than premiums in any one period, long-term insurers are more concerned that the valuation of their existing fund will adequately cover the estimated liabilities at some future date. Often the liability is known in advance or can be identified shortly before it becomes due — pensions, for example, are usually calculated on the basis of years of service and average or final salary levels.

On the basis of forecasting at what age a pensioner will die the insurance company or pension fund can calculate the amount that will be required to provide the pension. Difficulties in estimating this value will be greatly exacerbated by uncertainties in the rate of inflation, the final salary at retirement and the investment returns. During the 1970s, for example, many salaries increased dramatically with the unexpected inflation. Unfortunately this was not accompanied by an associated rise in the returns from investment so that in some cases actuaries found that the future liabilities of the long-term funds substantially exceeded the anticipated asset value. Consequently, funding contributions were increased in order to save the long-term fund from insolvency.

We discuss the investment implications of this problem later in this chapter and look more closely at the actuarial problems in the appendix to this chapter. With long-term funds, premiums may not always be paid over many years; *single premium* policies have been successfully marketed by insurance companies either to provide annuities or lump sum cash payments at the end of the specified period (or on death if earlier). For 1982, about 25% of the long-term insurance premium income was estimated (by the British Insurance Association) to be paid in single premiums. The bulk of the premium income (62%) was, however, received in annual premiums paid over a number of years. Most of the remaining 13% was paid to agents who make regular house-to-house visits, mainly for small policies. This business is referred to as *industrial life* insurance and a number of insurance companies and friendly societies specialise in this service.

There is a variety of long-term insurance policies which provide different cover to individuals. *Term policies* provide 'pure' insurance cover against death within a specified period of, say, five to ten years. The insured individual pays the premium for the period. If he or she survives no benefit is paid. On death in the period covered, a specified amount of cash is paid to the family or surviving dependants of the insured. The cost of this type of policy is cheap — for example, in February 1984 a sample of insurance companies quoted annual premiums of under £20 for a 30 year old man for a fifteen year term and a £10,000 cover.

In other cases, the policy contains a substantial savings element — the benefits from which may accrue either to the insured or their dependants. In the case of the *whole life* policy, the term is not specified but the insurance fund will always pay benefit on death of the insured. The premiums for this contract, of course, will be substantially higher than for the term policy because in *every* whole life policy the insurer will be committed to pay the agreed sum insured. For a 30 year old man, a whole life insurance policy providing £10,000 on death, cost (in February 1984) in the region of £165 annually; more than eight times greater than the term policy described above.

Another policy which has become popular with individuals is the *endowment* policy which combines the pure insurance feature of the term policy with the guaranteed payment of the whole life. Endowment policies cover a fixed period. If the insured person dies before the policy matures, the insurance policy pays the benefit; if however, the insured survives, the promised amount will be paid when the policy matures. Usually this type of policy is taken out on a 'with-profits' basis, by which the total amount payable rises over the period at a rate dependent upon the profitability of the insurance company.

Alternatively, a policy may be linked to a specific investment fund so that the insured individual can monitor the value of the insurance payment over the life of the policy. This type of policy is called 'unit-linked' since the fund is sometimes set up as a Unit Trust (see Chapter 13). In other cases, the investment is linked to an internal fund managed by the company.

The other major type of life insurance policy is the *annuity* which provides an income from a specified date until the death of the insured person. In some cases the payments can be made as long as either of two named people survive. Thus, for example, a married couple can arrange for an annuity to continue for as long as either survive. The premiums for this policy can be paid either as a single cash sum or as a series of payments over a number of years. In this latter case (which is termed a *deferred annuity*) the policy is usually sold as part of a pension scheme because there are substantial tax savings for this arrangement.

Pensions are organised in Britain either by the state or through schemes based on the occupation of the individual. Just under half of the workforce are members of an occupational pension scheme. The state scheme provides a basic flat rate benefit payable on retirement and an additional payment related to earnings.

Private occupational-based pensions can be either *funded* or *unfunded*. Unfunded pensions provide benefits for existing pensioners from the contributions paid by the employer and *existing* employees. Funded pension schemes, on the other hand, operate by setting up an investment fund into which contributions are paid by employees and the employer. These funds can be invested and profits made (either as income or capital gain) without incurring any tax liability. Thus for the pension fund contributor they represent a very efficient method of deferring income. On retirement, the employees will receive a pension generated from the investment contributions. In the private sector, most pensions are funded with the employer paying more into the fund than the employee, although some operate on a *non-contributory* basis in which the employee is not required to contribute anything. In the public sector, pensions such as those which cover policemen and civil servants are technically unfunded although some public sector pensions including teachers' pensions are funded.

The distinction between funded and unfunded pensions not only affects the cost of administering the scheme but also differs in impact on the capital markets. With unfunded schemes, there need be little if any financial investment since the contributions received will be almost immediately paid out in benefits. With funded schemes, however, the contributions paid into the fund will not be required until up to forty years later and there will be correspondingly large sums invested for long periods of time in order to ensure that adequate pensions can be paid. The investment decisions required in administering a pension scheme are considerable and often crucial in determining the level of contributions. For small pension schemes it may be difficult to acquire the professional expertise for this task and thus many corporate schemes are run by insurance companies offering specialist help in this area. Larger schemes may administer the benefits and contributions internally but hand over the investment decisions to professional investment advisors, including merchant banks (such as Barings or Warburgs), stock brokers (such as Grieveson Grant or Fielding Newson-Smith) or insurance companies (Legal & General or Prudential). Very large funds, such as that of the Post Office pension fund, may employ several professional managers each with instructions to manage part of their investment portfolios.

Principles of Investment Management

In order to safeguard the payment of pensions many years in the future, the funds generated either from pension schemes or from long-term insurance policies must be invested efficiently. In the case of pensions, actuaries regularly check that the value of the fund (containing accrued contributions and reinvested income) is sufficient to cover all the expected future benefits. To carry out this task, a number of assumptions have to be made since both the future contributions and benefits to be paid are uncertain. Typically, actuaries will assume specific rates of interest to be earned by the fund and also specific rates of inflation, growth of earnings (which will determine both the future contributions and benefits) and mortality rates.

One possible way in which investment managers could minimise the uncertainty in achieving a return would be by investing all the funds in fixed interest government bonds. This investment would clearly not be risky in the sense that the government is unlikely to default on the interest or capital repayment. However, if inflation suddenly accelerates the wisdom of investing in fixed term bonds would be questionable.

Indexed bonds were introduced to be attractive specifically to pension funds since the value of the interest payments increase when inflation rises. To a pension fund, therefore, indexed bonds provide (in the long term and if available in sufficient quantity over the years) a rock-bottom secure return against which it can evaluate its investment policy.

With large funds, investors believe that by diversifying amongst different types of investment, substantially greater returns can be achieved without incurring greater degrees of risk. This property of portfolio diversification is central to the investment management of long-term funds and has led to investment in assets as wide ranging as antiques, paintings and gold. Broadly, however, the investment portfolios of the long-term funds are classified into four main categories — short-term cash, long-term fixed interest, equities, and property.

Table 12.3 presents the main components in the institutional portfolios. As might be expected, the short-term investors — general insurance funds — hold much larger proportions of their fund in the form of short-term assets. More surprising is the difference between pension funds and long-term insurance funds in the holding of ordinary shares. Part of this difference can be explained by the explicit emphasis on the insurance funds' part of long-

Table 12.3   Component Portfolios held by Pension and Insurance Funds as at the end of 1983

	Percentage of portfolios					
	Cash and short-term assets[1]	Ordinary shares[2]	Fixed interest and government bonds[3]	Property[4]	Miscellaneous[5]	£m Total value
Pension funds	5.4	58.4	21.4	12.6	2.2	106,242
Long-term[6] insurance funds	6.2	41.2	29.9	22.1	0.6	95,862
General insurance funds	20.9	26.6	26.4	11.3	14.8	18,641

Source: *British Business,* 7 September 1984.

[1]   Including local authority securities and Government bonds with less than five years to maturity.
[2]   Including unit trust units and overseas company securities.
[3]   Including debentures, preference shares and overseas government securities.
[4]   Including mortgages, loans and property unit trust units.
[5]   For insurance companies, most of the miscellaneous category represents agents' balances.
[6]   Including insured pension business.

term fixed investment. In fact, the figures presented in the table understate the importance of bond-type investments held by insurance funds; about a fifth of the property investments are held in the form of mortgages and loans which might more properly be regarded as having the same characteristics as bonds. Reclassifying the assets on this assumption, the proportion of bonds in their portfolios could be re-estimated to be nearly 34%.

Long-term insurance funds have traditionally held property in their portfolios and over recent years they have invested consistently more in property than their pension fund counterparts. During the five years 1979–1983, the long-term insurance funds invested nearly 15% of their net cash flows in property (against just over 11% invested by pension funds). Critics of this involvement in the property market have argued that it has diverted resources away from more productive uses. From a financial viewpoint however, the property market has provided very profitable investment opportunities for the institutions, although during the mid-1970s property slump the market was shown to be riskier than many investors had previously believed.

More recently, because of the relaxation in the control of currency markets, the long-term funds have tended to invest overseas — in 1982, for example, the funds in aggregate bought nearly three times as much (by value) overseas shares as they had bought annually in the preceding four years. Again the competitive pressure to invest profitably encouraged this sharp change in policy, and again the trend has attracted considerable critical comment.

Because of the wide choice of assets open to fund managers it might seem difficult to monitor the efficiency of their investment decisions. In fact, *investment performance evaluation* is an important activity and has considerable influence on investment policies. There are several consulting actuarial firms and other specialist institutions which offer a performance evaluation service to institutional investors. Usually, the funds are analysed on the basis of asset-types (e.g. in the case of an ordinary share portfolio, the proportion of shares held in the various industrial sectors will be identified). For each asset-type, an average index is constructed and the hypothetical return from investing in the index is estimated. The fund's performance is then allocated to its constituent assets and each component's return is compared with that estimated for the appropriate index. There are thus two main criteria by which fund management can be judged — *timing* and *selection*.

For example, a fund manager may misjudge the potential profitability of investing in, say, oil company shares. Consequently, the fund may be holding little or no oil company shares during a period in which the oil sector rises in value. In 1974 many fund managers reduced their holdings of ordinary shares in the belief that ordinary share prices were generally declining. During the early part of 1975, share prices rose dramatically and some funds *underperformed* because of the mistake in timing.

Selection concerns the identification of individual companies or specific investments. Thus fund managers may correctly foresee that the shares of computer-orientated companies will rise in value but be unfortunate in buying the least profitable companies' shares. Similarly, a fund manager may recognise that office properties will generally rise in value but be unfortunate in buying particular offices that remain unaffected by the trend.

The quality of the investment performance of the fund manager can directly influence the competitive terms offered by the company on insurance policies (as well as having obvious implications for the provision of pensions by pension funds). Consider for example an individual who wishes to take out a life insurance policy covering a period of twenty years. The cheapest type of policy is, as discussed above, a *term* policy which might provide, say, £15,000 payable on the event of death of the insured within the insured period. The premiums quoted by the insurance company will take into account its assessment of the probable date of death of the insured, as well as the operating and administrative costs. However, when these factors are taken into account, the insurance contract will still effectively consist of a series of cash inflows terminated by one cash outflow. In setting its premiums, the company will have to take into account the rate at which the premiums will accumulate. In other words the company must assess the rate of return that it expects to earn on its investments, and the more successful investment returns, the more competitive can be the premiums quoted.

This issue is particularly important for insurance policies which contain a large savings element. For instance, an endowment insurance policy may be offered to a 35 year old man which would mature in 10 years time. For a guaranteed insured sum of £2000, the premiums might be in the region of £15 monthly. But in addition to the guaranteed sum of £2000, the maturity value of the policy will be linked to the profitability of the fund in which the premiums are invested. Estimations of the maturity value of the policies may be very variable but it is quite conceivable that the estimates would range from £2500 to £3500. To the insured individual, therefore, the investment performance of the fund manager could be vitally important in assessing the policy to be taken out. We can see this as follows. Suppose the cost of providing £3500 life cover during the same period amounts to monthly premiums of less than £1. The savings or investment component of the endowment policy, obtained from the net monthly premiums (£15 less the term policy premium of £1) paid over ten years, is the estimated terminal value (TV) of £3500. This is evaluated by compounding the annuity of £14 per month for a 10 year period and equating the terminal value of the annuity with the final sum. (Refer to the appendix to Chapter 5 for the formula for the terminal value of an annuity.) The implied return of the investment component (if the insured survives) is therefore given by i in the expression:

$$14\, s\,_{\overline{120}|\ i} \ = \ 3500$$

or in general terms, using the formula derived in the appendix to Chapter 5,

$$ms\,_{\overline{n}|\ i} \ = \ \text{TV}_n$$

where: n = the number of months; m = the monthly premium; TV_n = the estimated terminal value of the policy, and $s\,_{\overline{n}|\ i}$ = the TV of an ordinary annuity.

By trial and error, the monthly return is found to be 1.12% which implies an effective annual rate of over 14%. Even without taking into account the effect of taxation, this calculation provides the individual with some measure of the expectations of the various insurance companies. Bearing in mind the spread of investment between the types of assets held by the long-term fund, this investment can be compared with the performance which the individual could otherwise hope to achieve by investing directly in funds such as unit trusts and in National Savings or building societies.

Another comparison can be made between policies which offer only a specified sum and those which offer a 'with profits' payment. In the latter case, the insured is paying a higher premium in exchange for a benefit which will partly depend on the investment performance of the long-term funds.

One other point which should briefly be mentioned in discussing investment performance concerns the methods used in estimating returns. The problem arises because during the course of any period, the fund will receive cash inflows from premiums paid (or pension contributions) and will make cash payments (outflows) in the form of pension or insurance policy benefits. The value of the fund will therefore fluctuate simply because of those cash flows which are beyond the control of the fund manager. From the investor's viewpoint, the investment performance can be assessed in the same way as any other investment project by finding the rate of return which equates the cash flows. This approach — identified earlier in the text as finding the internal rate of return — is referred to in the investment literature as the *money-weighted* return.

From the fund manager's viewpoint, however, the more critical question concerns the performance of those aspects which are under the manager's control. Conventionally, therefore, the performance would be assessed by calculating the *average* return earned over each interval of time in which no cash flows were received or paid. Thus if a fund was valued on 1 January and received cash on 31 January and made cash payments on 1 June, we might calculate the return for the period by averaging the change in the value of the fund over the periods 1 January to 31 January, 31 January to 1 June, and 1 June to 31 December. In other words, the returns are calculated for periods, determined by the payment or receipt of cash. This method (which is called the *time-weighted* return) is implicit in the comparison of the fund with market indicators discussed earlier. Differences between the two methods may be substantial and most obvious when the returns are variable.

A simple demonstration of this would be the following case of a fund initially valued (at 1 January) at £100 million.

Date	£million	
	Cash flow	Value of fund
1 January	–	100
31 January	+100	200
28 February	–	300
31 March	–	200
30 April	−100	100
30 May	+100	250

Estimating first the money-weighted return, we solve for i in the following expression:

$$100 (1+i)^5 + 100 (1+i)^4 - 100 (1+i) + 100 = 250$$

The first £100 is invested for five months, the second cash flow of £100 is invested for 4 months whilst the third cash (out) flow occurs only one month before the end of the period. The final cash inflow of £100 occurs on the date at which the final valuation is made. Thus the final valuation can be thought of as the largest possible final cash outflow.

$$i = 0.056 \text{ or } 5.6\% \text{ per month}$$

Notice that in this example, the *value* of the fund is only taken into account at the beginning and end of the measurement period.

To find the time-weighted return we first calculate the return for the period between each time at which cash is received or paid. The return for each of these sub-intervals is given by

$$i_t \;=\; \frac{\text{value at } (t+1) - \text{value at } t - \text{net cash inflows}}{\text{value at } t}$$

in which the value at the end of the period includes any cash received or paid out on that date. Thus

$$i_{\text{Jan}} \;=\; \frac{200 \;-\; 100 - \; 100}{100} \qquad = 0\%$$

$$i_{\text{Feb}} \;=\; \frac{300 \;-\; 200}{200} \qquad = 50\%$$

$$i_{\text{Mar}} \;=\; \frac{200 \;-\; 300}{300} \qquad = -33.3\%$$

$$i_{\text{Apr}} \;=\; \frac{100 \;-\; 200 \;+\; 100}{200} \qquad = 0\%$$

$$i_{\text{May}} \;=\; \frac{250 \;-\; 100 \;-\; 100}{100} \qquad = 50\%$$

The average of these sub-interval returns is 13.33% per month which is nearly three times greater than the money-weighted return, but which, when analysed on a month-by-month basis, reveals the variability of the investment performance of the fund. From the trustee's point of view, therefore, the time-weighted return may be a more useful check on the fund managements' portfolio decisions than the money-weighted return.

Measurement of investment performance is an integral part of portfolio management. Although fund managers might argue that too much emphasis is thereby laid on short-term considerations, few would deny that some monitoring is essential. The importance of measuring the returns made by fund managers particularly arises when investment is predominantly an institutional activity. The increase in interest shown in performance measurement is thus a direct consequence of the development of institutional investors and is reflected most clearly in the area of life and pension business.

Public Policy Issues

The value of funds controlled by insurance companies and pension funds increased from £81 billion at the end of 1978 to £221 billion in 1983; the net cash investments during 1983 amounted to £15 billion. With this enormous spending power, it is not surprising that comment has frequently been made about the political and allocational effects of the institutional investors. One obvious way in which this investment power might be expected to be asserted is in influencing the management policies of the companies in which the insurance and pension funds hold shares. In some firms, for example, an insurance company may be the single most important shareholder; in others, a small group of institutional funds may jointly hold more than half the issued share capital and thus dominate the voting on any issue which affected shareholder interests. Critics of this potential power argue that the fund managers are in a position to exploit their specific interests, citing names of directors of insurance companies who also appear on the board of other companies in which shares are held. These interlocking directorships and other less formal links may adversely affect the interests of personal shareholders since decisions may be forced through the board more in the interests of the long-term insurance or pension funds and against the interests of the less knowledgeable private investor.

On the other hand, it is argued that the institutions are a welcome countervailing force to the policies and decisions made by the management of the company. Without institutional investors, the shareholders of any large company might be far too weak and badly organised to safeguard their own interests. Management would then be in a position to maintain inefficient policies which could never be effectively questioned. Furthermore, it is sometimes argued that institutional investors should intervene *more* in the managerial affairs of the companies in which they hold shares. Cases in the press are sometimes quoted, with approval, of companies agreeing to make managerial appointments under pressure from the 'institutional shareholders'. Similarly, the takeover bids which might be made for an inefficiently run company and which may contribute to the allocative efficienty of the market, can be facilitated if several large institutional investors approve of the proposed new management. Partly to control the potential power of institutional investors, proposals have sometimes been publicised to direct some (or all) of their investment funds. This direction may take the form of limits on the amount of overseas investment or more specifically, some restraints on investment into named companies or particular countries. Alternatively, it has been proposed to insist that a specific proportion of funds should be invested in specific types of asset such as Government bonds. These proposals have generally been made on political and ethical grounds but in some cases economic arguments are advanced to support the direction of institutional funds into particular industries, regions or activities.

The Wilson Committee considered the creation of an agency for directing investment. One proposals was to channel about 10% of the institutional investors' cash flow through a policy-committee comprising representatives of employers, employees and government departments. The purpose of the direction would be to stimulate investment in the UK by encouraging long term investment projects. The acceptability of the proposal to the investing institutions would be enhanced by a guaranteed minimum rate of return equal to the gilt edged rate.

However, the majority of the Wilson Committee rejected this proposal because they felt that the existing institutions and markets were sufficiently efficient and flexible to deal with the appraisal of any potentially profitable projects. Thus a subsidised institution would inevitably encourage investment in less successful projects. The Committee also felt that as no new funds would be created by setting up such an institution, the institutional investors themselves might react to the proposal by compensatory changes in their portfolios. Thus if a pension fund was compelled to invest 20% or 30% of its cash flow in UK industry, it might actually *increase* the proportion of its remaining funds invested overseas to compensate for the directed domestic participation. Since the publication of the Wilson Report, there has been no further movement towards directing investment although individual spokesmen continue to advocate such a policy.

Another issue concerning the provision of pensions involves employees who leave the employment of one firm in mid-career. Historically, 'early leavers' have been treated unfavourably. It was common to observe pension schemes in which employees merely had their contributions returned to them on leaving the firms' employment. A more equitable treatment exists for a fund which preserves the pension of an early leaver. Thus a pension scheme which provides 1/80 of the final salary for every year of service would pay a pension of ½ of the final salary for an employee who worked for 40 years. The same scheme would provide a pension of ¼ of the final salary for an employee who left after only 20 years. On the assumption that the leaver worked for another firm for a further 20 years, at retirement, this individual would receive two pensions, one from each employer.

If the salary were the same at the end of each 20 year period, the leaver's pension rights would be unaffected. However, if the salary increases during the time spent with the second firm, the leaver may be worse off at retirement. Suppose, for example. X works for firm A for 20 years, leaving with a final salary of £10,000, and joins firm B from which she retires after a further 20 years with a salary of £20,000. Further suppose that the final salary X would have obtained from A if she had continued with the company for the full forty years would also have been £20,000.

The pensions from A and B together would amount to:

$$\left[20 \times \frac{1}{80} \times £10,000 \right] + \left[20 \times \frac{1}{80} \times £20,000 \right] = £7500$$

Had X continued with firm A, her pension would have been:

$$40 \times \frac{1}{80} \times £20,000 = £10,000$$

Thus the pension derived from the two firms would be considerably below the level of her equivalent pension had she continued in employment with the same firm throughout her career.

Furthermore, it has been the practice of some corporate pension schemes to increase the benefits for pensioners after retirement in recognition of the problems caused by inflation — an enhancement not often covering early leavers. Since discrimination against early leavers might be expected to discourage labour mobility the labour market might be prevented from operating efficiently. Thus during 1982 and 1983 the pension funds have come under increasing pressure from the government to improve the benefits paid to early leavers and it is likely that in the course of the next few years discrimination will be reduced.

Summary

This chapter has discussed aspects of insurance and pension business and has shown how simple policies can be evaluated. The growth of the long-term insurance and pension funds introduced the theme of investment decisions and performance. Finally, we discussed some unresolved issues in public policy towards the institutional arrangements for insurance and pensions.

Further Reading

1. F. Ayres, *Mathematics of Finance* (McGraw-Hill, 1963) contains five chapters dealing with the derivation and application of insurance and annuity valuation equations.
2. P.J. Franklin and C. Woodhead, *The UK Life Assurance Industry* (Croom Helm, 1980). This rigorous and authoritative text provides an analysis of the microeconomics of life insurance. There is a useful account of the marketing and product policy of the industry during the sixties and seventies and an illuminating account of the mergers and takeover activity during the same period.
3. R. Minns, *Pension Funds and British Capitalism* (Heinemann Educational Books, 1980). This stimulating study of the relationship between the financial and industrial sectors of the economy examines the informal and formal control of pension fund portfolio investment. The author presents arguments for the direction of investment into British industrial activity.
4. *Committee to Review the Functioning of Financial Institutions* (The Wilson Report) (HMSO, 1980). As with issues discussed elsewhere in the book, the report covers the institutional background with a wealth of statistical detail. There is also a useful account of the debate on direction of investment.

Discussion Questions

12.1 Consider the costs of operating unfunded and funded pension schemes. In what circumstances will the unfunded scheme be (a) cheaper and (b) dearer in providing identical benefits. (Hint: you might first consider setting up a pension scheme for a company which experiences no net change in the number of its employees.)

12.2 Ms A is a 30 year old single parent of two children aged 4 and 6. What sort of factors do you think she ought to take into account in deciding whether she should take out a term insurance or whole-life policy?

12.3 Why do you think there is such a large difference in the premiums quoted by competing firms in the life insurance business?

12.4 There has been increasing merger activity and discussions between financial institutions of all types. In the light of this trend consider the similarities between insurance companies and (a) banks and (b) investment trusts.

Problems

12.5 Evaluate the investment return on the endownment implied by the following policies on the assumption that the insured survives the term. (Sum assured = £11,000.) Assume annual premiums paid at end of each year.
(a) A 15 year term policy for a 45 year old man; annual premium = £60.
(b) A 15 year endowment (non profit) policy for the same person; annual premium = £486.

12.6 A 30 year old woman is quoted the following premiums. On the assumption that she will die in 45 years time, estimate the return that is implicit in the 'with-profits' component of the life policy:
(a) Whole life, sum assured £5000, annual premium £30 (payable at the end of each year).
(b) Whole life with profit, sum assured £5000, expected total maturity value £24,300, annual premium £100 (payable at the end of each year).

12.7 A 75 year old woman can buy an annuity of £1940 (half-yearly in arrears) for £10,000. If she can invest the £10,000 in a bond at a nominal yield of 12%, to what age would she have to survive before the annuity was the 'better buy'? (Ignore the effect of taxation.)

12.8 A woman started employment on her 21st birthday and after 15 years was earning £8000 per year. She then left and worked for another firm for 10 years at £16,000 per year, after which she moved to a third firm at a salary of £24,000. Just before she retired at the age of 61 she heard from a friend working for her first employer that her graded salary would now have been £20,000 had she still been working for the firm. Calculate her present pension if each firm operated a contributory pension scheme in which the benefits amounted to 1/80 of the final salary for each year of service. Would her pension have been greater had she stayed with her original employer?

12.9 Mr Smith, a 50 year old man, has been working for company A for 10 years at a salary of £10,000 p.a. The pension scheme offers a pension of 1/80 of final salary per year worked. Mr Smith leaves firm A and joins Firm B which runs an identical pension scheme to A's. He expects to retire after ten years. Assume a final salary of £20,000, a discount rate of 10% p.a., and a life expectancy after retiring of 10 years. Calculate the present value, at the time of leaving A, of the loss in pension rights occasioned by Mr Smith in changing jobs, assuming that his final salary in A would have been identical to that in B.

12.10 A fund manager receives £100 million on the first day of January, February, March, April and May. On the last day of each month his fund is valued at £120m, £280m, £280m, £320m and £600m. Estimate the money-weighted and time-weighted returns for the fund. Assess his efficiency if the comparable market index moved from 100 on 1 January to 110, 132, 125, 120, 140 on the last day of successive months.

Actuarial Calculations

In the text it was stated that insurance companies analysed the statistics of mortality rates and adjusted their premiums so that a surplus was generated from their portfolios of policies. In this appendix, we illustrate how these statistics might be used in valuing simple policies.

If l_x = the number of people living at age x, then l_{x+1} will be the number of surviving for more than a year from the age x. The number of people dying within the year will therefore be given by $d_x = l_x - l_{x+1}$. Similarly, the *proportion* of people dying within the year will be given by $d_x \div l_x$ whereas the proportion of people surviving for *at least* one year will be given by $l_{x+1} \div l_x$.

Mortality tables are published but in this example we construct hypothetical statistics for a group of 18 year olds.

Age	Number living	Number dying
x	l_x	d_x
18	1000	3
19	997	3
20	994	3
21	991	3
22	988	3
23	985	3

Of the one thousand 18 year old people, 997 should be alive a year later; the probability therefore that an 18 year old will survive a year is 997/1000 or 0.997. Similarly, the probability that an 18 year old will survive two years will be 994/1000 or 0.994.

Temporary Annuity

Consider first an annuity which pays £1000 per annum to an 18 year old for a period of three years or until death (whichever is the earlier). Assume that payments are received at the *end* of each year, but that the single premium is paid at the beginning.

Thus the payments for a group of policy holders will depend on the numbers living at the end of the first and second years. From the table we expect that the proportion of 18 year olds who survive will be 997/100 (one year) and 994/1000 (two years). If all policy holders were *certain* to survive for two years, the present value of successive payments of £1 for two years would be:

$$a_{\overline{2}|i} = \frac{1}{1+i} + \frac{1}{(1+i)^2}$$

If we weight these £1 payments by the chances of their occurring we get:

$$a_{\overline{x:2}} = \left[\frac{l_{x+1}}{l_x} \frac{1}{(1+i)}\right] + \left[\frac{l_{x+2}}{l_x} \frac{1}{(1+i)^2}\right] \qquad (12A.1)$$

where $a_{\overline{x:n}}$ =   single premium for an n year temporary life annuity of £1 per
year for an individual aged x years
l_x =   the number living at age x
i =   the investment (discount) rate

If we take the investment rate i to be 5% then

$$a_{\overline{18:2}} = 0.9495 + 0.9016$$
$$= £1.851$$

Thus to provide a £1 annuity for two years to an 18 year old, a premium of at least £1.851 would be required (ignoring the expenses of commission etc). In general, the single premium for an n year temporary life annuity of £1 per year for an individual aged x years will be given by

$$a_{\overline{x:n}} = \sum_{t=1}^{n} \frac{l_{x+t}}{l_x} \frac{1}{(1+i)^t} \qquad (12A.2)$$

The premium required to pay the annuity of £1 for three years can be found to be:

$$\left[\frac{997}{100} \frac{1}{1.05}\right] + \left[\frac{994}{1000} \frac{1}{(1.05)^2}\right] + \left[\frac{991}{1000} \frac{1}{(1.05)^3}\right] = £2.71$$

The value of a whole life annuity can be found simply by extending the range of n to encompass the maximum expected life span of individuals covered by the policy. In fact in producing statistics of mortality, actuaries will usually construct tables summing the series

$$\frac{l_{x+1}}{(1+i)^1} \quad , \dots , \quad \frac{l_{x+n}}{(1+i)^n}$$

over the remaining life span of prospective customers, for selected rates of interest i.

Term Insurance

A term policy pays out the insured sum if the individual dies *within* a specified term. Thus the expected probabilities will be given by

$$\frac{d_x}{l_x} \quad , \quad \frac{d_{x+1}}{l_x} \quad , \dots$$

when d_x is the number of people dying between the ages of x and $x+1$. Taking into account the time value of the funds, the necessary single premium for a n year term will be given by

$$A_{\overline{x:n}} = \left[\frac{d_x}{l_x}\right]\left[\frac{1}{(1+i)}\right] + \left[\frac{d_{x+1}}{l_x}\right]\left[\frac{1}{(1+i)^2}\right] + \dots + \left[\frac{d_{x+n-1}}{l_x}\right]\left[\frac{1}{(1+i)^n}\right]$$

$$(12A.3)$$

For our 18 year olds, a two-year policy would be valued at

$$A_{\overline{18\,:\,2|}} = \frac{3}{1000}\,\frac{1}{1.05} + \frac{3}{1000}\,\frac{1}{(1.05)^2}$$

Therefore single premium = £0.00558 for a £1 policy, £5.58 for a £1000 policy.

For a whole-life insurance policy, this series can be extended over the expected life span of the insured. As with the annuity calculations, tables include information which facilitates the estimation of life insurance premiums.

Complications start to enter the actuarial calculation when evaluating policies for which annual premiums are payable. However we can illustrate the method by considering the evaluation of a term policy insurance promising £1 on death on which the premiums are paid annually at the beginning of each year.

At the start of the period the annual premium P will be paid by l_x individuals. At the end of the first year, d_x will be paid out and the premium will become due for the surviving l_{x+1} individuals . We therefore have

$$\left[\frac{l_x}{l_x}\right]\left[P\right] + \left[\frac{l_{x+1}}{l_x}\right]\left[\frac{P}{(1+i)}\right] + \left[\frac{l_{x+2}}{l_x}\right]\left[\frac{P}{(1+i)^2}\right] + \ldots + \left[\frac{l_{x+n}}{l_x}\right]\left[\frac{P}{(1+i)^n}\right]$$

$$= \left[\frac{d_x}{l_x}\right]\left[\frac{1}{(1+i)}\right] + \left[\frac{d_{x+1}}{l_x}\right]\left[\frac{1}{(1+i)^2}\right] + \ldots + \left[\frac{d_{x+n-1}}{l_x}\right]\left[\frac{1}{(1+i)^n}\right] \qquad (12A.4)$$

But the left-hand side of the equation is similar to the expression (12A.2), the single premium for an n year temporary life annuity. It can be rewritten in the form

$$P(1 + a_{\overline{x\,:\,n|}})$$

Similarly, the right-hand side can be seen to be like (12A.3), and can be written $A_{\overline{x:n|}}$. So

$$P(1 + a_{\overline{x:n|}}) = A_{\overline{x:n|}}$$

$$\text{or} \qquad P^1_{\,\overline{x:n|}} = \frac{A_{\overline{x:n|}}}{(1 + a_{\overline{x:n|}})} \qquad (12A.5)$$

where $P^1_{\overline{x:n|}}$ = net annual premium for an ordinary n year term insurance policy
      $A_{\overline{x:n|}}$ = net single premium for an n year term insurance policy
      $a_{\overline{x:n|}}$ = net single premium for an n year term life annuity

These expressions may be used in building and evaluating much more complicated policies — the interested reader should refer to the actuarial texts for more comprehensive and realistic applications.

Chapter Thirteen

Other Institutions in the Financial System

In the previous chapter, the major investing institutions were identified as the long-term insurance companies and the pension funds. There are, however, a number of other institutions which operate either as investment or as financial intermediaries. By their actions, information may be more quickly transmitted from one sector to another and the efficiency of the financial markets will thereby be improved. The objective of this chapter is to outline the functions of these other institutions.

Investment Intermediaries

Of the institutions which operate in the area of investment intermediation, the best known as far as the general reader is concerned, is the *unit trust*. Unit trusts are funds which are *open ended:* that is, the size of the fund and the number of shares issued depend directly upon the investors. If investors wish to place more money in the fund, the managers of the unit trust have to create and sell more shares (or *units* as they are more correctly termed). The price at which the units are sold or bought by the managers is dictated by the value of the fund. Thus to give an over-simplified example, if a unit trust is valued at £10m and has 10m units outstanding, further units will be offered for sale at (or slightly above) 100p each whilst units will be bought back by the management at slightly below 100p. If a further million units are sold to new investors, the value of the fund will be £11m but the number of units issued will also have increased to 11m and so the price of each unit will in principle remain unchanged by this transaction.

There will be administrative charges and legal costs which will lower the price at which units will be bought and raise the price at which units will be sold. Managers usually have some discretion in the method of calculating the price of units so that like the bid–offer quotation of the stock market jobber, the bid–offer prices of the unit trust will reflect the views and current stock position of the management. The bid prices will usually differ by about 5%–7% from the offer prices.

The organisation of the unit trust involves two institutions — the management and the trustees. The role of the trustee is to safeguard the interests of the unit holders and to ensure that the trust is operating on the lines laid down by the *trust deed* which has to be drawn up before the unit trust can exist. The role of the management company is to invest the assets of the unit holders. The assets will usually be invested in ordinary shares although some unit trusts invest in bonds and other securities. Sometimes the management company of the unit trust will act on the trustee's behalf in maintaining the register of unit holders, but in other cases the registration is carried out by companies which specialise in providing the register service.

The management company also advertises the sale of units, although the terms and claims made in the advertisement are monitored by the trustee to ensure that no misleading information is given to the investing public. There are units which are not allowed to advertise — these may be formed for specialist investment or for a group of private investors wishing to pool their resources. To distinguish between the types of unit trust, the term 'authorised' is used in respect of those trusts whose activities have been authorised by the Department of Trade. Authorisation involves acceptance of restraints on investment policy as regards the concentration of assets in one investment or the type of asset held.

Unit trusts are usually designed to provide an opportunity for individuals to invest relatively small amounts of money in a diversified portfolio. The managements of the unit trusts will sometimes be provided by banks such as Midland or Lloyds which offer investment advice to their personal customers. Other unit trusts are managed by companies which sell *unit linked* life insurance policies. The value of the sum paid when the policy matures will be determined by the price of the units. Managers of this type of trust include the Scottish Widows Fund Management and the Legal & General group. There are several general management groups such as M&G and Save and Prosper which manage a large number of unit trust funds created for a variety of different purposes and offering specialist funds for investment overseas or in particular sectors or markets. Finally stockbroking firms such as James Capel and Grieveson Grant also form unit trusts to provide a service for individual investors with relatively small portfolios.

The development of unit funds has been successful. Initiated in the 1930s, their size and number grew slowly until the early 1960s when, because of less restrictive legislation and buoyant equity markets, their growth accelerated. By the beginning of the 1970s there were over two hundred trusts with funds valued at nearly £1500 million; by 1980, the value of funds had more than trebled to nearly £5000 million and by mid-1983 there were more than five hundred trusts managing £10,000 million.

This represents a very wide choice to individual investors. Besides the various types of management group, unit trusts differ in their investment objectives. A number of categories are publicised but some indication of the range of specialities can be seen in Table 13.1.

More than half of the funds offer life insurance policies linked to their fund. Over the five year period it was estimated that unit trusts had on average made an annual profit for their unit holders of 16.8% compared with the 19% growth in the FT All Share Index over the same period. This would suggest that overall, small investors effectively pay something like 2% a year in charges to the unit trust management groups. In practice, annual charges are less than 1%. The remaining difference may partly be explained by unit trusts investing in assets outside the UK Stock Exchange — clearly the internationally orientated trusts should not be compared with the UK equity index. Also, as can be seen from Table 13.1, some trusts invest in bonds and short-term money markets: again, these funds should not be compared with an all-equity market index.

Table 13.1   Types of Unit Trusts and Their Performance

Category	No. of trusts	No. of trusts offering life policies	Average performance over last 5 years (% p.a.)
UK general	84	35	17.6
UK growth	93	44	18.1
UK equity	94	45	13.1
International	60	33	19.0
European	11	4	12.5
Far East	63	36	16.8
North American	54	32	19.8
Natural resources	29	18	17.9
Financial & property shares	13	10	17.2
Gilt & fixed interest shares	14	4	9.6
Gilt & fixed interest income	28	10	8.2
Investment trust units	7	3	18.6
Preference shares	6	3	17.3
FT All Share Index			19.0

Source: *Money Management and Unit Holder,* October 1983.

However even amongst these trusts almost wholly invested in UK equities, the *average* return seems slightly lower than might be expected although from one trust to another the results differ considerably. In the UK growth category, for example, the annual return varied from 26% at best to under 4%. Clearly with these examples of divergent profitability, management groups have considerable discretion as to the extent of diversification and the selection of shares. It is sometimes suggested that the apparent under-performance is caused by managers trying too hard to make profitable investment by excessive trading of securities. In response to this suggestion, from time to time unit trusts have been established with the aim of minimising transaction costs by simply holding a portfolio which matches as closely as possible the composition of one or other of the Financial Times — Actuaries Indices (such as the FT All Share Index). However, to date, the reasonableness of this objective does not seem to have been recognised by many unit trust investors and public attempts to create an 'index fund' have not been very successful. Although unit trusts have been established with a wide range of objectives, their portfolios in aggregate show a heavy proportion of ordinary shares. Table 13.2 compares their main holdings with those of the investment trusts. Over 50% of their assets are held in the form of UK equities.

Table 13.2   Portfolio Composition of Unit Trusts and Investment Trusts as at end 1983

Asset held	Unit trusts (%)	Investment trusts (%)
Net short-term assets	5.0	0.0
UK public sector securities	3.6	2.3
UK company securities	54.1	40.6
Overseas company securities	36.4	54.2
Miscellaneous assets	0.9	2.9
	100.0	100.0
Total value of portfolio	£11,412m	£13,407m

Source: *Financial Statistics,* August 1984.

Investment trusts are companies which issue shares and fixed interest securities, investing the proceeds in a managed portfolio. They are *closed end* funds: investors wishing to buy investment trust shares have to find other investors willing to sell. In other words, the investment trust is not directly involved in the buying and selling of its securities after the primary issue has been made. Correspondingly, the price of the investment trust shares does not depend directly on the value of the assets held by the investment trust; in practice the share price will usually be considerably below the corresponding value of the assets — a feature which is referred to as the investment trust *discount.*

Historically, investment trusts were first formed in the nineteenth century and have always emphasised the international aspects of investment. As can be seen from Table 13.2, their holdings of overseas securities account for over 50% of their portfolios (compared with 36% for the unit trusts). The restrictions imposed on unit trust investment policy do not apply to investment trusts, and they are more likely to invest in a wider range of assets including property and unlisted securities. Some investment trusts have emphasised this feature in recent years. The investment trusts are managed (like the unit trusts) by a group of managers. Although each investment trust is a separate company, many are controlled by management groups not unlike those controlling unit trusts. Amongst these management groups may be found Touche Remnant & Co., Investment Trust Services and Kleinwort Benson. There has also been a strong Scottish emphasis in the investment trust sector which has long traditions in both Edinburgh and Glasgow.

Investment trusts differ from unit trusts in a number of ways, other than the features mentioned above. One of the more obvious differences is the ability to borrow money. The effect of this borrowing is to increase the potential profitability but at an additional level of risk. For example, if the investment trust borrows money at 10%, the shareholders will receive proportionately more if the achieved profit is more than 10% but greatly reduced profits if the investment trust earns less than 10% on its investment. This 'gearing' is of potential benefit to private investors since the effect is to gear-up the performance of their investment in a way which could otherwise only be achieved by borrowing money with which to buy shares. Provided, therefore, that the trust can borrow at rates of interest *below* the rates which would be available to the investor, gearing may be of considerable benefit. However, for reasons discussed below, the gearing of the investment trusts has declined and is no longer a marked feature. At the end of 1982, for example, their loan and preference capital was estimated by the Bank of England to represent less than 9% of the total capital of the investment trusts.

Historically, the investment trust companies were aimed at individual investors but their shares have also attracted the attention of insurance companies. Recently, as observed in Chapter 2, the personal sector has been a net seller of shares to the institutional investors. This trend has also been reflected in the relative distribution of investment trust shares. The institutions have come increasingly to dominate the ownership of the investment trusts, and partly because the institutions already own diversified portfolios, there has been a shift in popularity towards more specialised investment trusts and away from trusts aiming for a general portfolio. In some cases, the management groups have responded by changing their investment policies. Touche Remnant, for example, announced in 1982 that nine of its eleven investment trusts were to be given more specialised objectives. It was hoped that in responding to the institutional preferences, the popularity of the trusts' shares would increase and the discount would thereby fall.

Of course, if the discount becomes unreasonably large, one would expect there to be demands for the trust to be liquidated in order to realise the full value of the underlying assets. It is not clear why this has not happened. Perhaps investors estimate that liquidation costs are high. Perhaps also, any small group of investors might find it prohibitively expensive to buy enough shares to gain control in order to push through the decision to liquidate. Certainly any news of possible liquidation tends to cause the share price to move quite sharply.

Liquidation has occurred to some extent though, in that some investment trusts have been *unitised,* that is, converted into unit trusts. The effect of this change is that the shareholders become unit holders; the price of the shares (units) is no longer determined by supply and demand but by the management (in accordance with the agreed procedures) estimating the equivalent asset value for each unit issued. Alternatively, as in the case of British Investment Trust, an institutional shareholder makes an open bid for the shares and gains control of the trust. Although the trust shares are still listed at a discount to the underlying assets, the controlling shareholder can now influence the investment and dividend policy of the trust towards its own interests.

It has been pointed out already that investment trusts are able to invest in a wider range of assets than the authorised unit trusts. In particular, it may be observed that investment trusts can be very similar to *property companies* which issue shares and debt, and invest the proceeds in land and buildings. (Indeed, from time to time some investment trusts have been classified within the property sector of the Stock Exchange.) The shares of property companies are not normally regarded in quite the same way as investment trusts since property companies emphasise their role as developers rather than as portfolio managers.

These companies do however have a unit trust equivalent in the *property unit trusts,* which provide an opportunity for tax-exempt institutional investors to invest in property. Property unit trusts became popular for smaller pension funds in the late 1960s during a period in which property investment by large funds increased dramatically. Thus the first major property unit trust, which was established in 1966 (The Pension Fund Property Unit Trust), was followed by four other trusts established within twelve months.

The property unit trusts respond more sensitively to the wishes of their unit holders than do other unit trusts. This responsiveness stems partly from the smaller number of unit holders — the largest property unit trust, for example, has fewer then seven hundred unit holders yet is worth nearly £1000 million. The number of unit holders will typically lie between 50 and 150. This concentration of interest in a few institutional hands thus enables much closer contact between the management of the trust and the unit holders. Another reason for the close link is the illiquidity of the underlying property asset which effectively prevents too large a proportion of unit holders from liquidating their unit holdings. Property unit trust holders therefore will always wish to have up-to-date information about the investments held by their management group.

The management group will try to avoid a situation in which they have to sell property in order to buy units from investors and may impose conditions about the length of notice required before buying back units. They may also impose other conditions that restrain the ease with which unit holders can realise their cash.

The size of the property unit trust sector is difficult to assess, but from statistics published by *Money Management* the value as at the end of 1982 exceeded £2000 million. Statistics from the Bank of England, which suggest a lower figure, indicate that only about 75% of the assets are held in the form of property — the balance being held on deposit or in short term securities.

For private investors, there are open-ended funds which invest in property. These funds are called *property bonds* and are invariably linked to a life insurance policy. This linkage minimises the risk of unexpected liquidation demands from the management group's viewpoint. Like the property unit trusts, however, the property bond funds minimise the risk of having to sell their property by maintaining a reserve of liquid assets. (In some cases the proportion of liquid assets can exceed 50%.) Thus if bond-holders wish to cancel their insurance policies and withdraw their investment, the managers can re-purchase the bond without difficulty.

One facet of the illiquidity of the underlying property investment is illustrated in the valuation of the property bond funds. Unlike unit trusts which have to value their investments by reference to their current market prices, the property bonds can assess the value of the property only if valued by professional property valuers. Since such an exercise is necessarily expensive, it is carried out at rather infrequent intervals. Thus if property values are rising, investors wishing to cash-in their investments may not receive the full value since the transaction will reflect the valuation at an earlier date.

Another feature which exacerbates the liquidity problem is the need to invest large sums of cash in property. Property investors have traditionally placed great emphasis on buying prime property (which has usually implied offices or shops in central city areas). However, such properties have often been developed on a large scale and their purchase has necessarily involved several millions of pounds. As a result, property funds have had to buy prime property at the cost of diversification. In smaller funds, one property may account for 20% or 30% of the portfolios; the investment performance of the fund therefore may be more risky than might be expected from the size of the fund. Despite these extra risks, they are relatively popular with investors and have been estimated to have attracted over £1500 million.

More flexibility is offered to private investors in the form of *managed bonds*. With these funds the management has the discretion to switch the investment from one asset type to another. Alternatively, the investor may specify the asset in which his or her money is invested and can change the type of asset held during the course of the year. Managed bonds, like property bonds, are invariably linked to insurance contracts and represent just one of a number of different types of investment scheme which are promoted by or in association with insurance companies. Other examples include *equity bonds, international bonds, fixed interest bonds* and *money bonds* (which specialise in investing in very liquid assets). In principle they fulfil the same function, offering opportunities for individuals to save in a tax-efficient way but in association with an insurance element. There is little official indication of the total size of the funds invested in these bonds but as at the end of 1983, statistics published by *Money Management* suggested the distribution shown in Table 13.3.

Table 13.3   Selected Statistics on Investment Intermediaries (October 1983)

	Number of funds	Total value £m	% value of funds accounted for by largest 3 funds
Property Bonds	61	1630	61
Managed Bonds	84	2360	37
Equity Bonds	96	1640	45
International Bonds	111	730	25
Fixed-Interest Bonds	60	490	27
Money Funds	55	190	53

Source: *Money Management and Unit Holder.*

The range in size of these funds is typically very large. Of the property bond funds, for example, three large funds account for more than 60% by value of the total sums invested by property bonds. At the other extreme, 11 funds are relatively small, accounting for less than £14 million — less than 1% of the total sums invested. The three largest money funds account for more than 50% of the funds invested. The fixed interest funds are less concentrated, the largest three funds only accounting for 27% of the total.

Apart from the specialist investment intermediaries described, there are a large number of funds established overseas. These off-shore funds may be registered in the Channel Islands, the Isle of Man, Bermuda or other areas in which their registration entails low or zero taxation. These funds are usually subject to less stringent accounting requirements than those registered within the UK, and the valuation of their assets may be accomplished in terms of US dollars, Swiss francs or sterling. It is therefore especially difficult to reach any estimate of the size of the off-shore sector with any degree of confidence. Analysis of the available statistics suggests that the aggregate value of the funds managed overseas but bought by UK investors might be in the region of £6 billion.

Financial Intermediaries

In the previous section, the activities of investment intermediaries have been briefly discussed. We should also refer to those institutions acting as intermediaries in channelling finance to borrowing institutions. As seen in the investment area, the process of intermediation inherently requires a flexible response to any market inefficiency. This inevitably leads to a large number of specialist activities being provided by competing institutions.

One common area in which financial intermediation can be observed is in providing finance to small companies. Historically, it has frequently been suggested that small companies have been hampered in their attempts to expand by the lack of finance. Very small companies, it was argued, can borrow money from banks in their normal course of business. Large companies, on the other hand, can tap the efficient markets associated with the Stock Exchange. Between the two sizes, however, companies might find it difficult to borrow or raise further equity capital.

There have been numerous responses to this identified gap in finance. Individual banks have set up subsidiary companies with the prime object of developing financing links with expanding companies. This financing will take various forms including loans made for periods of up to 5 or 7 years, instalment credit, leasing and loans made on the strength of trade debtors. The sums involved usually will be between £50,000 and £250,000 but may involve large sums for companies which can offer more security against the loan or which appear to have superior growth opportunities.

There are also similar institutions which specialise in offering finance in the form of participating equity. Flexibility is again emphasised in the packages of finance offered to firms but may consist of, say, £200,000 taken first as a preference share but with an option of converting into an ordinary share at some further date. This arrangement safeguards the income of the lending company in the short term but ensures that if the borrowing company expands as expected, the lender will be able to participate in the increased wealth generated by success.

Specialist funds have also been set up by the pension and long-term insurance funds as well as by those investment trusts which have the necessary discretion in investing their funds. Because the long-term investors naturally can afford to take a longer-term view, it is not surprising that their respective specialist intermediaries tend to take more equity interest than their banking counterparts. Alternatively, a long-term fund can provide finance by buying the property used by the expanding company. The company then 'repays' the fund by paying rent on the property being used. This type of financing is called 'sale and leaseback' since the borrower effectively obtains finance by leasing back a property previously owned.

Another type of financing intermediary is represented by Investors in Industry PLC otherwise known as the 3i Group which was set up by a group of institutions including the Bank of England, banks and long-term investors.

3i offers a number of specialist financing services ranging from its ventures division (which provides capital to companies expecting to expand very quickly) to the ICFC (Industrial and Commercial Finance Corporation) division. The role of the ICFC is to provide finance to medium and small businesses in the form either of loans or by buying shares.

The 3i Group obtains finance on behalf of the ICFC by issuing bonds, notes and shares. In addition the group accepts deposits for periods of between one and ten years. Because it has more than £1000 million lent or invested, the group has access to large scale economies that might be unavailable to the smaller firms that it finances. In this respect it is a successful example of financial intermediation. ICFC has expertise in helping to finance management 'buy-outs' in which the management of a division of a company effectively create a new company by buying the division from the previous owner. This has been a feature of the 1980s industrial environment as parent companies begin to regret their over-ambitious diversifying activity in earlier years.

Besides the many intermediaries set up by the private sector, there are also a number of institutions and schemes that have been established by and on behalf of the government. In some cases they have been designed to take investment decisions that would not otherwise be considered acceptable by private sector institutions. Thus, for example, the National Research and Development Corporation (NRDC) was established specifically to provide funds for technological innovation. The NRDC and the National Enterprise Board (NEB) are now linked under common partnership known as the British Technology Group. The NEB's role has changed substantially in response to current political views. At the time at which it was established (1975) it was viewed as being a major channel through which public funds could be directed towards industrial companies. At present its role seems to have been greatly curtailed and it has been relegated to acting as a temporary holding company before companies are resold to the public.

Other public sector financial services include a range of regionally-based financial facilities. Invariably, however, these schemes are administered by or on behalf of the Department of Industry and cannot therefore be classified as financial intermediaries, in that capital is *not* raised from market sources.

International Institutions

The enormous growth in the number of overseas banks participating in the UK financial markets has led to a substantial increase in intermediation between British institutions and overseas supplies of investment funds.

Besides the large number of overseas banks which now operate in the UK, there are a number of agencies set up under international agreements. Most of these, such as the International Monetary Fund, operate by lending currency to countries. The funds for these loans are provided by subscriptions from member countries and so do not come within our consideration. In some cases, such as the problems arising from the effect of oil revenues accruing to a small number of countries, the solution has involved the cooperation of market-orientated institutions (including banks) with the IMF and the member governments. In this instance the excess supply of dollars accruing to the oil-exporting countries was recycled into the world investment markets (including the UK stock and monetary markets).

In other cases, the IMF has, with the agreement of its members, created extra liquidity in the world monetary markets by creating a new monetary unit — the Special Drawing Right (SDR). The aim was to effect the same kind of changes in the international sphere as the introduction of bank credit had within the domestic financial system. More credit would, it was hoped, increase the efficient operation of the system. The SDR is a compendium of currencies (US dollars, West German mark, sterling, French francs and Japanese yen) against which other currencies can be compared. Not only are bonds denominated in SDRs now issued and traded, but UK banks have also been offering SDR-denominated deposit facilities and Certificates of Deposit.

Another international agency which has acted as an intermediary affecting operations in the UK markets, is the European Investment Bank (EIB). The EIB was set up in 1958 with capital subscribed from the members of the EEC and with the power to raise capital on domestic and international capital markets. Most of the loans made by the EIB help to finance regional development projects and concern 'infra-structure' such as the provision of roads, water supply and sewage treatment. In 1983, for example, the EIB made loans for road schemes in Strathclyde and Lothian, for improvements to Manchester Airport and a £30 million loan to Barclays and ICFC for financing of small and medium-sized tourism enterprises.

The economic significance of operations such as the EIB is that the projects financed can be very large, and are financed by an international intermediary raising capital from domestic markets with the security provided by the institution rather than the specific project. It is almost impossible to categorise large projects into domestic, international, private or public since a prominent feature of this type of intermediation is cooperation between different types of institution. The EIB can cooperate with private sector intermediaries and may lend sterling, dollars or mixtures of currencies as the specific case requires. Loans may involve fixed or floating intererst rates and be repaid in specified (or a range of) currencies.

Conclusion

The operations of capital markets have been markedly affected by the intermediation of institutions. In the case of unit trusts and investment trusts, the intermediation has been between large numbers of individual investors and the secondary capital market. These types of institution have been popular and have encouraged more specialised intermediary vehicles to be set up in the markets for property, bonds and short-term monetary instruments. Besides these investing intermediaries, an associated financing intermediation has developed in which perceived gaps in the market or market failures have been filled by financial institutions. In some cases these institutions have received official support; in others international organisations have supplied finance. Finally, we would stress that the field of financial and investing intermediation is characterised by innovation and flexibility. This feature suggests, by itself, that the market allocative process is operating with commendable efficiency.

Further Reading

1. D.C. Corner and D.C. Stafford; *Open-End Investment Trusts in the EEC and Switzerland* (Macmillan, 1977) and D.C. Corner and H. Burton, *Investment and Unit Trusts in Britain and America* (Elek, 1968) provide authoritative reviews of investment groups and policies with international comparisons.
2. For information on the activities of the European Investment Bank and other EEC institutions, *European Economy* is a useful quarterly publication of the Commission of the European Communities.
3. A.A. Arnaud, *Investment Trusts Explained* (Woodhead-Faulkner, 1983) is a professionally written account of the investment trust sector concentrating on the institutional features of the companies as a method of investment.
4. J. Freear, *The Management of Business Finance* (Pitman, 1980) provides some useful information and discussion on private and public sector financing institutions, including the ICFC and the ECGD.

Discussion Questions

13.1 How might you evaluate the investment performance of unit trusts?

13.2 Discuss the reasons which might lead to the price of investment trust shares falling below the value of their net assets per share.

13.3 Advise an individual, who has recently retired, on the factors he or she should take into account in placing a lump sum in selected unit trusts.

13.4 What kind of investors would you suggest might reasonably consider investing in property via property bonds?

13.5 Is it necessary to have any public-sector-supported financial intermediaries? Will the market fill the gap if public sector support is not forthcoming?

13.6 Discuss the ways in which either the investing or financial intermediaries described in this chapter, help to 'complete' the markets, by providing investors with opportunties and facilities for more efficient investments.

Part Four

THE FUTURE

─────────── *Chapter Fourteen* ───────────
New Developments in the
Financial System

During the period in which this book has been written, the financial markets and institutions have changed rapidly. Hardly a month has passed without there being announced some change in regulation, operation or organisation of the financial institutions. In this final chapter we therefore discuss some of the most recent changes and tentatively suggest ways in which the process will continue.

New Markets in Financial Instruments

The intermediation process can involve either market participants or instruments. Much of our discussion has emphasised the role of institutions acting as intermediaries between borrowers and lenders (or deficit and surplus sectors). We have mentioned in Chapter 9 the establishment of the traded options market which, in trading another type of security, contributed to market completeness. In this section we refer to the financial futures market which likewise enables investors to trade in novel types of financial asset.

In the financial futures market, the traded assets are related as closely as possible to interest rates (or other specific financial variables such as exchange rates). However, although the future may be associated with an interest rate, it is invariably priced as a security or a bill. Thus when investors buy a financial future in, say, the euro-dollar rate, if interest rates rise, the value of the futures contract will fall, whilst if interest rates fall, the futures contract will appreciate in value. By appropriate calculation, investors can buy a sufficient number of contracts in financial futures to insulate their portfolios from the effect of changing rates over the period for which the futures contract is held.

Unlike options which give buyers the choice of whether to exercise their contract, the buyer of a futures contract must either take delivery or sell the contract before or on the expiry date. In the case of the long-term gilts contract, for example, the seller contracts to deliver £50,000 (nominal value) of a long-term (more than 15 years maturity) government bond with a 12% coupon; but the conditions of delivery enable a seller to deliver one of a number of government bonds. Thus the price of the futures contract will be affected by the price of the bond which can be estimated to be the cheapest as far as the seller is concerned.

Futures contracts oblige investors to deposit money (termed the 'margin') at the outset of the contract. Subsequent price movements are thus credited or debited daily to their accounts, which are settled when the contract is closed.

The pricing of the futures contract is designed to make trading simple. For the 12% 20 year gilt contract, a price of 100 would equate with a redemption yield of 12%. Correspondingly, a price of 86 would imply a nominal redemption yield of about 14% interest. The price is calculated by finding the redemption yield on a hypothetical 20 year gilt with a 12% coupon paid in equal half-yearly instalments. However, since delivery may involve other stocks, the London International Financial Futures Exchange (LIFFE) publishes tables which enable investors to calculate the amount of specific stocks which would have to be delivered to fulfil the conditions of a contract.

Futures contracts were initially available in a range of foreign currencies, and three interest rates (dollars, short sterling and the aforementioned gilt). Delivery months are specified as March, June, September and December with up to five different series being traded at any one time. This variety of maturities and underlying securities is designed to make the financial futures market attractive to a variety of investors. LIFFE has vigorously promoted the use of financial futures and argues that users may include (a) companies expecting to raise new loan capital, (b) companies expecting to receive payment in foreign currency, (c) fund managers receiving known cash flows over the passage of several months, and (d) banks committed to making loans to their own customers. As with other futures trading, the arguments for using LIFFE depend on the depth and efficiency of the market, in addition to the costs of participation. In addition to the named contracts, LIFFE has introduced futures in a broad Stock Exchange Index which might be attractive to investors wishing to hedge against market variability.

The development of a market in financial futures has in other countries signalled the creation of a wide range of options and futures instruments including options on financial futures. In 1984, for example, an option on and a futures contract on a Stock Exchange Index were established on the London Stock Exchange and LIFFE respectively. There was no strong indication that company treasurers or fund managers were likely to play a dominant role in these new markets, but the creation of these new instruments has aroused considerable interest in the financial community.

Competitive Processes

One of the underlying themes in the report of the Wilson Committee was the distortion in the operations of the financial markets caused by government intervention by way of tax or tax relief. One lasting effect of the report has been the continuing movement towards 'fiscal neutrality'. In particular, this has been discussed with reference to the competitive process between banks and building societies.

Throughout the years in which the building societies greatly expanded, the banks argued that the taxation arrangements favoured the building societies. First, the composite rate arrangements provided some effective tax relief. Depositors earning interest from bank deposits were subject to tax determined entirely by their own circumstances, whilst those depositing money in building societies received interest net of a rate of tax set by the average tax rate of building society depositors. Thus if 25% of depositors were liable to no tax and the remaining 75% were liable at the standard rate of 30%, the composite rate would be set at 22.5%. By this process, of course, the tax-exempt are subsidising the tax-paying depositors and it is only because of the administrative convenience that such a policy could be supported. In the 1984 Budget, however, the Chancellor announced that the composite rate system would be extended to the clearing banks — a change partly justified by the saving in administrative costs of tax collection and partly also by a move towards the establishment of fiscal neutrality between banks and building societies.

The same argument could also justify the move in early 1984 by the Inland Revenue to change the tax ruling on building societies short-term investments. It had previously been held that building societies were exempt from tax arising from profits made on the sale and purchase of gilts. This ruling, however, was changed in February 1984, when the Inland Revenue announced that capital gains made by building societies from trading in short-term government securities would be subject to capital gains tax; a ruling that had always applied to the capital gains made by banks.

It is quite clear that as the building societies and banks continue to compete, the government will reconsider the other characteristics in their tax and market arrangements which inhibit or bias the competitive process. In the long run, the chief difference which distinguishes building societies from banks is their objectives. Banks are, like other companies, owned by equity-holding shareholders. In any decision involving future policy, the bank management can refer to the shareholders' interests for the appropriate criteria. Thus in the long run, banks should engage in areas which would maximise shareholder wealth. By contrast, building societies are not companies but non-profit making institutions. The shareholders in building societies do not buy and sell shares in the secondary market at prices which reflect the future profitability of the societies. The objectives of building societies are therefore not viewed in terms of shareholders' wishes but in terms of *activities* such as lending money for home purchase, or implicitly by *targets* of growth in assets or growth in loans made. It is not clear that trying to alter any of these objectives will necessarily lead to an increase in efficiency of the markets in which the societies operate.

Although much debate has been activated by the increasing competition between banks and building societies, it has been dwarfed by the controversies surrounding the competitive developments in the *stock market*. Following an agreement in the summer of 1983 between the government and the Stock Exchange, there was rapid and widespread recognition that many of the established trading practices in the Stock Exchange would be revolutionised.

It was originally expected that the Office of Fair Trading would, with the encouragement of the government, reform the operation of the Stock Exchange by taking legal action against the restrictive practices of the Stock Exchange. Specifically, it was intended to question the efficacy of 'single capacity' (discussed in Chapter 7) and to open up the London securities market by abandoning the fixed commissions on security transactions and by allowing non-member institutions to trade in the financial markets.

The Stock Exchange negotiated with the government and agreed (a) to abandon fixed commissions, and (b) to allow non-members to be part owners of broking and jobbing firms on the understanding that the Office of Fair Trading would take no further action against the alleged restrictive policies of the Stock Exchange. It quickly became apparent that substantial changes would be caused by the ending of minimum commissions. As early as November 1983, the Capital Markets Committee (set up by the Bank of England) reported that negotiated commissions would effectively destroy the single capacity system. The Committee argued that some dealers operating outside the market (and therefore able to both hold and trade shares with institutional investors) would be able to negotiate a very low commission with a rate-cutting broker. Hence one would observe net prices quoted by external dealers which might be more favourable than those obtained by non-specialist brokers dealing for their clients on the Stock Exchange. In these circumstances, the Committee suggested, other brokers would demand the right to act in dual capacity, whilst jobbers would demand direct access to investors.

Following the publication of arguments such as these, there appeared within the City widespread recognition that changes would come rapidly. One reaction has been to encourage the merging of institutions. In the US when the New York Stock Exchange abandoned minimum commissions in 1975, the effect was to damage the medium-sized broking firms and to help the very large and the specialist firms to expand. A fear that similar processes have been set under way in London has caused a number of Stock Exchange firms to be sympathetic to the suggestion of merger or takeover.

Merchant banks have initially joined with jobbers as one step towards achieving economies of scale: Warburgs with Akroyd & Smithers, Rothschild with Smith Brothers. Similar links were established between Citicorp (an American bank) and Vickers da Costa, a London stockbroking firm with a speciality in international trading. With broking and jobbing firms looking outside the Stock Exchange for expansive (or defensive) opportunities, the economic climate in the City seemed to be similarly affected. Clearing banks, discount houses and money brokers were all reported in the press as candidates for takeover or merger. In late 1983 and early 1984 overseas trading and investment firms such as Goldman Sachs and

Merrill Lynch were reported in the press either to be recruiting personnel or to be considering the purchase of London-based dealing firms.

It is impossible to forecast with any confidence the outcome of these changes, but many observers of the financial markets expect to see a small number of international institutions emerging, each offering a wide range of financial and investment services, with facilities either to make markets or to have direct access to the securities markets. Beside this 'first eleven' (to go by US experience) there will also survive a secondary tier of institutions offering a restricted range of services, probably with special expertise in one or more of the services offered. Thus some brokers will offer cut-price dealing, others high quality research whilst smaller firms may even offer special knowledge of particular sectors of the market.

This situation, whilst attractive to the large institutional investors, may prove hostile to the interests of the small investors who are unable to negotiate low commissions. Thus a key issue in the development of the financial markets over the next few years will be the attitude towards individual investors and in particular the regulation and control of the changing markets.

Changes in Regulation

The problem of regulation has always been controversial within the financial market system. In preceding chapters, we have referred to the ways in which the regulatory system has responded to specific inequitable practice such as 'dawn raiding'. At the heart of the debate there have been two broad opposing views. The first, which has cited the operations of the SEC in the US, has argued for legally enforceable regulations. Only a centralised authority, it is argued, can be given sufficient resources to investigate and enforce the necessary regulations. Although the tradition in the UK has been based on self-regulation, the Wilson Committee noted that there had been a noticeable shift towards more statutory regulation but that in contrast with other countries, the UK was still informally regulated and that this informality had been attractive to international market operators.

The debate was advanced in January 1984 by the publication of a review on investor protection (The Gower Report). The recommendations of the Gower Report fall firmly within the traditional argument for self-regulation in that it envisages the setting up of a number of self-regulatory agencies, each responsible for disciplinary control of their members but each in turn responsible to and given statutory support by the Council for Securities Industry. Although the report received comment that was generally favourable, the weakness of its argument lies in the new developments that have been described above. Financial institutions are always changing in response to market pressures and opportunities and the speed of change seems likely to increase in the mid-1980s. In time there may be types of institutions that differ markedly from those dominating their respective markets today, and the creation of self-regulatory agencies in 1985 or 1986 may result in anachronistic controls in 1988 or 1989.

Gower recognised this problem and recommended that the overseeing Council for Securities industry should have the power to persuade the self-regulatory agencies to merge or to expand their regulatory cover into areas which were seen to develop within the investment market. In addition, Gower emphasised the protection of individual investors by recommending registers for investment advisors, deposit or fund insurance schemes to protect investors' money, and the prior approval of advertisements or sales promotion literature concerned with investment schemes or advice.

Whatever the specific government responses to the Gower Report, it is clear that in a period of rapid change, effective supervision will be particularly difficult to maintain. At present it is hoped that more competition will create some of the benefits that would otherwise have to be obtained through regulation. Only time will reveal whether this view is reasonable.

Future Shocks to the Financial Market System

We have observed that one of the major characteristics of the financial system over the last twenty years has been the growth of the long-term investing intermediaries. The growth has been caused partly by a larger number of employees and partly by wider coverage, of those employed, by corporate or employer-based pension schemes. Correspondingly, a change that has profound significance in the long term is the slowing down in the growth rate of pension funds. This would result from the changing age distribution of the population, caused both by a low birthrate and an increased life expectancy. Although long-term demographic prediction can be notoriously inaccurate, it is clear that the growth in pension funds is unlikely to persist. It is possible that at some stage the pension funds may be net sellers of securities, and that individual or corporate investors will once again be net purchasers. The burden of maintaining the dependent population will inevitably fall on those working. In some cases, the burden will be directly observed, as would be the case of increased national insurance contributions. In other cases, it would not be so obvious: the pension schemes of a particular company, for example, would grow as the company expanded and only suffer a net cash loss as the number of new contributions became outweighed by the benefits paid to former employees. The cash flow into the funded schemes will thus depend on a number of factors including the growth of companies in which employees are pension scheme members, the retirement age, the incentives given by legislation and regulation to saving by other means, and not least on the returns generated by the funds from investment in the securities markets.

The debate on the future development of pension provision will increasingly take into account the effects of an ageing population; it would be naive to expect that the institutions which dominate pension provision will remain unchanged. One obvious change which has already been advocated is to unitise the value of pension contributions so that at any point, a contributor can monitor the present value of his pension entitlement. Furthermore, it has been suggested that the beneficiaries' position could be strengthened by allowing them to transfer their entitlement into alternative forms of investment — to switch their pension holdings from, say, securities to deposits, or to hold units in a unit trust portfolio. These changes would obviously affect the concentration of investment power to some extent but again we forbear to offer any firm prediction of the extent of the changes.

Another type of shock which may dramatically affect the operations of the financial system derives from international events. One can point to the sudden change in oil prices in the 1970s as one example of an international economic event which had profound implications for the domestic markets. In the 1980s and 1990s, developing countries may find it impossible to repay the large amounts of capital borrowed in earlier years. Since many of these loans were made by private-sector banks and other financial institutions, the prospect of large scale default threatens the stability of the financial system. Defaults which involve countries would usually involve the cooperation of the central banks if the damage to the international market system is to be minimised. In the short term, one would expect that continuing preventative and supporting action would be taken by cooperative countries under the aegis of the International Monetary Fund or other transnational agencies.

It is, perhaps, in the area of international financial markets that much of the future development will be made. Whilst the operations of domestic capital markets have been closely studied, their international counterparts have received much less analysis. To some extent, this neglect can be attributed to the relative lack of data. It also partly stems from the lack of regulation and official intervention. However, market forces are persistent and, in time, the competitive pressures from competing institutions and markets will lead to more information and more analysis of the pricing process. The next decade is likely to witness a much greater degree of internationalisation of financial markets, and in turn this will lend weight to the arguments for increasing harmonisation of regulations across national frontiers.

Conclusion

Nothing dates more quickly than a forecast. This chapter, in suggesting how the financial system will develop, many aptly demonstrate this statement. Although we do not claim to be any less myopic than other observers of the financial system, we argue that the analysis in this book will continue to be useful regardless of whether institutions survive in their present form. At the heart of every financial market is the valuation of a stream of cash, whether it be dividends, interest or a single capital sum. In many cases, relatively simple analysis will, as we have demonstrated, illuminate the valuation and pricing of quite complicated assets.

The other central feature of our analysis concerns the discussion of efficiently operating markets. Whilst there may be much disagreement about the nature and the exercising of power within society, we feel it is uncontentious that if markets exist, they should be encouraged to operate efficiently. It is therefore a useful and important task to consider the ways in which efficiency can be analysed and encouraged. Whilst in the coming months and years much regulation may be announced, we hope that by reference to the concepts of market efficiency, readers will be able to interpret both the purposes and the possible effects.

Further Reading

1. B. Brown and C.R. Geisst, *Financial Futures Markets* (Macmillan, 1983) provides a comprehensive discussion of the new developments in financial futures.
2. J. Plender, *That's the Way the Money Goes: The Financial Institutions and the Nation's Savings* (Andrew Deutsch, 1982) is an aggressive investigation of some of the more dubious activities of institutional investors, fund managers, trustees and other individuals in the investing community.
3. *The Bank of England Quarterly Bulletin* is a source of articles and reports of speeches reflecting both government policy and changes in the financial markets.
4. L.C.B. Gower, *Review of Investor Protection, Part I,* Cmnd 9125 (HMSO, 1984) contains a detailed treatment of the City's arrangements for protecting the interests of investors, with proposals for reform.

Discussion Questions

14.1 Why might companies wishing to borrow money for a capital project starting in six months' time be interested in using the financial futures market?

14.2 Compare the characteristics of futures contracts in (a) commodities (b) a share index.

14.3 What do you understand by the term 'fiscal neutrality'? Illustrate your answer by reference to the legislation announced in 1984.

14.4 Suggest ways in which managers of non-profit institutions could be evaluated. Are they similar in some respects to professional occupations such as doctors or solicitors?

14.5 Why might legally employed regulation be less effective than self-regulation in ensuring market efficiency?

14.6 Consider the effects of a fall in the size of pension funds caused by a persistent outflow of cash. (Refer to the flow of funds data in Chapter 2.)

14.7 What kind of portfolio would you select if you had complete control of the investment policy of your own pension contributions? On what principles would you select particular assets?

Glossary

* Denotes an institution or market for which further information is provided in the appendices to Chapter 1.

* **Accepting houses** Banks which have the distinctive function of guaranteeing or 'accepting' bills of exchange.

Acceptance credit A type of bill of exchange created by an institution or company owing money.

Annuity A series of cash flows paid at the end of each of a specified number of periods. The cash flows may be equal each period or they may grow or decline in a mathematically regular fashion.

Arbitrage Buying and selling securities in order to profit from price differences without incurring risk.

Ask price The price at which a dealer is prepared to sell a security.

Asset stripping The practice of taking over a company and selling some or all of its assets. The term has been mainly used in a perjorative sense.

Bank bill A bill of exchange guaranteed or accepted by a bank.

Bank of England The central bank of the UK, responsible for carrying out the government's monetary policy and regulating the British financial system.

Barter The process of exchanging goods or services without using money.

Bear An investor who trades on the expectation that prices in the market will fall. Also used to describe a period in which prices have fallen.

Beta A measure of risk of a security: the covariation between the returns from the security and the returns from a market index.

Bid price The price at which a dealer is prepared to buy a security.

Bill of exchange A certificate containing a promise to pay a specified amount of money, which is created by the creditor company or institution and 'accepted' by or on behalf of the debtor. It can subsequently be traded as a financial asset.

Bond rating The classification of a bond into risk categories denoted by alphabetical characters.

Broker An individual or firm acting as an agent on behalf of an investor to buy or sell securities or other assets.

* **Building society** A financial institution which borrows and accepts deposits with the objective of providing loans for house purchase.

Bull An investor who trades in the expectation that prices in the market will rise. Also used to describe a period in which prices have risen.

Bulldog bond A bond, denominated in sterling, issued on behalf of foreign companies or institutions.

Capital budgeting The process by which a firm identifies and chooses capital investments to hold — usually involving the purchase of real assets, e.g., machinery, property.

Call option A security which gives the holder the right to buy a number of shares at a specified price sometime before the expiry date.

Call over A system of trading on securities markets in which securities are traded during specific periods by dealers trading directly with each other.

Capitalisation rate A multiplier, used to derive a valuation by applying it to a current benefits flow, e.g., dividends or profits.

Captive insurance companies Subsidiaries of industrial or commercial groups established to handle the insurance needs of the group.

Certificate of deposit A security traded in the short-term financial markets and created by a bank certifying that a specified sum of money has been deposited and will be repaid with interest at a specific date.

* **Clearing bank** A retail bank accepting deposits from the personal and corporate sectors and offering a wide range of financial services to individual customers.

* **Commercial bank** A financial institution that borrows money or accepts deposits which are invested in financial markets or lent to borrowers. See also *Accepting house, Clearing bank*.

Commercial bill Bill of exchange issued either by a commercial or financial institution.

Composite rate An average rate of tax deducted at source by building societies and banks on interest earned by depositors. The composite rate is determined by reference to the average tax liability of depositors.

Compound interest The amount by which a sum of money will grow in each of a number of periods when the amount deposited plus the interest already earned attracts interest at a given rate.

Consols Certain UK government stocks for which no date by which they will be redeemed is specified. The term is sometimes used as a general description for any undated or irredeemable bonds.

Convertible stock Fixed interest loans or preference shares which can be converted at some specified time into ordinary shares of the same company.

Coupon The interest payable on a fixed interest investment, the rate of interest payable being specified in terms of the nominal value of a security.

Debenture stock A type of fixed interest bond which effectively acts as a mortgage on assets owned by the issuer.

Discount house A company which specialises in trading in money market instruments and has lender-of-last-resort facilities at the Bank of England.

* **Discount market** The market in which bills of exchange and Treasury bills are bought and sold.

Discount rate The amount over £1 which £1 now is deemed to be worth one period hence. Can be expressed either in terms of present value or future value.

Dividend Cash paid to shareholders, usually twice a year — interim dividend and final dividend.

Dividend yield Dividends divided by the share price.

Drop-lock A bond in which the interest rate is initially variable but which in specified circumstances is 'locked' into a fixed rate.

Earnings yield The profits available for shareholders divided by the share price.

Effective rate of interest The rate of interest earned over the course of a year taking into account any compounding of interest that might be appropriate.

Endowment policy An insurance policy offering a payment at the end of the contracted period or on death of the insured, if earlier.

Entity A company, institution, individual or group which can be distinguished from its economic environment for the purpose of analysis. A legal entity has the capacity to enter into contracts.

Equity In the context of capital markets, equity refers to an ordinary share. In accounting and legal terms, it refers to the financial interest in a firm's assets after prior claims have been met.

Euro-bond An international bond that may be issued in any currency and subsequently traded in international markets — usually by dealers buying and selling on their own or clients' accounts. London is an important centre for euro-bond trading.

Euro-currency Any currency which is traded, lent or repaid by market participants outside the country of origin.

Euro-dollars Dollar-denominated euro-currency.

Ex div Shares (bonds) are traded ex div shortly before dividends (interest) are due to be paid. The purchase of an ex div security does not entitle the purchaser to receive the next dividend (interest) payment which accordingly is paid to the seller of the share (bond).

Exercise price The specified price at which options can be taken up or exercised.

Expectations hypothesis A model of the term structure of interest rates that predicts that the future short-term rates of interest can be estimated by reference to the differences between current long-term interest rates.

* **Export Credits Guarantee Department** A government established institution providing insurance in international trade (especially to UK exporters).

Factoring Raising finance either by selling trade debts or using them as security for borrowing.

* **Finance house (Finance company)** A financial institution which accepts deposits and finances leasing and hire purchase agreements.

Financial futures A standardised financial security enabling investors to contract a future investment at a specified price or rate.

Fiscal policy Government policy concerned with taxation and public spending.

Flow of funds Analysis of economic activity based on the movements of financial assets and liabilities between entities and sectors in the economy.

Focal date A point in time, chosen for convenient estimation, to which future (or past) cash flows are discounted (or compounded).

Forward-forward Trading in financial futures so as to arbitrage with exchange or interest rates in a later period.

Forward rate The rate of interest covering a period which is implied by the current prices of securities of the same type. Thus a two year and a three year bond can together imply a forward one year rate between the second and third years.

Fundamental analysis The valuation of shares based on the analysis of corporate and economic information.

Fund manager Individual who manages monies placed with an investment intermediary.

Futures Standardised contracts involving either commodities or financial assets (or indices). See *Financial futures*.

Gilt, gilt edged A bond issued on behalf of (or backed up by) the government.

Hedging The avoidance of risk by arranging a contract at specified prices which will yield a known return.

Hire purchase   The purchase of an asset by a formal agreement involving a number of payments spread out over a period.

Indemnity   The principle of replacing in an insurance claim only the value of what has been lost.

Index   An indicator of the general movements in prices, quantities or values of goods or services. Used extensively in reporting of prices in financial markets.

Index fund   A fund or unit trust that aims to maintain a portfolio that will match the investment performance of a broad based stock market index such as the FT Actuaries All-Share Index.

Index-linked gilt   A government bond for which the interest and redemption value is directly linked to the Index of Retail Prices.

Insider   A person who has access to unpublished or privileged information and who uses it to trade at un unfair advantage in the capital market.

* **Insurance company**   A financial institution which is involved in general and/or long-term insurance business. In general insurance the insurance company will compensate their insured clients for loss caused by specific accidents or events. Long-term business mainly concerns 'life' or pension provision.

Intermediary   An intermediary links borrowers and lenders either by acting as an agent, or by bringing together potential traders, or by acting in place of a market.

Inter-bank   Usually refers to the short-term loans traded between banks on the parallel money markets.

Internal rate of return   A measure of profitability of an investment project.

Introduction   A method by which existing securities become traded on the Stock Exchange.

* **Investment trust**   A company which performs the task of fund manager on behalf of its shareholders.

Irredeemable   A security which does not specify to holders any date at which it will be redeemed (repaid) by the issuer.

* **Issuing house**   A financial institution (e.g. bank, stockbroker) which advises on and arranges the issuance of securities.

Jobber   A firm, or individual, in the Stock Exchange responsible for quoting prices to and trading securities via brokers.

Lease   A method of obtaining the use of an asset by contracting a series of payments (e.g. rents) over a specified period.

Lender of last resort   The understanding that the Bank of England will always stand ready to lend money to a limited number of financial institutions if they are unable to obtain finance from market sources.

Lessee   The entity, in a lease, which agrees to pay the leasing payments in exchange for use of the asset.

Lessor   The entity, in a lease, which finances the purchase of the asset in return for receipt of leasing payments.

Lifeboat   An operation, set up by the Bank of England, designed to save a number of financially embarassed institutions.

* **LIFFE**   The London International Financial Futures Exchange.

Limit order   An order to buy or sell securities at a price specified to be above or below the current prices quoted in the market.

Liquid asset   An asset which may easily be turned into cash at short notice.

Liquidity preference The explanation of the term structure of interest rates based on the assumption that lenders prefer securities which have shorter maturities (i.e. which are more liquid). The preference will be reflected in the lower returns on short-term securities.

Listed securities Securities which are authorised to be traded on a particular financial market.

* **Lloyds** A market for insurance.

Loan stock A long-term bond issued by a company or public sector body.

Macmillan Gap A structural defect in the primary market for corporate finance whereby small to medium-sized companies found it difficult to raise finance. (Identified by the Macmillan Committee in 1931.)

Margin The proportion or amount of funds that has to be deposited by an investor when trading options or futures contracts.

Maturity The length of time elapsing before a debt is to be redeemed by the issuer.

* **Merchant bank** A non-consumer orientated bank which will provide funds, arrange and advise on corporate finance.

Merger The combination of two or more firms into a single entity.

Minimum lending rate (MLR) A specified rate of interest at which the Bank of England might offer assistance to the discount market.

Monetary policy Economic policy acting through the supply of money, interest rates and the availability of credit within the economy.

* **Money market** A short-term financial market usually involving assets with less than a year to maturity.

Money multiplier The extent to which the financial system can create credit from its reserve assets (e.g. cash and government short-term securities).

Money-weighted return A measure of investment performance equivalent to the internal rate of return in a fund over a specified period.

Moral hazard The problem caused by the incentive of the insured (a) to mislead the insurer by providing false information or making false claims and (b) to take little care to avoid loss.

Negotiable securities Securities which, when traded, give the buyer the same rights as those previously enjoyed by the seller.

Net present value (NPV) The value of an investment's cash flows discounted to a focal date at the beginning of the project.

Net terminal value (NTV) The value of an investment's cash flows compounded to a focal date at the end of the project.

Nominal interest The calculation of interest which assumes that interest accrues only at the end of each year.

Nominal value The price which was denominated for coupon payment purposes at the time of issue — not necessarily the issue price. With bonds which are to be redeemed, the nominal value will generally coincide with the redemption price.

Numeraire A commodity (such as money) which is used to express the values of other commodities or services.

Offer price The price at which a dealer (or jobber) is prepared to sell securities.

Offer for sale A method of issuing securities by offering to potential investors a specified number of securities at a specified price.

Opportunity cost   The benefits foregone by the adoption of a particular action, e.g. the opportunity costs of investing in a project is the return that could have been obtained in the best comparable investment.

Option   The right to undertake a transaction on prespecified terms. Thus traded options on the Stock Exchange give the right to buy specified ordinary shares at a known price.

Ordinary share   The security representing the claim to the residual ownership of a company (see *Equity*).

Overdraft   The facility to obtain credit from a bank by withdrawing more from the bank account than has been previously deposited.

Over-the-counter (OTC) market   An informal dealer-based market.

Overfunding   The policy of selling long-term government bonds in excess of the amount required to finance the public sector borrowing requirement.

Par (bond)   The nominal value of a bond, or a bond which is currently quoted at a price equal to its nominal value.

Parallel markets   A number of markets in which short-term instruments are traded without lender-of-last-resort facilities.

*   **Pension fund**   An institution or arrangement which accepts contributions from members in order to pay out pensions on retirement.

Perpetuity   An endless annuity.

Placing   A method of selling securities, subsequently to be traded in the secondary market, by selling the securities to a selected number of investors.

Preference share   A share which pays a fixed dividend and ranks prior to the ordinary shares in liquidation.

Price/earnings (P/E) ratio   The ratio of the price of a share to either the most recent or forecasted profits per share.

Primary market   A market in which securities are traded between issuers and investors, thereby raising additional funds for the issuing entity.

Prime (property)   Property which, by nature of its size, location and tenants, affords the owner a very secure growth in rental income.

Property bond   A fund, linked to insurance schemes, which invests the net premiums in property.

Prospectus   The advertisement, used in issuing shares, carrying financial and investment details of interest to potential investors.

Public sector borrowing requirement (PSBR)   The amount of money required by the public sector, not otherwise raised by taxation.

Published accounts   Financial statements circulated by companies giving the latest balance sheet (details of their assets, liabilities and equities) and profit and loss statement, and various other data on their operations and prospects.

Put–call parity theorem   A relationship based on the principles of arbitrage, relating the prices of the call option, the put option, the rate of interest and the price of the underlying share.

Put option   A security which gives the holder the right to sell a specified share at a specified price sometime before the end of the contract.

Put through   The arrangement whereby a broker sells and buys shares through a jobber in order to complete a transaction between the broker's own clients.

Random walk   In the context of share price behaviour, prices follow a random walk if past changes are of no help in predicting future changes.

Real return   The return on an investment after taking into account the effects of changes in purchasing power.

Redemption (maturity)   The repayment of a stock at a specified date and price.

Redemption yield   An indicator of the return earned on buying a stock and holding it until maturity.

Re-insurance   The practice of reducing the risks of bearing insurance by re-contracting some, or all, of the insurance with another insurer.

Reserve assets   Financial assets, such as cash, Treasury bills and deposits at the Bank of England, required to be held by banks.

Rights issue   The offer by a company of additional shares to its existing shareholders at a specially low price.

Riskless, riskfree, rate   A return which is certain to materialise if a security is bought and held over a specified investment horizon (e.g. Treasury bills bought and held over their three month lives.)

Roll-over   An agreement whereby a loan is prolonged at specified terms.

Round-tripping   A type of arbitrage trade involving borrowing from one source and lending in another market at a higher rate of interest.

Running yield   Bond interest divided by price.

Sale and leaseback   The provision of finance whereby a company sells a property to an institution on the agreement that it can lease the premises, thereby converting a capital value into an immediate cash inflow at the cost of future lease payments.

* **Savings bank**   An incorporated society providing savings facilities for the personal sector.

Scrip issue   The issuing, without charge, of additional shares to existing shareholders.

Secondary market   The market in which existing securities and financial claims are bought and sold.

Segmentation hypothesis   The explanation of the term structure of interest rates by identification of investors/borrowers with specific investment horizons.

Short   A bond with less than five years to run before maturity.

Simple interest   The calculation of simple interest allows only for interest to be charged on the principal sum, not on any interest accruing from previous periods.

Specialist   A member of the New York Stock Exchange whose responsibility is to maintain an orderly market by dealing and monitoring share transactions in particular stocks.

Spot rate   The rate of interest to maturity currently offered on a particular class of bond or bill.

Stag   An investor who applies for securities at the time of issue on the expectation that the market price will be greater than the price at which they are issued.

Stockbroker   A member (firm or individual) of the Stock Exchange who deals on behalf of clients with jobbers.

Striking price   The price at which securities will be sold as a result of an issue by tender. Sometimes also used to describe the exercise price of an option.

Syndicate   The groups into which the underwriting members of Lloyds are organised, and on whose behalf the underwriting agents accept insurance business.

Tender   An issue of securities for which the issue price is determined by the various prices offered by investors wishing to buy the stock.

Term insurance   A life policy which expires worthless if the insured survives the term covered by the policy.

Term structure of interest rates   The pattern of interest rates currently available for bonds of different maturities (terms).

Time-weighted return   The average rate of return earned on an investment between the receipt or payment of cash flows.

Trade bill   A Bill of Exchange issued by a company and accepted by another company (not a bank).

Transfer payment   A payment or gift of money made without a corresponding service or commodity.

Transmutation of claims   The change in form or maturity of one financial claim into another.

Treasury bill   A short-term loan taken out by the government in the form of a Bill of Exchange.

Trustee Savings Bank (TSB)   Banks which evolved from institutions set up to channel personal savings in to financing the PSBR, but which now operate in a commercial framework.

Underwriter   An individual or institution agreeing either to buy or insure an event such as a share issue or a range of insurance risks.

* **Unit trust**   An open-ended fund which sells units to investors and invests the proceeds in a range of investments (usually equities).

Unlisted security   A security which is traded by dealers but not listed (quoted) on the Stock Exchange.

Warrant   A security which gives the holder the right to buy, during a specified period, a number of ordinary shares in the issuing company at a specified price.

Whole life   An insurance contract which will pay a specified sum of money on the death of the insured in return for a regular premium.

Yield   A rate of return.

Yield curve   A curve describing the pattern of redemption yields of similar bonds of differing maturities.

Zero coupon bond   A bond which offers return only in the form of capital gain. (Usually seen in practice only for short-term issues, e.g. Treasury Bills.)

——Financial Tables——

1. Present Value of £1
2. Present Value of £1 per Period
3. Terminal Value of £1 per Period

Present Value of £1

PERIOD   % I N T E R E S T   R A T E   P E R   P E R I O D

PERIOD	1	2	3	4	5	6	7	8	9	10	11	12
1	.9901	.9804	.9709	.9615	.9524	.9434	.9346	.9259	.9174	.9091	.9009	.8929
2	.9803	.9612	.9426	.9246	.9070	.8900	.8734	.8573	.8417	.8264	.8116	.7972
3	.9706	.9423	.9151	.8890	.8638	.8396	.8163	.7938	.7722	.7513	.7312	.7118
4	.9610	.9238	.8885	.8548	.8227	.7921	.7629	.7350	.7084	.6830	.6587	.6355
5	.9515	.9057	.8626	.8219	.7835	.7473	.7130	.6806	.6499	.6209	.5935	.5674
6	.9420	.8880	.8375	.7903	.7462	.7050	.6663	.6302	.5963	.5645	.5346	.5066
7	.9327	.8706	.8131	.7599	.7107	.6651	.6227	.5835	.5470	.5132	.4817	.4523
8	.9235	.8535	.7894	.7307	.6768	.6274	.5820	.5403	.5019	.4665	.4339	.4039
9	.9143	.8368	.7664	.7026	.6446	.5919	.5439	.5002	.4604	.4241	.3909	.3606
10	.9053	.8203	.7441	.6756	.6139	.5584	.5083	.4632	.4224	.3855	.3522	.3220
11	.8963	.8043	.7224	.6496	.5847	.5268	.4751	.4289	.3875	.3505	.3173	.2875
12	.8874	.7885	.7014	.6246	.5568	.4970	.4440	.3971	.3555	.3186	.2858	.2567
13	.8787	.7730	.6810	.6006	.5303	.4688	.4150	.3677	.3262	.2897	.2575	.2292
14	.8700	.7579	.6611	.5775	.5051	.4423	.3878	.3405	.2992	.2633	.2320	.2046
15	.8613	.7430	.6419	.5553	.4810	.4173	.3624	.3152	.2745	.2394	.2090	.1827
16	.8528	.7284	.6232	.5339	.4581	.3936	.3387	.2919	.2519	.2176	.1883	.1631
17	.8444	.7142	.6050	.5134	.4363	.3714	.3166	.2703	.2311	.1978	.1696	.1456
18	.8360	.7002	.5874	.4936	.4155	.3503	.2959	.2502	.2120	.1799	.1528	.1300
19	.8277	.6864	.5703	.4746	.3957	.3305	.2765	.2317	.1945	.1635	.1377	.1161
20	.8195	.6730	.5537	.4564	.3769	.3118	.2584	.2145	.1784	.1486	.1240	.1037
21	.8114	.6598	.5375	.4388	.3589	.2942	.2415	.1987	.1637	.1351	.1117	.0926
22	.8034	.6468	.5219	.4220	.3418	.2775	.2257	.1839	.1502	.1228	.1007	.0826
23	.7954	.6342	.5067	.4057	.3256	.2618	.2109	.1703	.1378	.1117	.0907	.0738
24	.7876	.6217	.4919	.3901	.3101	.2470	.1971	.1577	.1264	.1015	.0817	.0659
25	.7798	.6095	.4776	.3751	.2953	.2330	.1842	.1460	.1160	.0923	.0736	.0588
26	.7720	.5976	.4637	.3607	.2812	.2198	.1722	.1352	.1064	.0839	.0663	.0525
27	.7644	.5859	.4502	.3468	.2678	.2074	.1609	.1252	.0976	.0763	.0597	.0469
28	.7568	.5744	.4371	.3335	.2551	.1956	.1504	.1159	.0895	.0693	.0538	.0419
29	.7493	.5631	.4243	.3207	.2429	.1846	.1406	.1073	.0822	.0630	.0485	.0374
30	.7419	.5521	.4120	.3083	.2314	.1741	.1314	.0994	.0754	.0573	.0437	.0334
31	.7346	.5412	.4000	.2965	.2204	.1643	.1228	.0920	.0691	.0521	.0394	.0298
32	.7273	.5306	.3883	.2851	.2099	.1550	.1147	.0852	.0634	.0474	.0355	.0266
33	.7201	.5202	.3770	.2741	.1999	.1462	.1072	.0789	.0582	.0431	.0319	.0238
34	.7130	.5100	.3660	.2636	.1904	.1379	.1002	.0730	.0534	.0391	.0288	.0212
35	.7059	.5000	.3554	.2534	.1813	.1301	.0937	.0676	.0490	.0356	.0259	.0189

Present Value of £1

PERITOD   % I N T E R E S T   R A T E   P E R   P E R I O D

PERIOD	13	14	15	16	18	20	22	24	26	28	30	35
1	.8850	.8772	.8696	.8621	.8475	.8333	.8197	.8065	.7937	.7813	.7692	.7407
2	.7831	.7695	.7561	.7432	.7182	.6944	.6719	.6504	.6299	.6104	.5917	.5487
3	.6931	.6750	.6575	.6407	.6086	.5787	.5507	.5245	.4999	.4768	.4552	.4064
4	.6133	.5921	.5718	.5523	.5158	.4823	.4514	.4230	.3968	.3725	.3501	.3011
5	.5428	.5194	.4972	.4761	.4371	.4019	.3700	.3411	.3149	.2910	.2693	.2230
6	.4803	.4556	.4323	.4104	.3704	.3349	.3033	.2751	.2499	.2274	.2072	.1652
7	.4251	.3996	.3759	.3538	.3139	.2791	.2486	.2218	.1983	.1776	.1594	.1224
8	.3762	.3506	.3269	.3050	.2660	.2326	.2038	.1789	.1574	.1388	.1226	.0906
9	.3329	.3075	.2843	.2630	.2255	.1938	.1670	.1443	.1249	.1084	.0943	.0671
10	.2946	.2697	.2472	.2267	.1911	.1615	.1369	.1164	.0992	.0847	.0725	.0497
11	.2607	.2366	.2149	.1954	.1619	.1346	.1122	.0938	.0787	.0662	.0558	.0368
12	.2307	.2076	.1869	.1685	.1372	.1122	.0920	.0757	.0625	.0517	.0429	.0273
13	.2042	.1821	.1625	.1452	.1163	.0935	.0754	.0610	.0496	.0404	.0330	.0202
14	.1807	.1597	.1413	.1252	.0985	.0779	.0618	.0492	.0393	.0316	.0254	.0150
15	.1599	.1401	.1229	.1079	.0835	.0649	.0507	.0397	.0312	.0247	.0195	.0111
16	.1415	.1229	.1069	.0930	.0708	.0541	.0415	.0320	.0248	.0193	.0150	.0082
17	.1252	.1078	.0929	.0802	.0600	.0451	.0340	.0258	.0197	.0150	.0116	.0061
18	.1108	.0946	.0808	.0691	.0508	.0376	.0279	.0208	.0156	.0118	.0089	.0045
19	.0981	.0829	.0703	.0596	.0431	.0313	.0229	.0168	.0124	.0092	.0068	.0033
20	.0868	.0728	.0611	.0514	.0365	.0261	.0187	.0135	.0098	.0072	.0053	.0025
21	.0768	.0638	.0531	.0443	.0309	.0217	.0154	.0109	.0078	.0056	.0040	.0018
22	.0680	.0560	.0462	.0382	.0262	.0181	.0126	.0088	.0062	.0044	.0031	.0014
23	.0601	.0491	.0402	.0329	.0222	.0151	.0103	.0071	.0049	.0034	.0024	.0010
24	.0532	.0431	.0349	.0284	.0188	.0126	.0085	.0057	.0039	.0027	.0018	.0007
25	.0471	.0378	.0304	.0245	.0160	.0105	.0069	.0046	.0031	.0021	.0014	.0006
26	.0417	.0331	.0264	.0211	.0135	.0087	.0057	.0037	.0025	.0016	.0011	.0004
27	.0369	.0291	.0230	.0182	.0115	.0073	.0047	.0030	.0019	.0013	.0008	.0003
28	.0326	.0255	.0200	.0157	.0097	.0061	.0038	.0024	.0015	.0010	.0006	.0002
29	.0289	.0224	.0174	.0135	.0082	.0051	.0031	.0020	.0012	.0008	.0005	.0002
30	.0256	.0196	.0151	.0116	.0070	.0042	.0026	.0016	.0010	.0006	.0004	.0001
31	.0226	.0172	.0131	.0100	.0059	.0035	.0021	.0013	.0008	.0005	.0003	.0001
32	.0200	.0151	.0114	.0087	.0050	.0029	.0017	.0010	.0006	.0004	.0002	.0001
33	.0177	.0132	.0099	.0075	.0042	.0024	.0014	.0008	.0005	.0003	.0002	.0001
34	.0157	.0116	.0086	.0064	.0036	.0020	.0012	.0007	.0004	.0002	.0001	.0000
35	.0139	.0102	.0075	.0055	.0030	.0017	.0009	.0005	.0003	.0002	.0001	.0000

Present Value of £1 per Period

PERIOD	% I N T E R E S T		R A T E	P E R	P E R I O D						
	1	2	3	4	5	6	7	8	9	10	11	12
1	0.990	0.980	0.971	0.962	0.952	0.943	0.935	0.926	0.917	0.909	0.901	0.893
2	1.970	1.942	1.913	1.886	1.859	1.833	1.808	1.783	1.759	1.736	1.713	1.690
3	2.941	2.884	2.829	2.775	2.723	2.673	2.624	2.577	2.531	2.487	2.444	2.402
4	3.902	3.808	3.717	3.630	3.546	3.465	3.387	3.312	3.240	3.170	3.102	3.037
5	4.853	4.713	4.580	4.452	4.329	4.212	4.100	3.993	3.890	3.791	3.696	3.605
6	5.795	5.601	5.417	5.242	5.076	4.917	4.767	4.623	4.486	4.355	4.231	4.111
7	6.728	6.472	6.230	6.002	5.786	5.582	5.389	5.206	5.033	4.868	4.712	4.564
8	7.652	7.325	7.020	6.733	6.463	6.210	5.971	5.747	5.535	5.335	5.146	4.968
9	8.566	8.162	7.786	7.435	7.108	6.802	6.515	6.247	5.995	5.759	5.537	5.328
10	9.470	8.983	8.530	8.111	7.722	7.360	7.024	6.710	6.418	6.145	5.889	5.650
11	10.37	9.790	9.250	8.760	8.306	7.887	7.499	7.139	6.805	6.495	6.207	5.938
12	11.26	10.58	9.950	9.390	8.863	8.384	7.943	7.536	7.161	6.814	6.492	6.194
13	12.13	11.35	10.63	9.990	9.390	8.853	8.358	7.904	7.487	7.103	6.750	6.424
14	13.00	12.11	11.30	10.56	9.900	9.290	8.745	8.244	7.786	7.367	6.982	6.628
15	13.87	12.85	11.94	11.12	10.38	9.710	9.110	8.559	8.061	7.606	7.191	6.811
16	14.72	13.58	12.56	11.65	10.84	10.11	9.450	8.851	8.313	7.824	7.379	6.974
17	15.56	14.29	13.17	12.17	11.27	10.48	9.760	9.120	8.544	8.022	7.549	7.120
18	16.40	14.99	13.75	12.66	11.69	10.83	10.06	9.370	8.756	8.201	7.702	7.250
19	17.23	15.68	14.32	13.13	12.09	11.16	10.34	9.600	8.950	8.365	7.839	7.366
20	18.05	16.35	14.88	13.59	12.46	11.47	10.59	9.820	9.130	8.514	7.963	7.469
21	18.86	17.01	15.42	14.03	12.82	11.76	10.84	10.02	9.290	8.649	8.075	7.562
22	19.66	17.66	15.94	14.45	13.16	12.04	11.06	10.20	9.440	8.772	8.176	7.645
23	20.46	18.29	16.44	14.86	13.49	12.30	11.27	10.37	9.580	8.883	8.266	7.718
24	21.24	18.91	16.94	15.25	13.80	12.55	11.47	10.53	9.710	8.985	8.348	7.784
25	22.02	19.52	17.41	15.62	14.09	12.78	11.65	10.67	9.820	9.080	8.422	7.843
26	22.80	20.12	17.88	15.98	14.38	13.00	11.83	10.81	9.930	9.160	8.488	7.896
27	23.56	20.71	18.33	16.33	14.64	13.21	11.99	10.94	10.03	9.240	8.548	7.943
28	24.32	21.28	18.76	16.66	14.90	13.41	12.14	11.05	10.12	9.310	8.602	7.984
29	25.07	21.84	19.19	16.98	15.14	13.59	12.28	11.16	10.20	9.370	8.650	8.022
30	25.81	22.40	19.60	17.29	15.37	13.76	12.41	11.26	10.27	9.430	8.694	8.055
31	26.54	22.94	20 00	17.59	15.59	13.93	12.53	11.35	10.34	9.480	8.733	8.085
32	27.27	23.47	20.39	17.87	15.80	14.08	12.65	11.43	10.41	9.530	8.769	8.112
33	27.99	23.99	20.77	18.15	16.00	14.23	12.75	11.51	10.46	9.570	8.801	8.135
34	28.70	24.50	21.13	18.41	16.19	14.37	12.85	11.59	10.52	9.610	8.829	8.157
35	29.41	25.00	21.49	18.66	16.37	14.50	12.95	11.65	10.57	9.640	8.855	8.176

Present Value of £1 per Period

PERIOD	% I N T E R E S T R A T E P E R P E R I O D											
	13	14	15	16	18	20	22	24	26	28	30	35
1	0.885	0.877	0.870	0.862	0.847	0.833	0.820	0.806	0.794	0.781	0.769	0.741
2	1.668	1.647	1.626	1.605	1.566	1.528	1.492	1.457	1.424	1.392	1.361	1.289
3	2.361	2.322	2.283	2.246	2.174	2.106	2.042	1.981	1.923	1.868	1.816	1.696
4	2.974	2.914	2.855	2.798	2.690	2.589	2.494	2.404	2.320	2.241	2.166	1.997
5	3.517	3.433	3.352	3.274	3.127	2.991	2.864	2.745	2.635	2.532	2.436	2.220
6	3.998	3.889	3.784	3.685	3.498	3.326	3.167	3.020	2.885	2.759	2.643	2.385
7	4.423	4.288	4.160	4.039	3.812	3.605	3.416	3.242	3.083	2.937	2.802	2.508
8	4.799	4.639	4.487	4.344	4.078	3.837	3.619	3.421	3.241	3.076	2.925	2.598
9	5.132	4.946	4.772	4.607	4.303	4.031	3.786	3.566	3.366	3.184	3.019	2.665
10	5.426	5.216	5.019	4.833	4.494	4.192	3.923	3.682	3.465	3.269	3.092	2.715
11	5.687	5.453	5.234	5.029	4.656	4.327	4.035	3.776	3.543	3.335	3.147	2.752
12	5.918	5.660	5.421	5.197	4.793	4.439	4.127	3.851	3.606	3.387	3.190	2.779
13	6.122	5.842	5.583	5.342	4.910	4.533	4.203	3.912	3.656	3.427	3.223	2.799
14	6.302	6.002	5.724	5.468	5.008	4.611	4.265	3.962	3.695	3.459	3.249	2.814
15	6.462	6.142	5.847	5.575	5.092	4.675	4.315	4.001	3.726	3.483	3.268	2.825
16	6.604	6.265	5.954	5.668	5.162	4.730	4.357	4.033	3.751	3.503	3.283	2.834
17	6.729	6.373	6.047	5.749	5.222	4.775	4.391	4.059	3.771	3.518	3.295	2.840
18	6.840	6.467	6.128	5.818	5.273	4.812	4.419	4.080	3.786	3.529	3.304	2.844
19	6.938	6.550	6.198	5.877	5.316	4.843	4.442	4.097	3.799	3.539	3.311	2.848
20	7.025	6.623	6.259	5.929	5.353	4.870	4.460	4.110	3.808	3.546	3.316	2.850
21	7.102	6.687	6.312	5.973	5.384	4.891	4.476	4.121	3.816	3.551	3.320	2.852
22	7.170	6.743	6.359	6.011	5.410	4.909	4.488	4.130	3.822	3.556	3.323	2.853
23	7.230	6.792	6.399	6.044	5.432	4.925	4.499	4.137	3.827	3.559	3.325	2.854
24	7.283	6.835	6.434	6.073	5.451	4.937	4.507	4.143	3.831	3.562	3.327	2.855
25	7.330	6.873	6.464	6.097	5.467	4.948	4.514	4.147	3.834	3.564	3.329	2.856
26	7.372	6.906	6.491	6.118	5.480	4.956	4.520	4.151	3.837	3.566	3.330	2.856
27	7.409	6.935	6.514	6.136	5.492	4.964	4.524	4.154	3.839	3.567	3.331	2.856
28	7.441	6.961	6.534	6.152	5.502	4.970	4.528	4.157	3.840	3.568	3.331	2.857
29	7.470	6.983	6.551	6.166	5.510	4.975	4.531	4.159	3.841	3.569	3.332	2.857
30	7.496	7.003	6.566	6.177	5.517	4.979	4.534	4.160	3.842	3.569	3.332	2.857
31	7.518	7.020	6.579	6.187	5.523	4.982	4.536	4.161	3.843	3.570	3.332	2.857
32	7.538	7.035	6.591	6.196	5.528	4.985	4.538	4.162	3.844	3.570	3.333	2.857
33	7.556	7.048	6.600	6.203	5.532	4.988	4.539	4.163	3.844	3.570	3.333	2.857
34	7.572	7.060	6.609	6.210	5.536	4.990	4.540	4.164	3.845	3.571	3.333	2.857
35	7.586	7.070	6.617	6.215	5.539	4.992	4.541	4.164	3.845	3.571	3.333	2.857

Terminal Value of £1 per Period

PERIOD	% I N T E R E S T R A T E P E R P E R I O D											
	1	2	3	4	5	6	7	8	9	10	11	12
1	1.000	1.000	1.000	1.000	1.000	1.000	1.000	1.000	1.000	1.000	1.000	1.000
2	2.010	2.020	2.030	2.040	2.050	2.060	2.070	2.080	2.090	2.100	2.110	2.120
3	3.030	3.060	3.091	3.122	3.152	3.184	3.215	3.246	3.278	3.310	3.342	3.374
4	4.060	4.122	4.184	4.246	4.310	4.375	4.440	4.506	4.573	4.641	4.710	4.779
5	5.101	5.204	5.309	5.416	5.526	5.637	5.751	5.867	5.985	6.105	6.228	6.353
6	6.152	6.308	6.468	6.633	6.802	6.975	7.153	7.336	7.523	7.716	7.913	8.115
7	7.214	7.434	7.662	7.898	8.142	8.394	8.654	8.923	9.200	9.487	9.783	10.09
8	8.286	8.583	8.892	9.214	9.549	9.897	10.26	10.64	11.03	11.44	11.86	12.30
9	9.369	9.755	10.16	10.58	11.03	11.49	11.98	12.49	13.02	13.58	14.16	14.78
10	10.46	10.95	11.46	12.01	12.58	13.18	13.82	14.49	15.19	15.94	16.72	17.55
11	11.57	12.17	12.81	13.49	14.21	14.97	15.78	16.65	17.56	18.53	19.56	20.65
12	12.68	13.41	14.19	15.03	15.92	16.87	17.89	18.98	20.14	21.38	22.71	24.13
13	13.81	14.68	15.62	16.63	17.71	18.88	20.14	21.50	22.95	24.52	26.21	28.03
14	14.95	15.97	17.09	18.29	19.60	21.02	22.55	24.21	26.02	27.97	30.09	32.39
15	16.10	17.29	18.60	20.02	21.58	23.28	25.13	27.15	29.36	31.77	34.41	37.28
16	17.26	18.64	20.16	21.82	23.66	25.67	27.89	30.32	33.00	35.95	39.19	42.75
17	18.43	20.01	21.76	23.70	25.84	28.21	30.84	33.75	36.97	40.54	44.50	48.88
18	19.61	21.41	23.41	25.65	28.13	30.91	34.00	37.45	41.30	45.60	50.40	55.75
19	20.81	22.84	25.12	27.67	30.54	33.76	37.38	41.45	46.02	51.16	56.94	63.44
20	22.02	24.30	26.87	29.78	33.07	36.79	41.00	45.76	51.16	57.27	64.20	72.05
21	23.24	25.78	28.68	31.97	35.72	39.99	44.87	50.42	56.76	64.00	72.27	81.70
22	24.47	27.30	30.54	34.25	38.51	43.39	49.01	55.46	62.87	71.40	81.21	92.50
23	25.72	28.84	32.45	36.62	41.43	47.00	53.44	60.89	69.53	79.54	91.15	104.6
24	26.97	30.42	34.43	39.08	44.50	50.82	58.18	66.76	76.79	88.50	102.2	118.2
25	28.24	32.03	36.46	41.65	47.73	54.86	63.25	73.11	84.70	98.35	114.4	133.3
26	29.53	33.67	38.55	44.31	51.11	59.16	68.68	79.95	93.32	109.2	128.0	150.3
27	30.82	35.34	40.71	47.08	54.67	63.71	74.48	87.35	102.7	121.1	143.1	169.4
28	32.13	37.05	42.93	49.97	58.40	68.53	80.70	95.34	113.0	134.2	159.8	190.7
29	33.45	38.79	45.22	52.97	62.32	73.64	87.35	104.0	124.1	148.6	178.4	214.6
30	34.78	40.57	47.58	56.08	66.44	79.06	94.46	113.3	136.3	164.5	199.0	241.3
31	36.13	42.38	50.00	59.33	70.76	84.80	102.1	123.3	149.6	181.9	221.9	271.3
32	37.49	44.23	52.50	62.70	75.30	90.89	110.2	134.2	164.0	201.1	247.3	304.8
33	38.87	46.11	55.08	66.21	80.06	97.34	118.9	146.0	179.8	222.3	275.5	342.4
34	40.26	48.03	57.73	69.86	85.07	104.2	128.3	158.6	197.0	245.5	306.8	384.5
35	41.66	49.99	60.46	73.65	90.32	111.4	138.2	172.3	215.7	271.0	341.6	431.7

Terminal Value of £1 per Period

PERIOD   % I N T E R E S T   R A T E   P E R   P E R I O D

	13	14	15	16	18	20	22	24	26	28	30	35
1	1.000	1.000	1.000	1.000	1.000	1.000	1.000	1.000	1.000	1.000	1.000	1.000
2	2.130	2.140	2.150	2.160	2.180	2.200	2.220	2.240	2.260	2.280	2.300	2.350
3	3.407	3.440	3.472	3.506	3.572	3.640	3.708	3.778	3.848	3.918	3.990	4.173
4	4.850	4.921	4.993	5.066	5.215	5.368	5.524	5.684	5.848	6.016	6.187	6.633
5	6.480	6.610	6.742	6.877	7.154	7.442	7.740	8.048	8.368	8.700	9.043	9.954
6	8.323	8.536	8.754	8.977	9.442	9.930	10.44	10.98	11.54	12.14	12.76	14.44
7	10.40	10.73	11.07	11.41	12.14	12.92	13.74	14.62	15.55	16.53	17.58	20.49
8	12.76	13.23	13.73	14.24	15.33	16.50	17.76	19.12	20.59	22.16	23.86	28.66
9	15.42	16.09	16.79	17.52	19.09	20.80	22.67	24.71	26.94	29.37	32.01	39.70
10	18.42	19.34	20.30	21.32	23.52	25.96	28.66	31.64	34.94	38.59	42.62	54.59
11	21.81	23.04	24.35	25.73	28.76	32.15	35.96	40.24	45.03	50.40	56.41	74.70
12	25.65	27.27	29.00	30.85	34.93	39.58	44.87	50.89	57.74	65.51	74.33	101.8
13	29.98	32.09	34.35	36.79	42.22	48.50	55.75	64.11	73.75	84.85	97.63	138.5
14	34.88	37.58	40.50	43.67	50.82	59.20	69.01	80.50	93.93	109.6	127.9	188.0
15	40.42	43.84	47.58	51.66	60.97	72.04	85.19	100.8	119.3	141.3	167.3	254.7
16	46.67	50.98	55.72	60.93	72.94	87.44	104.9	126.0	151.4	181.9	218.5	344.9
17	53.74	59.12	65.08	71.67	87.07	105.9	129.0	157.3	191.7	233.8	285.0	466.6
18	61.73	68.39	75.84	84.14	103.7	128.1	158.4	196.0	242.6	300.3	371.5	630.9
19	70.75	78.97	88.21	98.60	123.4	154.7	194.3	244.0	306.7	385.3	484.0	852.7
20	80.95	91.02	102.4	115.4	146.6	186.7	238.0	303.6	387.4	494.2	630.2	1152
21	92.47	104.8	118.8	134.8	174.0	225.0	291.3	377.5	489.1	633.6	820.2	1556
22	105.5	120.4	137.6	157.4	206.3	271.0	356.4	469.1	617.3	812.0	1067	2102
23	120.2	138.3	159.3	183.6	244.5	326.2	435.9	582.6	778.8	1040	1388	2839
24	136.8	158.7	184.2	214.0	289.5	392.5	532.8	723.5	982.3	1332	1806	3833
25	155.6	181.9	212.8	249.2	342.6	472.0	651.0	898.1	1238	1706	2348	5176
26	176.9	208.3	245.7	290.1	405.3	567.4	795.2	1114	1561	2185	3054	6989
27	200.8	238.5	283.6	337.5	479.2	681.9	971.1	1383	1968	2798	3971	9436
28	227.9	272.9	327.1	392.5	566.5	819.2	1185	1716	2481	3583	5164	—
29	258.6	312.1	377.2	456.3	669.4	984.1	1447	2128	3127	4587	6714	—
30	293.2	356.8	434.7	530.3	790.9	1181	1767	2640	3942	5873	8729	—
31	332.3	407.7	501.0	616.2	934.3	1419	2156	3275	4967	7518	—	—
32	376.5	465.8	577.1	715.7	1103	1704	2632	4062	6260	9624	—	—
33	426.5	532.0	664.7	831.3	1303	2045	3212	5039	7889	—	—	—
34	482.9	607.5	765.4	965.3	1538	2456	3920	6249	9941	—	—	—
35	546.7	693.6	881.2	1120	1816	2948	4783	7750	—	—	—	—

Index

A

Acceptance credit, 85, 89, 219
Accepting house, 15, 152, 163, 219
Account
    Stock Exchange, 102
    Lloyds, 177
Actuarial calculations, 194–196
Adverse selection, 45, 179–180
Agency costs, 169
Annuity, 78, 194–195, 219
    deferred, 182
    factor, 69
Annuity factor, 69
Arbitrage, 43, 45, 89, 219
Arnaud, A.A., 208
Ask price, 219
Asset stripping, 106, 219
Asymmetry of information, 45, 169
Ayres, F., 74, 191

B

Bain, A.D., 29, 30, 48, 58
Balance sheet, 6, 7, 12, 19, 20, 30, 131
Baltic Exchange, 153
Bank bill, 85, 219
Banking, joint stock origins, 152, 154
Bank lending to industry, 167–168
Bank of England, 9, 10, 13, 22, 29, 51,
    54, 83, 89, 92, 105, 107, 155, 156,
    162, 203, 205, 214, 219
    Quarterly Bulletin, 18, 22, 81, 92,
    123, 125, 174, 218
Banks (*see also* DTIs, LDTs)
    clearing, 15, 48, 162–3, 213, 220
    commercial, 10, 15, 156–7, 161,
    162–164, 166, 220
    overseas, 15
Barter, 4, 5, 8, 12, 219
Bear, 219
Beta, 147–148, 219
Bid price, 97, 98, 106, 197, 219
Bill discounting, 80–83
Bill of exchange, 85–86, 152, 163, 219

B (second column)

Bill
    commercial, 13, 220
    local authority, 13, 82, 86
Blue chip, 168
Bonds
    issues of, 107–109
    managed, 2
    money, 204
    rating, 110, 123, 219
Brealey, R.A., 74
British Technology Group, 206
Broker, 13, 14, 37, 95, 177, 219
    Insurance, 179
Bromwich, M., 74
Brown, B., 218
Building societies, 9, 10, 15, 23, 35, 47,
    122, 153, 154, 155, 156, 159, 162,
    164, 166, 174, 186, 213, 219
    development of, 164–165
    objectives of, 213
Bull, 219
Bulldog bond, 109, 219
Burton, H., 208
Business sector, 3, 4
Buy-outs, 206

C

Cairncross, C.K., 160
Cairncross, F., 12
Call option, 14, 219
Call over, 92, 220
Capitalisation rate, 134, 220
Capital budgeting, 219
Captive insurance companies, 220
Central Statistical Office, 22, 30
Certificate of deposit, 55, 93, 220
    euro-dollar, 90–91, 93
    SDR, 207
    sterling, 87–89, 93
Chan, L.G., 106
*Cissell, R., Cissell, H., and Flaspohler,
    D.C.,* 74
City code, 105
City, criticisms of, 46–48, 188–191
Clark, T.M., 174
Clarke, W.M., 12

Cleary, E.J., 174
Clientele, 121, 122, 139
Closed ended fund, 16
Competition between financial
    institutions, 156–157
Composite rate, 220
Compound interest, 67–71, 220
    mathematics of, 76–79
Consols *(see* Undated stocks), 220
Contractual saving, effect of, 158–159
Convertible stock, 96, 108–9, 139, 140,
    144, 220
Corner, D.C., 208
Council for the Securities Industry, 99,
    105, 157, 215–216
Coupon, 112, 113, 114, 220
Crockett, A.D., 58
Crouzet, F., 168
Currency, 14
Curry, S.J., 106

D

Dawn-raiding, 98–99, 157
Dealers, 95
Debenture stock, 108–109, 220
Dennis, G.J., 106
Department of Trade, 10
Deposits, local authority, 87, 89
    bank, 15, 50
    creation of, 50–54
Deposit-taking institutions (DTIs), *(see
    also* Banks, LDTs), 159–173, 174
Development agencies, 17
Discount house, 13, 37, 54, 85–86, 92,
    163, 174, 220
Discount market, 13, 37, 83–87, 220
Discount rate, 80, 81, 135, 142, 220
Diversifying, 43, 44, 45, 138, 183–184
Dividend, 19, 31, 39, 57, 96, 131, 132,
    133, 136, 138, 142–144, 220
    interim/final, 132
    policy, 144
    yield, 132–133, 220
Drop-lock, 108–109, 220
Dufey, G., 92
Dundas Hamilton, J., 106
Durkin, T.A., 29, 48, 123

E

Earnings quality, 134
Earnings yield, 133, 220
Economies of scale, 34
    in insurance, 153
Edwards, J.S.S., 173–174

Endowment policy, 181–182, 220
    with profits, 181
    unit linked, 182
Entity, 6, 7, 9, 221
Equilibrium, 45
Equity *(see also* Ordinary shares), 6, 27,
    57, 140, 159, 183–184, 221
Equity bonds, 203, 204
Euro-bond, 13, 90, 109, 221
Euro-currency, 13, 90, 221
Euro-currency units (ECUs), 109
Euro-dollars, 14, 90, 221
Euro-markets, 11, 90
    inter-bank, 91
European Investment Bank, 207
Ex div, 112, 221
Exercise price, 14, 141, 142, 221
Expectations hypothesis, 120, 221
Export Credits Guarantee Department,
    17, 168, 221

F

Factoring, 15, 16, 221
Finance for Industry (FFI), 168
Finance house (finance company), 10,
    15, 16, 165, 166, 221
Financial futures, 14, 89, 90, 95, 211,
    218, 221
Financial institutions
    development of, 151–154, 156–158
    classification of, 158–159
Financing of small companies, 205
Financial intermediary, 12, 205–206
Fiscal neutrality, 212, 218
Fiscal policy, 11, 54, 221
Fixed interest bonds, 204
Flow of funds, 18–31, 221
Focal date, 69, 221
Foreign currency, 26
Foreign exchange (market), 13, 44, 90,
    184
Forward, 14, 89
Forward rate, 73–74, 118, 119, 120, 221
Forward-forward, 90, 221
Franklin, P.J., 191
Freear, J., 208
French Bourse, 96
Fundamental analysis, 134, 221
Fund manager, 221
Futures, 44, 221
Future shocks to the financial market
    system, 216–218

G

Gearing, 201
Geisst, C.R., 218
General insurance, 16, 177–179
  and risk management, 179–180
Giddy, I.H., 92
Gilt, gilt-edged, 13, 107, 110–114, 121,
  123, 221
Goff, T.G., 123
Goodhert, C.A.E., 58
Government, impact of (*see also* Tax),
  10, 11, 52–53, 154–156
Government securities
  characteristics of, 110–114
  issues of, 107–108
  trade in, 39
Gower, L.C.B., 215–216, 218
Gross domestic product (GDP), 27

H

Hagin, R., 143
Heaton, H., 168
Hedging, 43, 44, 45, 221
Hire purchase, 15, 16, 165, 222
Household sector, 3, 4, 5, 6, 7, 12, 15

I

Indemnity, 180, 222
Index, 222
Index fund, 138, 200, 222
Index-linked gilt, 100, 108, 110, 124,
  222
Industrial & Commercial Finance
  Corporation (ICFC), 206
Industrial life insurance, 181
Industry PLC (3i Group), 205–206
Inflation, 27
  impact of, 57, 173, 183
Insider, 222
Institute of actuaries, 110
Insurance, 14, 36, 153, 154, 157
Insurance agent, 179
Insurance companies (*see also* Life
  assurance companies), 155–157,
  177–183, 188–189, 222
  cash flows of, 175–176
  composites, 179
  long-term, general, 175
Inter-bank, 14, 87, 89, 222
Inter-bank deposits, 87, 89
Inter-bank market, 87, 89, 91
Intermediary, 222
  investment, 197

Internal rate of return, 66, 67, 69, 70,
  222
International bonds, 204
International institutions, 206–207
International Monetary Fund (IMF)
  206–207, 217
Introduction, 222
Investment by institutions, 188–191
Investment management, 183–188
Investment trust, 10, 16, 122, 200–202,
  205, 208, 222
  discount, 200, 201–202
  unitised, 202
Irredeemable, 113, 222
Irving, J., 12
Issuing house, 129, 222

J

Jobber, 97–98, 102, 106, 131, 154, 222

K

Kay, J.A., 160
Keynesians, 53
  versus monetarists, 53–54, 58
  view of gov't policy, 54–55
King, M.A., 160

L

Labour Party, 48
  government, 47, 49
Lease, 15, 222
  finance, 170
  operating, 170
Leasing, 154, 155, 165, 170–172
Lender of last resort, 86, 155, 156, 222
Lessee, 222
Lessor, 222
LIBOR, 91, 92
Life assurance, 16, 24, 27, 175–176
  investment policy, 184–185
  and pensions, 180–183
Life assurance companies, 121–205
  and risk reduction, 176
  types of policies, 175, 181–183, 186
Lifeboat, 156, 222
LIFFE, 14, 212, 222
Limit order, 95, 222
Liquid asset, 222
Liquidity, 9, 13, 16, 40, 89
Liquidity preference, 121, 223
Listed security, 223
Lloyds, 14, 177, 178, 179, 223
  profitability and regulation, 177–179

Loan stock, 13, 223
  priority, 110
Long-term insurance (*see* life assurance)

M

McCrae, H., 12
Macmillan Committee, 46
  Gap, 47, 223
Margin, 223
Market efficiency (*see* Primary market
  and Secondary market)
Market failure, 46, 47
Market model, 138, 147–148
Market orders, 95
Mason, S., 12, 29
Maturity, 16, 34, 56, 82, 83, 85, 86,
  110, 223
Mayer, C.P., 173, 174
Merchant bank (*see also* Accepting
  houses), 152, 214, 223
Merger, 15, 223
Minimum lending rate (MLR), 54–55,
  223
Minns, R., 191
Monetary policy, 11, 53–54, 84, 155,
  223
  CCC, 55, 157
Money
  creation of, 50–54
  and credit, 50–59
  commodities, 5, 8
  definitions, 9, 50–51, 55, 162
  effect of gov't on, 54, 55, 56
  functions of, 8, 12, 43
  weighted return, 187–188, 223
Moral hazard, 45, 179–180, 223
Morgan, E.V., 48
Mortgage, starvation, 36
Myers, S.C., (*see Brealey, R.A.*)

N

National Enterprise Board (NEB) (*see
  also* British Technology Group) 17,
  206
National Research & Development
  Corporation (NRDC) (*see also*
  British Technology Group), 206
National Savings Bank, 15, 164, 186
National Savings Stock Register, 100
Negotiable securities, 40, 223
Net assets, 19, 208
Net financial assets, 19, 21
Net present value, 66, 67, 69, 72, 77,
  223

Net terminal value, 66–67, 70, 76, 78,
  223
Net worth, 19, 20, 30, 31
New markets, 211–212
New York Stock Exchange, 95, 214
Nominal interest, 70–71, 109, 115, 223
Nominal value, 223
Numeraire, 4, 5, 223

O

Occupational Pensions Board, 10
Offer for sale, 129, 223
Offer price, 97, 98, 106, 129, 223
Off-shore bonds, 204
Open ended fund, 16, 197
Open market operations, 28
Opportunity cost, 53, 224
Options, 13, 14, 96, 139, 141–142, 224
  call, put, 141, 142, 144
  expiration of, 144
  traded v share, 97, 221
Ordinary shares, 13, 14, 16, 28, 44, 96,
  108, 126–139, 140, 141, 224
  discounted values of, 135–136,
  145–146
Other licensed deposit-taking
  institutions (LDTs), (*see also* Banks,
  DTIs), 161, 164–165
Overdraft, 89, 168, 224
Overfunding (PSBR), 84–85
Over-the-counter, 224

P

Parallel markets, 13, 87–90, 224
Pensions, 16, 27, 175, 180–183
  and contractual saving, 159
Pension funds, 16, 23, 39, 47, 108, 121,
  153–154, 157, 176, 183–184, 205,
  218, 224
Pension schemes, 182, 191
Perfect markets, 46
Performance evaluation, 185–188
  of unit trusts, 199–200
Perpetuity, 224
Phillips, P., 123
Placing, 224
Plender, J., 218
Polakoff, M.E., 29, 48, 123
Portfolio, 16, 36, 137–138, 140, 142,
  147–148, 183–184, 200
Portfolios of DTIs, 166–167
Post Office, 36
Preference share (stock), 13, 224
Premium, 16

Price/earnings (P/E) ratio, 133, 134, 146, 224
Primary market, 10, 36, 37, 38, 39, 40–41, 48, 224
  allocational efficiency of, 40–41
Prime (property), 224
Property, 16, 104, 183
  bonds, 203, 224
  companies, 104, 202
  invested by long-term funds, 184
  liquidity, 203
  unit trusts, 202–203
  valuation, 203
Prospectus, 126, 129, 224
Public sector borrowing requirement (PSBR), 28, 55, 59, 155, 160, 164, 224
Published accounts, 224
Put–call parity theorem, 142, 224
Put option, 14, 141, 142, 224
Put-through, 98, 224

R

Radcliffe Committee, 18
Random walk, 224
Rate of interest, 9, 33, 40
  defintion of, 56–57
  effective, 70–71, 78, 115, 220
Real assets, 6, 19, 20, 31, 33, 52
Real return, 33, 59, 225
Redemption (maturity), 96, 108, 110–114, 115, 118, 124, 225
  yield, 114–117, 118, 120, 124, 125–126, 225
Registrar of Friendly Societies, 10
Reilly, F.K., 143
Re-insurance, 157, 177–178, 225
Reserve assets, 52, 55, 225
Reserve ratios, 51–52, 156
Revell, J., 7, 12, 48
Richards, P., 106
Richards, R.D., 159
Rights issue, 126–129, 143, 225
Riskless rate, 36, 142, 225
Roden, D.H., 106
Roll-over, 88, 225
Round-tripping, 89, 225
Running yield, 114, 132, 133, 225
Rutterford, J., 123, 143
Rybczynski, T.M., 160

S

Sale and leaseback, 205, 225
Savings bank (*see also* NSB, TSB), 10, 15, 166, 225

Scrip issue, 225
Secondary bank, 15
Secondary market, 10, 36–43, 48, 225
  breadth of, 41–42, 49, 95, 158
  completeness of, 97, 210
  depth of, 41, 49, 95, 158
  efficiency, 42–43, 49, 102, 104
Segmentation hypothesis, 120–121, 225
Share issues, 126–132
Sharpe, W.F., 143
Shaw, E.R., 92
Short, 110–113, 114, 225
  sell, 46
Simple interest, 71, 81, 88, 132, 225
Single capacity, 98, 214
Single premium policies, 181
Society of Investment Analysts, 101, 110
Special drawing right (SDR) (*see* Certificate of deposit)
Specialist, 95
Spot rate, 14, 73–74
Stafford, D.C., 208
Stag, stagging, 129
Stapleton, R.C., 106
Stigum, M., 92
Stockbroker, 29, 97–99, 102, 106, 110, 113
Stock Exchange, 13, 28, 37, 94, 97, 98, 99, 101, 104–105, 121, 126, 129, 131, 132, 141–142, 200, 202, 205, 212
  accounts, 102
  changes in, 214
  commission structure, 105
  Fact Book, 121, 125
  rules for non-quoted companies, 100
Striking price, 129
Syndicate, 177, 225

T

Take-over, 10, 189
Tax, 11, 20, 27
  composite, 213
  effects of, 112–114, 116, 122, 133, 139, 154, 171–172
Tender, 129, 225
Term insurance, 181, 185, 195–196, 226
Term structure, 117–121, 123, 226
Time preference, 64–65
Time value of money, 63–66, 75
Time-weighted return, 187–188, 226
Trade bill, 226
Trading post, 95

Transaction costs, 34, 40, 45, 46, 57, 113
Transfer payment, 19, 226
Transmutation, 35, 226
Treasury, 29
Treasury bill, 13, 82–84, 85, 86, 92, 163, 226
Treasury bill tender, 83–84
Trustee Savings Bank (TSB), 9, 15, 164, 226

U

Undated stocks (*see* Consols), 113
Underwriter, 226
  insurance, 177
  leading underwriter, 177
  Stock Exchange, 129, 154
Unit trust, 10, 16, 157, 197–200, 203, 208, 226
  link with insurance, 182, 198
Unlisted security, 99
USM, 99–100, 106, 157

V

Volatility, 42, 158

W

Warrant, 13, 96, 139, 140, 226
Wendt, P.F., 143
Weston, R., 173
Whiting, D.P., 173
Whole life, 181, 226
Wilson, K.W., 58, 160, 173
Wilson Report, 11, 12, 47, 48, 58, 189, 212, 216
Winfield, R.G., 106
Wojnilower, A.M., 123
Woodhead, C., 191

Y

Yamovsky, M., 30
Yield curve, 120, 123, 226

Z

Zero coupon bond, 226